THE CONCEPT OF ANXIETY

KIERKEGAARD'S WRITINGS, VIII

THE CONCEPT OF ANXIETY

A SIMPLE PSYCHOLOGICALLY ORIENTING DELIBERATION ON THE DOGMATIC ISSUE OF HEREDITARY SIN

by Søren Kierkegaard

*Edited and Translated
with Introduction and Notes by*

Reidar Thomte

in collaboration with

Albert B. Anderson

PRINCETON UNIVERSITY PRESS
PRINCETON, NEW JERSEY

Library of Congress Cataloging in Publication Data will be
found on the last printed page of this book

Editorial preparation of this work has been assisted by a grant from
Lutheran Brotherhood, a fraternal benefit society, with headquarters
in Minneapolis, Minnesota

Clothbound editions of Princeton University Press books
are printed on acid-free paper, and binding materials are
chosen for strength and durability

Designed by Frank Mahood

Printed in the United States of America
by Princeton University Press, Princeton, New Jersey

CONTENTS

III Anxiety as the Consequence of that Sin which
Is Absence of the Consciousness of Sin
81

IV Anxiety of Sin or Anxiety as the Consequence
of Sin in the Single Individual
111

V Anxiety as Saving through Faith
155

HISTORICAL INTRODUCTION

Among those attending W.F.J. Schelling's series of lectures on the philosophy of mythology and revelation (*Philosophie der Mythologie und Offenbarung*) at the University of Berlin in the winter of 1841-1842 were both Friedrich Engels and Søren Kierkegaard.[1] After the second lecture Kierkegaard wrote: "I am so happy to have heard Schelling's second lecture—indescribably. I have been pining and thinking mournful thoughts long enough. The embryonic child of thought leapt for joy within me, as in Elizabeth, when he mentioned the word 'actuality' in connection with the relation of philosophy to actuality."[2] Although this initial enthusiasm declined rapidly, Kierkegaard continued to attend the lectures and took copious notes. What interested him in particular was Schelling's criticism of Hegel's rationalistic system, and upon his return to Copenhagen in 1842 he turned to the study of Leibniz, Descartes, and Aristotle, as well as to the anti-Hegelian writings of Adolph Trendelenburg[3] and portions of W. G. Tennemann's history of philosophy.[4] Each of these studies helped him to shape his own philosophical position and also furnished him with an arsenal for his relentless battle with Hegel and speculative idealism.

Leibniz's review of arguments pertaining to the problem of freedom interested Kierkegaard especially. In response to Leibniz's point in the *Theodicy* that the connection between

[1] Paul Tillich, "Existential Philosophy," *Journal of the History of Ideas*, V (1944), 44.

[2] See p. 229, note 51.

[3] Adolph Trendelenburg, *Logische Untersuchungen* (Berlin: 1840; *ASKB* 842); *Die logische Frage in Hegel's System. Zwei Streitschriften* (Leipzig: 1843; *ASKB* 846). See Niels Thulstrup, *Kierkegaards Forhold til Hegel* (Copenhagen: Gyldendal, 1967), pp. 241, 269.

[4] W. G. Tennemann, *Geschichte der Philosophie*, I-XII (Leipzig: 1798-1819; *ASKB* 815-26). See Thulstrup, *Kierkegaards Forhold til Hegel*, pp. 241, 243, 245-46, 249-50.

judgment and will is not as necessary as one might think, Kierkegaard asked: "In what relationship does the will stand to the last act of the understanding. . . ?"[5] He agreed with Leibniz that a completely indifferent will (*æquilibrium*) is an absurdity and a chimera.[6] In another journal entry he noted that Leibniz mentions two difficulties that have disturbed man: the relation between freedom and necessity, and the continuity of matter and its separate parts. The first problem has engaged all men; the second, only the philosophers.[7] Subsequently, Kierkegaard dealt with the problem of freedom in three of his pseudonymous works: *Philosophical Fragments* defines the ontological ground of freedom and its realm, whereas *The Concept of Anxiety* and *The Sickness unto Death* consider the anthropological aspects of freedom.

In response to Descartes's idea of freedom, Kierkegaard noted in his papers that: "In freedom I can emerge only from that into which I have entered in freedom. . . . If I am going to emerge from doubt in freedom, I must enter into doubt in freedom. (Act of Will.)"[8] Therefore, Descartes, according to Kierkegaard, had inverted the relationship between thought and will:

> Incidentally, it is noteworthy that Descartes, who himself in one of the meditations explains the possibility of error by recalling that freedom in man is superior to thought, nevertheless has construed thought, not freedom, as the absolute. Obviously this is the position of the elder Fichte—not *cogito ergo sum*, but I act *ergo sum*, for this *cogito* is something derived or it is identical with "I act"; either the consciousness of freedom is in the action, and then it should not read *cogito ergo sum*, or it is the subsequent consciousness.[9]

[5] *JP* II 1241 (*Pap*. IV C 39).
[6] *JP* II 1241 (*Pap*. IV C 39); Leibniz, *Theodicy*, §§311ff., 319; *God. Guil. Leibnitii Opera philosophica* . . . , ed. J. E. Erdmann (Berlin: 1840; *ASKB* 620), pp. 595-98. See also *JP* III 2361, 3340; IV 4419; V 5581-85 (*Pap*. IV A 12, 14-18, 22, 35).
[7] *JP* III 2360 (*Pap*. IV A 11).   [8] *JP* I 777 (*Pap*. IV B 13:21).
[9] *JP* II 2338 (*Pap*. IV C 11).

In a marginal notation Kierkegaard added: "This transition is manifestly a *pathos-filled* transition, not dialectical, for dialectically nothing can be derived. To me this is important. A pathos-filled transition can be achieved by every man if he wills it, because the transition to the infinite, which consists in pathos, takes only courage."[10]

Kierkegaard criticized the Cartesian principle of methodical doubt because it mistakenly gives more weight to reflection (thought) than it does to act (will).

> What skeptics should really be caught in is the ethical. Since Descartes they have all thought that during the period in which they doubted they dared not to express anything definite with regard to knowledge, but on the other hand they dared to act, because in this respect they could be satisfied with probability. What an enormous contradiction! As if it were not far more dreadful to do something about which one is doubtful (thereby incurring responsibility) than to make a statement. Or was it because the ethical is in itself certain? But then there was something which doubt could not reach![11]

Descartes's apparently epistemological problem is for Kierkegaard an existential one; that is, the solution of doubt lies not in reflection but in resolution.[12]

The remainder of Kierkegaard's studies during the fall of 1842 centered on Trendelenburg and Tennemann, and from them Kierkegaard gained insights into Aristotle's thought. References in his papers indicate that he also made use of primary sources. In a discussion of Aristotle's doctrine of motion, Tennemann wrote: "Because possibility and actuality are distinguishable in all things, change, *insofar as it is change*, is *the actualization of the possible.* . . . The transition from possibility to actuality is a change, κίνησις. This could be expressed more precisely by saying: *change*, motion, is *the*

[10] *JP* III 2339 (*Pap*. IV C 12).   [11] *JP* I 774 (*Pap*. IV A 72).
[12] *JP* I 776 (*Pap*. IV B 5:13).

actualization of the possible as far as it is possible."[13] This conception of change held great significance for Kierkegaard, and he made Tennemann's interpretation of κίνησις the point of departure for his own theory of transition—what in *The Concept of Anxiety* is referred to as the "qualitative leap."

Kierkegaard found support for his conception of the qualitative leap in Trendelenburg's idea that the highest principles can be demonstrated only indirectly (negatively). Yet he reproached Trendelenburg for his failure to recognize the necessity of a qualitative leap in order to recognize the validity of such principles.[14]

Kierkegaard's primary criticism of Aristotle centers on his view that the real self resides ultimately in the thinking part of man, and that consequently the contemplative life constitutes man's highest happiness. Kierkegaard found in Aristotle an understanding that ethics will not admit of the precision required for scientific knowledge: "The definition of science that Aristotle gives in 6,3 is very important. The objects of science are things that can be only in a single way. What is scientifically knowable is therefore the necessary, the eternal, for everything that is absolutely necessary is also absolutely everlasting."[15] He does then agree with Aristotle that, strictly speaking, there is no scientific knowledge of human existence, since its essential qualification is one of freedom and not of necessity. However, from Kierkegaard's point of view, "Aristotle has not understood this self deeply enough, for only in the esthetic sense does contemplative thought have an entelechy, and the felicity of the gods does not reside in contemplation but in eternal communication."[16] For Kierkegaard, therefore, Aristotle falls short in his understanding that the consummation of man's ethical life lies in the contemplative posture.

[13] Tennemann, *Geschichte der Philosophie*, III, pp. 126-27. For Kierkegaard's use of κίνησις see *Philosophical Fragments*, *KW* VII (*SV* IV 236-39).
[14] *JP* III 2341 (*Pap.* V A 74).
[15] *JP* II 2281 (*Pap.* IV C 23). The reference is to *Nicomachean Ethics*, 1115 b, 18 ff.
[16] *JP* IV 3892 (*Pap.* IV C 26).

Following his studies of Leibniz, Descartes, and Aristotle, Kierkegaard began to delve deeper into the study of Hegel, centering on the *Phenomenology of Mind* and the *Encylopædia of the Philosophical Sciences*. Where Hegel and his followers proclaimed the harmonious relationship of philosophical idealism and Christianity, Kierkegaard argued that Christianity and philosophy (Hegel's speculative idealism) present an irreconcilable opposition.[17] Thus, however else Kierkegaard may be classified in the history of thought, he stands in direct opposition to the philosophical idealism of his day.

There is no question but that Kierkegaard's thought was influenced by Hegel's; however, there is some disagreement as to the degree and nature of that influence. Per Lønning writes:

It has usually been maintained that Hegel's philosophy was a decisive influence in the formulation of Kierkegaard's thought, especially his conception of history and of the paradox in relation to history. . . . Such a view seems to be rooted in a complete failure to recognize fully how Kierkegaard's interpretation stands entirely independent of the Hegelian philosophy of religion. However, many of Kierkegaard's conceptual formulations may be due to a relation to Hegel.[18]

The views of Stephen Crites and Mark Taylor would have Kierkegaard considerably more indebted to Hegel, and as evidence they indicate the similarities between Kierkegaard's concept of the self in *The Sickness unto Death* and a passage in Hegel's *Phenomenology of Mind*.[19] However, Niels Thulstrup

[17] *JP* III 3245 (*Pap*. I A 94), October 17, 1835.

[18] Per Lønning, *"Samtidighedens Situation"* (Oslo: Forlaget Land og Kirke, 1954), p. 285.

[19] Stephen Crites, *In the Twilight of Christendom: Hegel vs. Kierkegaard on Faith and History* (Chambersburg, Pa.: American Academy of Religion, 1972), p. 70; Mark C. Taylor, *Kierkegaard's Pseudonymous Authorship: A Study of Time and the Self* (Princeton: Princeton University Press, 1975), p. 104. See *The Sickness unto Death*, KW XIX (*SV* XI 127-28); G.W.F. Hegel, *Phänomenologie des Geistes, Georg Wilhelm Friedrich Hegel's Werke, vollständige Ausgabe*, I-XVIII, ed. Ph. Marheineke et al. (Berlin: 1832-40; *ASKB* 549-65),

warns against being misled by verbal or terminological corre-
spondences between Kierkegaard and Hegel, particularly
with reference to Kierkegaard's triadic conception of selfhood
in *The Concept of Anxiety* and other works.[20]

The Concept of Anxiety was published on June 17, 1844, the
year in which Nietzsche was born and Kierkegaard was
thirty-one years old. On the same day, Kierkegaard also published a book called *Prefaces*, and four days earlier *Philosophical
Fragments* had appeared. In addition to these works, he published in the same year *Two Upbuilding Discourses, Three Upbuilding Discourses*, and *Four Upbuilding Discourses*.

According to Jens Himmelstrup,[21] *Philosophical Fragments*,
Prefaces, and *Four Upbuilding Discourses* received contemporary reviews; the last work was honored with a review by
Bishop J. P. Mynster, the primate of the Danish Church.
However, there were no reviews of *The Concept of Anxiety*; in
other words, this book, one of the most significant and possibly the most difficult of Kierkegaard's works, apparently
caused no stir among scholars of the day.

The Concept of Anxiety has deep roots in the personal history of its author. That Kierkegaard lived intimately with
anxiety is reflected in the numerous references to this idea in
his journals and works both before and after he wrote *The
Concept of Anxiety*. In a journal entry for 1837, he speaks of
certain presentiments that seem to precede everything that
will happen and of an anxious consciousness by which "innocent but fragile souls can easily be tempted to believe themselves guilty."[22] However, to Kierkegaard anxiety is clearly
more pervasive and basic than simple presentiment.[23] On

II, pp. 14-18; *Sämtliche Werke, Jubiläumsausgabe* [*J.A.*], I-XXVI, ed. Hermann
Glockner (Stuttgart: Fr. Fromans Verlag, 1927-40), II, pp. 23-26; *The Phenomenology of Mind*, tr. J. P. Baillie (New York: Harper Torchbook, 1967), pp.
80-84.

[20] Thulstrup, *Kierkegaards Forhold til Hegel*, p. 305. For the relation of Kierkegaard to Hegel and idealism, see the numerous references in the editorial
Notes to *The Concept of Anxiety*.

[21] *Søren Kierkegaard International Bibliografi* (Copenhagen: Gyldendals Forlag, 1962), p. 10.

[22] See Supplement, p. 169 (*Pap.* II A 18).   [23] See pp. 42-43.

May 12, 1839, he wrote, "All existence [*Tilværelsen*], from the smallest fly to the mysteries of the Incarnation, makes me anxious."²⁴ Three years after the publication of *The Concept of Anxiety*, he observed: "Deep within every human being there still lives the anxiety over the possibility of being alone in the world, forgotten by God, overlooked by the millions and millions in this enormous household."²⁵ Again, in an 1848 entry he reflected upon his own upbringing and the anxiety with which his father had filled his soul, upon his frightful melancholy, and upon his anxiety over Christianity, to which he was nevertheless drawn.²⁶ Finally, in 1850 he spoke of a "melancholy anxiety" and an "inborn anxiety."²⁷ The idea of anxiety and its relation to his own life was therefore a lifelong and pervasive concern.

The first published indication of Kierkegaard's deep interest in anxiety appears in his treatment of Mozart's *Don Giovanni* in *Either/Or*, where the concept is explored in its relation to sensuousness. Don Giovanni's anxiety, Kierkegaard suggests, is a substantial or prototypical kind,²⁸ whereas that of Antigone is tragic,²⁹ and Nero's anxiety is psychopathic.³⁰ However, it is in *The Concept of Anxiety* that Kierkegaard deals for the first time with "anxiety over nothing"—that pregnant anxiety that is directed toward the future and that is a pristine element in every human being.³¹

The psychological concern that fostered *The Concept of Anxiety* figures in many of Kierkegaard's other works. *Repetition* is "A Venture in Experimenting³² Psychology"; the subtitle of " 'Guilty?'/'Not Guilty?' " in *Stages on Life's Way* is

²⁴ See Supplement, p. 170 (*Pap.* II A 420).
²⁵ See Supplement, p. 171 (*Pap.* VIII¹ A 363).
²⁶ See Supplement, pp. 170-72 (*Pap.* IV A 107; III A 164; IX A 411).
²⁷ See Supplement, pp. 172-73 (*Pap.* X² A 493).
²⁸ *Either/Or*, I, *KW* III (*SV* I 107-08).
²⁹ *Either/Or*, I, *KW* III (*SV* I 131-32).
³⁰ *Either/Or*, II, *KW* IV (*SV* II 168-69).
³¹ For the numerous references to anxiety in Kierkegaard's works, see *Søren Kierkegaard-Register, Sag- og Forfatterregister*, by A. Ibsen, *Terminologisk Register*, by I. Himmelstrup (Copenhagen: Gyldendalske Boghandel, Nordisk Forlag, 1936).
³² Danish: *experimenterende*. On this word in its various forms, see *Fear and*

"An Imaginary Psychological Construction"; the subtitle of *The Sickness unto Death* is "A Christian Psychological Exposition for Upbuilding and Awakening"; and *The Concept of Anxiety* has as its subtitle, "A Simple Psychologically Orienting Deliberation on the Dogmatic Issue of Hereditary Sin." These subtitles reflect the history of Kierkegaard's personal experience and the extent to which these works represent an analysis of his own self.

His contribution to psychological thought did not go unnoticed. In 1881 Georg Brandes,[33] a celebrated writer and literary critic, wrote in a letter to Nietzsche, "In my opinion, he [Kierkegaard] is one of the most profound psychologists who ever lived."

Historically, the psychology with which Kierkegaard worked is quite different from present-day psychological research. His is a phenomenology that is based on an ontological view of man, the fundamental presupposition of which is the transcendent reality of the individual, whose intuitively discernible character reveals the existence of an eternal component. Such a psychology does not blend well with any purely empirical science and is best understood by regarding soma, psyche, and spirit as the principal determinants of the human structure, with the first two belonging to the temporal realm and the third to the eternal.

From the positivistic point of view, the psychology of *The Concept of Anxiety* was attacked by the philosopher Harald Høffding,[34] whose criticism was directed especially against the idea of the "qualitative leap." He maintained that the sciences, including the science of psychology, are based on the assumption that there is an unbroken continuity in the passage from possibility to actuality and that every new state is

---

Trembling and *Repetition, KW* VI, Historical Introduction, notes 30-55 and related texts; note on subtitle.

[33] *Correspondence de Georg Brandes*, I-VI, ed. Paul Krüger (Copenhagen: Rosenkilde og Bagger, 1966), III, p. 448 (ed. tr.).

[34] *Søren Kierkegaard som Filosof* (Copenhagen: Gyldendalsk Boghandels Forlag, 1877; 2 ed., 1919), pp. 70-82.

thereby the simple consequence of a previous state. For Høffding, a presuppositionless leap would abrogate the strict continuity required in every science. Yet this is precisely Kierkegaard's point, namely, that the "qualitative leap" is a category outside the scope of scientific procedures and that its confirmation is therefore not reducible to the principles of verification assumed by the sciences. Kierkegaard expressed this difference by positing not only psychosomatic dimensions in human existence but also a dimension of spirit, distinguishing the "outwardness" of scientific observation from the "inwardness" of spiritual experience. A psychology that does not account for the determining and transforming activity of spirit in the self-conscious subject will not accurately reflect what grounds and generates the quality of man's becoming. *The Concept of Anxiety* then suggests that the psychologist could analyze this notion and its relation to the "qualitative leap" produced in the dialectic of freedom in order to work toward a more adequate grasp of man's nature and the ontological determinants that shape the human condition.

In recent years *The Concept of Anxiety* has been recognized by philosphers, theologians, and psychologists as one of Kierkegaard's major works. Kierkegaard's method is keyed to the principle *unum noris omnes*,[35] which actually expresses the same as the Socratic "know yourself," provided that *unum* is understood to be the observer himself, who does not look for an *omnes* but determinedly holds fast to himself, the one who actually is all. Thus every human being possesses, or is within himself, a complete expression of humanness, whose essential meaning cannot be gained from scientific studies. That is, neither rational speculation nor natural science will disclose to the existing individual his essential nature and purpose. Self-knowledge is attained by man in existing; that is, self-knowledge is coordinate with the actualizing of one's potentiality to become oneself.[36]

[35] See p. 79.
[36] See *Concluding Unscientific Postscript, KW* XII (*SV* VII 307-09).

Kierkegaard's principle of *unum noris omnes* has created interest among thinkers who draw heavily upon existential psychology. Martin Heidegger "denies that it is possible to approach Being through objective reality, and insists that 'Existential Being,' *Dasein*, self-relatedness, is the only door to Being itself. The objective world (*Das Vorhandene*) is a late product of immediate personal experience."[37] According to Karl Jaspers, personal existence ("Existential Subjectivity") is the center and aim of reality. No being who lacks such personal experience "can ever understand existence."[38] In this connection, it is only proper to state that Kierkegaard's principle of *unum noris omnes* refers to self-knowledge. The task of the subjective thinker is to understand himself in his existence. "Know yourself" is to be understood in the Greek way as the Greeks would have understood it if they had possessed Christian presuppositions.[39]

Paul Tillich's view of anxiety somewhat parallels that of Kierkegaard. He defines anxiety as "finitude in awareness": "Anxiety is the self-awareness of the finite self as finite." Like finitude, anxiety is ontological; it cannot be derived from anything. Anxiety differs from fear in that the object of anxiety is "nothingness," and nothingness is not an "object." Fear relates itself to objects—for example, a danger, a pain, an enemy—for it is psychological and can be conquered. Anxiety cannot be conquered, for no finite being can conquer its finitude. Anxiety is always present, although it may be latent. Because it is ontological, anxiety expresses finitude from the inside. Tillich also speaks of "the anxiety of losing our ontological structure," which is "the anxiety of not being what we essentially are. It is anxiety about disintegrating and falling into non-being through existential disruption," with "the consequent destruction of the ontological structure." In a very significant footnote, Tillich says: "Psychotherapy cannot remove ontological anxiety, because it cannot change the structure of finitude. But it can remove compulsory forms of

[37] Quoted by Tillich, "Existential Philosophy," p. 57.
[38] Ibid.   [39] See p. 79.

anxiety and can reduce the frequency and intensity of fears. It can put anxiety 'in its proper place.' "[40]

Kierkegaard's concepts of the self and of anxiety are basic to Reinhold Niebuhr's doctrine of man. Man stands at the juncture of nature and spirit; he is involved both in freedom and necessity; he is both limited and limitless. "Anxiety is the inevitable concomitant of freedom and finiteness in which man is involved. . . . It is the inevitable spiritual state of man, standing in the paradoxical situation of freedom and finiteness."[41] Anxiety is the permanent internal preconditioning of sin as well as of creativity.

Similarly, Rollo May emphasizes that anxiety is not an affect among other affects, such as pleasure and sadness. It is an ontological characteristic of man, rooted in his very existence. Fear is a threat to the periphery of one's existence and can be studied as an affect among other affects. Anxiety is a threat to the foundation and center of one's existence. It is ontological and can be understood only as a threat to *Dasein*. If the individual did not have some measure of freedom, there could be no experience of anxiety.[42]

Kierkegaard emphatically affirms the religious dimension of the self: "The formula that describes the state of the self when despair is completely rooted out is this: in relating itself to itself and in willing to be itself, the self rests [or, has its ground] transparently in the power that established it."[43] For Kierkegaard this power is God.[44] The God-relation is an ontological quality of the self, apart from which the self cannot fully actualize itself or know itself as the infinite self.

Although Kierkegaard's ontological structure of the self has influenced philosophers like Heidegger and Sartre and psychologists of the existential-analytical school, these thinkers

---

[40] Paul Tillich, *Systematic Theology*, I-III (Chicago: University of Chicago Press, 1959-64), I, pp. 191-92, 199.
[41] Reinhold Niebuhr, *The Nature and Destiny of Man*, I-II (New York: Charles Scribner's Sons, 1947), I, p. 182.
[42] Rollo May et al., *Existence* (New York: Simon & Schuster, 1958), pp. 50-51.
[43] *The Sickness unto Death*, KW XIX (*SV* XI 128). [44] *Pap.* VIII² B 170:2.

do not accept the God-relation of the self. Thus Ludwig Binswanger acknowledges his indebtedness to Kierkegaard and draws upon *aspects* of his thought, but he rejects the God concept, which in Kierkegaard's structure of the self is the ultimate.[45]

Kierkegaard's style is different from that of contemporary writers, and readers may think this translation both stilted and long-winded. *The Concept of Anxiety* does not read like a popular book on psychological problems. There is an inordinate number of categorical terms and substantive phrases, and clause upon clause in sentence upon sentence leaves the reader breathless. However, to break up some of Kierkegaard's longer sentences would probably obscure rather than clarify his meaning.

Although every translation leaves something to be desired by comparison with the original, in this one every effort has been made to emulate what was done in a studied and deliberate manner by the author of *The Concept of Anxiety*. The work, by the pseudonymous Vigilius Haufniensis, is original and seminal and therefore demands new and arresting classifications. His expression is the result of an exacting analysis of concepts, which he carries on without apology in the need to drive home vital distinctions. Moreover, if the style used for this purpose is relentless and often overwhelming, from Kierkegaard's point of view this mood is essential. Although the tone is more direct and didactic than in his other pseudonymous works, the magnitude of the reflection surrounding the concept of anxiety requires the reader to examine every pertinent implication in order to arrive at an increasingly profound and multidimensioned awareness of what anxiety is. Such is the kind of reflection that provides the approach to self-knowledge, and such, therefore, is the character of Kierkegaard's dialectic.

[45] Ludwig Binswanger, "Insanity as Life-Historical Phenomenon and as Mental Disease: The Case of Ellen Ilse," and "The Case of Ellen West, an Anthropological-Clinical Study," in May et al., *Existence*, pp. 236, 297-98.

THE CONCEPT OF ANXIETY

A SIMPLE PSYCHOLOGICALLY
ORIENTING DELIBERATION
ON THE DOGMATIC ISSUE
OF HEREDITARY SIN

by Vigilius Haufniensis

The age of making distinctions is past. It has been vanquished by the system. In our day, whoever loves to make distinctions is regarded as an eccentric whose soul clings to something that has long since vanished. Be that as it may, yet Socrates still is what he was, the simple wise man, because of the peculiar distinction that he expressed both in words and in life, something that the eccentric Hamann first reiterated with great admiration two thousand years later: "For Socrates was great in 'that he distinguished between what he understood and what he did not understand.' "

In my opinion, one who intends to write a book ought to consider carefully the subject about which he wishes to write. Nor would it be inappropriate for him to acquaint himself as far as possible with what has already been written on the subject. If on his way he should meet an individual who has dealt exhaustively and satisfactorily with one or another aspect of that subject, he would do well to rejoice as does the bridegroom's friend who stands by and rejoices greatly as he hears the bridegroom's voice.[2] When he has done this in complete silence and with the enthusiasm of a love that ever seeks solitude, nothing more is needed; then he will carefully write his book as spontaneously as a bird sings its song,[3] and if someone derives benefit or joy from it, so much the better. Then he will publish the book, carefree and at ease and without any sense of self-importance, as if he had brought everything to a conclusion or as if all the generations of the earth were to be blessed[4] by his book. Each generation has its own task and need not trouble itself unduly by being everything to previous and succeeding generations. Just as each day's trouble is sufficient for the day,[5] so each individual in a generation has enough to do in taking care of himself and does not need to embrace the whole contemporary age with his paternal solicitude or assume that era and epoch[6] begin with his book, and still less with the New Year's torch[7] of his promise or with the intimations of his farseeing promises or with the referral of his reassurance to a currency of doubtful value.[8] Not everyone who is stoop-shouldered is an Atlas, nor did he become such by supporting a world. Not everyone who says Lord, Lord, shall enter the kingdom of heaven.[9] Not everyone who offers himself as surety for the whole contemporary age proves by such action that he is reliable and can vouch for himself. Not everyone who shouts Bravo, schwere Noth, Gottsblitz, bravissimo[10] has therefore understood himself and his admiration.

Concerning my own humble person,[11] I frankly confess that as an author I am a king without a country and also, in fear and much trembling,[12] an author without any claims. If to a noble envy or jealous criticism it seems too much that I bear a Latin name, I shall gladly assume the name Christen Madsen. Nothing could please me more than to be regarded as a layman who indeed speculates but is still far removed from speculation, although I am as devout in my belief in authority as the Roman was tolerant in his worship of God. When it comes to human authority, I am a fetish worshipper and will worship anyone with equal piety, but with one proviso, that it be made sufficiently clear by a beating of drums that he is the one I must worship and that it is he who is the authority and *Imprimatur*[13] for the current year. The decision is beyond my understanding, whether it takes place by lottery or balloting, or whether the honor is passed around so that each individual has his turn as authority, like a representative of the burghers on the board of arbitration.

Beyond this I have nothing to add except to wish everyone who shares my view and also everyone who does not, everyone who reads the book and also everyone who has had enough in reading the Preface, a well meant farewell.

Copenhagen

Respectfully,
VIGILIUS HAUFNIENSIS

The sense in which the subject of our deliberation is a task of psychological interest and the sense in which, after having been the task and interest of psychology, it points directly to dogmatics.

The view that every scientific issue within the larger compass of science has its definite place, its measure and its limit, and thereby precisely its harmonious blending in the whole as well as its legitimate participation in what is expressed by the whole, is not merely a *pium desiderium* [pious wish] that ennobles the man of science by its enthusiastic and melancholy infatuation. This view is not merely a sacred duty that commits him to the service of the totality and bids him renounce lawlessness and the adventurous desire to lose sight of the mainland; it also serves the interest of every more specialized deliberation, for when the deliberation forgets where it properly belongs, as language often expresses with striking ambiguity, it forgets itself and becomes something else, and thereby acquires the dubious perfectibility of being able to become any thing and everything. By failing to proceed in a scientific manner and by not taking care to see that the individual issues do not outrun one another, as if it were a matter of arriving first at the masquerade, a person occasionally achieves a brilliance and amazes others by giving the impression that he has already comprehended that which is still very remote. At times he makes a vague agreement with things that differ. The gain is always avenged, as is every unlawful acquisition, which cannot be owned legally or scientifically.

IV
282

Thus when an author entitles the last section of the *Logic* "A c t u a l i t y,"[14] he thereby gains the advantage of making it appear that in logic the highest has already been achieved, or if one prefers, the lowest. In the meantime, the loss is obvious, for neither logic nor actuality is served by placing actuality in the *Logic.* Actuality is not served thereby, for contingency, which is an essential part of the actual, cannot be admitted within the realm of logic. Logic is not served thereby, for if logic has thought actuality, it has included something that it cannot assimilate, it has appropriated at the beginning what it should only *praedisponere* [presuppose]. The penalty is obvious. Every deliberation about the nature of actuality is rendered difficult, and for a long time perhaps made impossible, since the word "actuality" must first have time to collect itself, time to forget the mistake.

Thus when in dogmatics *faith* is called the *immediate*[15] without any further qualification, there is gained the advantage that everybody is convinced of the necessity of not stopping with faith. The admission may be elicited even from one who subscribes to orthodoxy, because at first he perhaps does not discern the misunderstanding, that it does not have its source in a subsequent error but in that πρῶτον ψεῦδος [fundamental error]. The loss is quite obvious. Faith loses by being regarded as the immediate, since it has been deprived of what lawfully belongs to it, namely, its historical presupposition. Dogmatics loses thereby, because it does not begin where it properly should begin, namely, within the scope of an earlier beginning. Instead of presupposing an earlier beginning, it ignores this and begins without ceremony, just as if it were logic. Logic does indeed begin with something produced by the subtlest abstraction, namely, what is most elusive: the immediate. What is quite proper in logic, namely, that immediacy is *eo ipso* canceled, becomes in dogmatics idle talk. Could it ever occur to anyone to stop with the immediate (with no further qualification), since the immediate is annulled[16] at the very moment it is mentioned, just as a somnam-

bulist wakes up at the very moment his name is mentioned? Thus when one sometimes finds, and almost solely in propaedeutic investigation, the word "reconciliation"[17] [*Forsoning*] used to designate speculative knowledge, or to designate the identity of the perceiving subject and the object perceived, or to designate the subjective-objective, etc., it is obvious that the author is brilliant and that by means of this

brilliance he has explained every riddle, especially to all those
who even in matters of science use less care than they do in
daily life, where they listen carefully to the words of the riddle before they attempt to guess its meaning. Otherwise he
gains the incomparable reputation of having posed by virtue
of his explanation a new riddle, namely, how it could ever
occur to any man that this might be the explanation. The notion that thought on the whole has reality was assumed by all
ancient and medieval philosophy. With Kant, this assumption
became doubtful. If it is now assumed that Hegelian philosophy has actually grasped Kant's skepticism[18] thoroughly
(something that might continue to remain a great question
despite all that Hegel and his school have done with the help
of the slogan "method and manifestation"[19] to conceal what
Schelling[20] with the slogan "intellectual intuition and construction" openly acknowledged as a new point of departure)
and now has reconstructed the earlier in a higher form and in
such a way that thought does not possess reality by virtue of a
presupposition—does it therefore also follow that this reality,
which is consciously brought forth by thought, is a reconciliation? In that case, philosophy has only been brought back to
where the beginning was made in the old days, when reconciliation did in fact have enormous significance. There is an
old, respectable philosophical terminology: thesis, antithesis,
synthesis. A more recent terminology has been chosen in
which "mediation" takes the third place. Is this such an extraordinary advance? "Mediation" is equivocal, for it suggests simultaneously the relation between the two and the result of the relation, that in which the two relate themselves to
each other as well as the two that related themselves to each
other. It indicates movement as well as repose. Whether this
is a perfection must be determined by subjecting mediation to
a more profound dialectical test, but, unfortunately, this is
something for which we still must wait. One rejects synthesis
and says "mediation." Very well. Brilliance, however, demands more—one says "reconciliation" [*Forsoning*], and what
is the result? The propaedeutic investigations are not served
by it, for naturally they gain as little in clarity as does the

IV
284

truth, as little as a man's soul gains in salvation by having a title conferred upon him. On the contrary, two sciences, ethics and dogmatics, become radically confused, especially when after the introduction of the term "reconciliation" it is further pointed out that logic and λóγος [the dogmatical] correspond to each other, and that logic is the proper doctrine of λóγος.[21] Ethics and dogmatics struggle over reconciliation in a *confinium* [border area] fraught with fate. Repentance and guilt torment forth reconciliation ethically, while dogmatics, in its receptivity to the proffered reconciliation, has the historically concrete immediacy with which it begins its discourse in the great dialogue of science. And now what will be the result? Presumably language will celebrate a great sabbatical year in which speech and thought may be at rest so that we can begin at the beginning.

In logic, *the negative*[22] is used as the impelling power to bring movement into all things. One must have movement in logic no matter how it is brought about, and no matter by what means. The negative lends a hand, and what the negative cannot accomplish, play on words and platitudes can, just as when the negative itself becomes a play on words.* In

* *Exempli gratia: Wesen ist was ist gewesen; ist gewesen* is a *tempus præteritum* of *seyn, ergo, Wesen* is *das aufgehobene Seyn,* the *Seyn* that has been [For example: Essence is what has been; "has been" is past tense of "to be," *ergo,* essence is annulled being, being that has been].[23] This is a logical movement! If anyone would take the trouble to collect and put together all the strange pixies and goblins who like busy clerks bring about movement in Hegelian logic (such as this is in itself and as it has been improved by the [Hegelian] school), a later age would perhaps be surprised to see that what are regarded as discarded witticisms once played an important role in logic, not as incidental explanations and ingenious remarks but as masters of movement, which made Hegel's logic something of a miracle and gave logical thought feet to move

on, without anyone's being able to observe them. Just as Lulu[24] comes running without anyone's being able to observe the mechanism of movement, so the long mantle of admiration conceals the machinery of logical movement. To have brought movement into logic is the merit of Hegel. In comparison with this, it is hardly worth mentioning the unforgettable merit that was Hegel's, namely, that in many ways he corrected the categorical definitions and their arrangement, a merit he disdained in order to run aimlessly.[25]

logic, no movement must *come about*, for logic is, and whatever is logical only *is*.* This impotence of the logical consists in the transition of logic into becoming, where existence [*Tilværelse*]²⁶ and actuality come forth. So when logic becomes deeply absorbed in the concretion of the categories, that which was from the beginning is ever the same. Every movement, if for the moment one wishes to use this expression, is an immanent movement, which in a profound sense is no movement at all. One can easily convince oneself of this by considering that the concept of movement is itself a transcendence that has no place in logic. The negative, then, is immanent in the movement, is something vanishing, is that which is annulled. If everything comes about in this manner, nothing comes about at all, and the negative becomes an illusion. Nevertheless, precisely in order to make something come about in logic, the negative becomes something more; it becomes that which brings forth the opposition, not a negation but a contraposition. And thus the negative is not the stillness of the immanent movement; it is *"the necessary other,"*²⁷ indeed, something that may be very necessary for logic in order to bring about movement, but it is something that the negative is not. Turning from logic to ethics, we find again the same indefatigable negative that is active in the entire Hegelian philosophy. Here one is astonished to discover that the negative is the evil.²⁸ As a result, confusion is in full swing and there are no limits to cleverness, and what Mme Staël-Holstein²⁹ has said of Schelling's philosophy, namely, that it makes a man clever for his whole life, applies in every way to Hegelianism. One can see how illogical the movements must be in logic, since the negative is the evil, and how unethical they must be in ethics, since the evil is the negative. In logic they are too much and in ethics too little. They fit nowhere if they are supposed to fit both. If ethics has no other transcendence, it is essentially logic. If logic is to have as

IV
286

* The eternal expression for the logical is what the Eleatics through a misunderstanding transferred to existence: nothing comes into being [*opkommer*], everything is.

IV
285

much transcendence as common propriety requires of ethics, it is no longer logic.

What has been developed here is probably too complicated in proportion to the space that it occupies (yet, considering the importance of the subject it deals with, it is far from too lengthy); however, it is in no way extraneous, because the details are selected in order to allude to the subject of the book. The examples are taken from a greater realm, but what happens in the greater can repeat itself in the lesser, and the misunderstanding is similar, even if there are less harmful consequences. He who presumes to develop the system[30] is responsible for much, but he who writes a monograph can and also ought to be faithful over a little.[31]

The present work has set as its task the psychological treatment of the concept of "anxiety," but in such a way that it constantly keeps *in mente* [in mind] and before its eye the dogma of hereditary sin. Accordingly, it must also, although tacitly so, deal with the concept of sin. Sin, however, is no subject for psychological concern, and only by submitting to the service of a misplaced brilliance could it be dealt with psychologically. Sin has its specific place, or more correctly, it has no place, and this is its specific nature. When sin is treated in a place other than its own, it is altered by being subjected to a nonessential refraction of reflection. The concept is altered, and thereby the mood that properly corresponds to the correct concept* is also disturbed, and instead of the endurance of the true mood there is the fleeting phantom of false moods. Thus when sin is brought into esthetics, the mood becomes either light-minded or melancholy, for the category in which sin lies is that of contradiction, and this is either comic or

* That science, just as much as poetry and art, presupposes a mood in the creator as well as in the observer, and that an error in the modulation is just as disturbing as an error in the development of thought, have been entirely forgotten in our time, when inwardness has been completely forgotten, and also the category of appropriation, because of the joy over all the glory men thought they possessed or in their greed have given up as did the dog that
preferred the shadow.[32] Yet every error gives birth to its own enemy. Outside of itself, the error of thought has dialectics as its enemy, and outside of itself, the absence or falsification of mood has the comical as its enemy.

tragic. The mood is therefore altered, because the mood that corresponds to sin is earnestness. The concept of sin is also altered, because, whether it become comic or tragic, it becomes in any case something that endures, or something nonessential that is annulled, whereas, according to its true concept, sin is to be overcome. In a deeper sense, the comic and the tragic have no enemy but only a bogeyman at which one either weeps or laughs.

If sin is dealt with in metaphysics, the mood becomes that of dialectical uniformity and disinterestedness, which ponder sin as something that cannot withstand the scrutiny of thought. The concept of sin is also altered, for sin is indeed to be overcome, yet not as something to which thought is unable to give life, but as that which is, and as such concerns every man.

If sin is dealt with in psychology, the mood becomes that of persistent observation, like the fearlessness of a secret agent, but not that of the victorious flight of earnestness out of sin. The concept becomes a different concept, for sin becomes a state. However, sin is not a state. Its idea is that its concept is continually annulled. As a state (*de potentia* [according to possibility]), it is not, but *de actu* or *in actu* [according to actuality or in actuality] it is, again and again. The mood of psychology would be antipathetic curiosity, whereas the proper mood is earnestness expressed in courageous resistance. The mood of psychology is that of a discovering anxiety, and in its anxiety psychology portrays sin, while again and again it is in anxiety over the portrayal that it itself brings forth. When sin is dealt with in this manner, it becomes the stronger, because psychology relates itself to it in a feminine way. That this state has its truth is certain; that it occurs more or less in every human life before the ethical manifests itself is certain. But in being considered in this manner sin does not become what it is, but a more or a less.

Whenever the issue of sin is dealt with, one can observe by the very mood whether the concept is the correct one. For instance, whenever sin is spoken of as a disease, an abnormality, a poison, or a disharmony, the concept is falsified.

Sin does not properly belong in any science,[33] but it is the subject of the sermon, in which the single individual speaks as the single individual to the single individual. In our day, scientific self-importance has tricked pastors into becoming something like professorial clerks who also serve science and find it beneath their dignity to preach. Is it any wonder then that preaching has come to be regarded as a very lowly art? But to preach is really the most difficult of all arts and is essentially the art that Socrates praised, the art of being able to converse. It goes without saying that the need is not for someone in the congregation to provide an answer, or that it would be of help continually to introduce a respondent. What Socrates criticized in the Sophists, when he made the distinction that they indeed knew how to make speeches but not how to converse,[34] was that they could talk at length about every subject but lacked the element of appropriation. Appropriation is precisely the secret of conversation.

Corresponding to the concept of sin is earnestness. Now ethics should be a science in which sin might be expected to find a place. But here there is a great difficulty. Ethics is still an ideal science, and not only in the sense that every science is ideal. Ethics proposes to bring ideality into actuality. On the other hand, it is not the nature of its movement to raise actuality up into ideality.* Ethics points to ideality as a task and assumes that every man possesses the requisite conditions. Thus ethics develops a contradiction, inasmuch as it makes clear both the difficulty and the impossibility. What is said of the law[35] is also true of ethics: it is a disciplinarian that demands, and by its demands only judges but does not bring forth life. Only Greek ethics made an exception, and that was because it was not ethics in the proper sense but retained an esthetic factor. This appears clearly in its definition of virtue[36] and in what Aristotle frequently, also in *Ethica Nicomachea*,

---

* If this is considered more carefully, there will be occasions enough to notice the brilliance of heading the last section of the *Logic* "Actuality," inasmuch as ethics never reaches it. The actuality with which logic ends means, therefore, no more in regard to actuality than the "being" with which it begins.

states with amiable Greek naiveté, namely, that virtue alone does not make a man happy and content, but he must have health, friends, and earthly goods and be happy in his family. The more ideal ethics is, the better. It must not permit itself to be distracted by the babble that it is useless to require the impossible. For even to listen to such talk is unethical and is something for which ethics has neither *time* nor *opportunity*. Ethics will have nothing to do with bargaining; nor can one in this way reach actuality. To reach actuality, the whole movement must be reversed. This ideal characteristic of ethics is what tempts one to use first metaphysical, then esthetic, and then psychological categories in the treatment of it. But ethics, more than any other science, must resist such temptations. It is, therefore, impossible for anyone to write an ethics without having altogether different categories in reserve.

Sin, then, belongs to ethics only insofar as upon this concept it is shipwrecked with the aid of repentance.* If ethics is

IV
290

* In his work *Fear and Trembling* (Copenhagen: 1843), Johannes de Silentio makes several observations concerning this point. In this book, the author several times allows the desired ideality of esthetics to be shipwrecked on the required ideality of ethics, in order through these collisions to bring to light the religious ideality as the ideality that precisely is the ideality of actuality, and therefore just as desirable as that of esthetics and not as impossible as the ideality of ethics. This is accomplished in such a way that the religious ideality breaks forth in the dialectical leap and in the positive mood—"Behold all things have become new"[37] as well as in the negative mood that is the passion of the absurd to which the concept "repetition" corresponds. Either all of existence [*Tilværelsen*] comes to an end in the demand of ethics, or the condition is provided and the whole of life and of existence begins anew, not through an immanent continuity with the former existence, which is a contradiction, but through a transcendence. This transcendence separates repetition from the former existence [*Tilværelse*] by such a chasm that one can only figuratively say that the former and the latter relate themselves to each other as the totality of living creatures in the ocean relates itself to those in the air and to those upon the earth. Yet, according to the opinion of some natural scientists, the former as a prototype prefigures in its imperfection all that the latter reveals. With regard to this category, one may consult *Repetition* by Constantin Constantius (Copenhagen: 1843). This is no doubt a witty book, as the author also intended it to be. To my knowledge, he is indeed the first to have a lively understanding of "repetition" and to have allowed the preg-

IV
289

IV
290

to include sin, its ideality comes to an end. The more ethics remains in its ideality, and never becomes so inhuman as to lose sight of actuality, but corresponds to actuality by presenting itself as the task for every man in such a way that it will make him the true and the whole man, the man κατ' ἐξοχήν

---

nancy of the concept to be seen in the explanation of the relation of the ethnical and the Christian,[38] by directing attention to the invisible point and to the *discrimen rerum* [turning point] where one science breaks against another until a new science comes to light. But what he has discovered he has concealed again by arraying the concept in the jest of an analogous conception. What has motivated him to do this is difficult to say, or more correctly, difficult to understand. He himself mentions that he writes in this manner so "that the heretics would not understand him."[39] Since he wanted to occupy himself with repetition only esthetically and psychologically, everything had to be arranged humorously so as to bring about the impression that the word in one instant means everything and in the next instant the most insignificant of things, and the transition, or rather the constant falling down from the clouds, is motivated by its farcical opposite. In the meantime, he has stated the whole matter very precisely on page 34:[40] "repetition is the interest [*Interesse*] of metaphysics, and also the interest upon which metaphysics comes to grief; repetition is the watchword [*Løsnet*] in every ethical view; repetition is *conditio sine qua non* [the indispensable condition] for every issue of dogmatics." The first statement has reference to the thesis that metaphysics as such is disinterested, something that Kant[41] had said about esthetics. As soon as interest steps forth, metaphysics steps aside. For this reason, the word is italicized. In actuality, the whole interest of subjectivity steps forth, and now metaphysics runs aground. If repetition is not posited, ethics becomes a binding power. No doubt it is for this reason that the author states that repetition is the watchword in every ethical view. If repetition is not posited, dogmatics cannot exist at all, for repetition begins in faith, and faith is the organ for issues of dogma. In the realm of nature, repetition is present in its immovable necessity. In the realm of the spirit, the task is not to wrest a change from repetition or to find oneself moderately comfortable during the repetition, as if spirit stood only in an external relation to the repetition of spirit (according to which good and evil would alternate like summer and winter), but to transform repetition into something inward, into freedom's own task, into its highest interest, so that while everything else changes, it can actually realize repetition. At this point the finite spirit despairs. This is something Constantin has suggested by stepping aside himself and by allowing repetition to break forth in the young man by virtue of the religious. For this reason Constantin mentions several times that repetition is a religious category, too transcendent for him, that it is the movement by virtue of the absurd, and on page 142[42] it is further stated that eternity is the true repetition. All of this Professor Heiberg failed to notice. Instead, through his learn-

[in an eminent sense], the more it increases the tension of the difficulty. In the struggle to actualize the task of ethics, sin shows itself not as something that belongs only accidentally to the accidental individual, but as something that withdraws deeper and deeper as a deeper and deeper presupposition, as a presupposition that goes beyond the individual. Then all is lost for ethics, and ethics has helped to bring about the loss of all. A category that lies entirely beyond its reach has appeared. *Hereditary sin* makes everything still more desperate, that is, it removes the difficulty, yet not with the help of ethics but with the help of *dogmatics.* As all ancient knowledge and speculation was based on the presupposition that thought has reality [*Realitet*], so all ancient ethics was based on the presupposition that virtue can be realized. Sin's skepticism is altogether foreign to paganism. Sin is for the ethical consciousness what error is for the knowledge of it—the particular exception that proves nothing.

With dogmatics begins the science that, in contrast to that science called ideal *stricte* [in the strict sense], namely, ethics, proceeds from actuality. It begins with the actual in order to raise it up into ideality. It does not deny the presence of sin; on the contrary, it presupposes it and explains it by presupposing hereditary sin. However, since dogmatics is very seldom treated purely, hereditary sin is often brought within its confines in such a way that the impression of the heterogeneous originality of dogmatics does not always come clearly

IV
292

ing, which like his *New Year's Gift*[43] is superbly elegant and neat, he kindly wished to help this work [*Repetition*] to become a tasteful and elegant triviality by pompously bringing the matter to the point where Constantin begins, or, to recall a recent work, by bringing the matter to the point where the esthete in *Either/Or* had brought it in "The Rotation of Crops." If Constantin had actually felt himself flattered by enjoying the singular honor of having been brought into such undeniably select company in this manner, he must, in my opinion, since he wrote the book, have gone stark mad. But if, on the other hand, an author such as he, writing to be misunderstood, forgot himself and did not have ataraxia enough to count it to his credit that Professor Heiberg had failed to understand him, he must again be stark mad. This is something I need not fear, since the circumstance that hitherto he has made no reply to Professor Heiberg indicates sufficiently that he understands himself.

into view but becomes confused. This also happens when one finds in it a dogma concerning angels,[44] concerning the Holy Scriptures, etc. Therefore dogmatics must not explain hereditary sin[45] but rather explain it by presupposing it, like that vortex about which Greek speculation concerning nature had so much to say,[46] a moving something that no science can grasp.

That such is the case with dogmatics will readily be granted if once again time is taken to understand Schleiermacher's immortal service[47] to this science. He was left behind long ago when men chose Hegel. Yet Schleiermacher was a thinker in the beautiful Greek sense, a thinker who spoke only of what he knew. Hegel, on the contrary, despite all his outstanding ability and stupendous learning, reminds us again and again by his performance that he was in the German sense a professor of philosophy on a large scale, because he à *tout prix* [at any price] must explain all things.

So the new science begins with dogmatics[48] in the same sense that immanental science begins with metaphysics. Here ethics again finds its place as the science that has as a task for actuality the dogmatic consciousness of actuality. This ethics does not ignore sin, and it does not have its ideality in making ideal demands; rather, it has its ideality in the penetrating consciousness of actuality, of the actuality of sin, but note carefully, not with metaphysical light-mindedness or with psychological concupiscence.

It is easy to see the difference in the movements, to see that the ethics of which we are now speaking belongs to a different order of things. The first ethics was shipwrecked on the sinfulness of the single individual. Therefore, instead of being able to explain this sinfulness, the first ethics fell into an even greater and ethically more enigmatic difficulty, since the sin of the individual expanded into the sin of the whole race.[49] At this point, dogmatics came to the rescue with hereditary sin. The new ethics presupposes dogmatics, and by means of hereditary sin it explains the sin of the single individual, while at the same time it sets ideality as a task, not by a movement from above and downward but from below and upward.

It is common knowledge that Aristotle used the term πρώτη φιλοσοφία [first philosophy][50] primarily to designate metaphysics, though he included within it a part that according to our conception belongs to theology. In paganism it is quite in order for theology to be treated there. It is related to the same lack of an infinite penetrating reflection that endowed the theater in paganism with reality as a kind of divine worship. If we now abstract from this ambiguity, we could retain the designation and by πρώτη φιλοσοφία* understand that totality of science which we might call "ethnical," whose essence is immanence and is expressed in Greek thought by "recollection," and by *secunda philosophia* [second philosophy] understand that totality of science whose essence is transcendence or repetition.**

The concept of sin does not properly belong in any science; only the second ethics can deal with its manifestation, but not with its coming into existence [*Tilblivelse*]. If any other science were to treat of it, the concept would be confused. To get closer to our present project, such would also be the case if psychology were to do so.

The subject of which psychology treats must be something in repose that remains in a restless repose, not something restless that always either produces itself or is repressed. But this abiding something out of which sin constantly arises, not by necessity (for a becoming by necessity is a state, as, for example, the whole history of the plant is a state) but by freedom—this abiding something, this predisposing presupposition, sin's real possibility, is a subject of interest for psychology. That which can be the concern of psychology and

IV
294

---

* Schelling[51] called attention to this Aristotelian term in support of his own distinction between negative and positive philosophy. By negative philosophy he meant "logic"; that was clear enough. On the other hand, it was less clear to me what he really meant by positive philosophy, except insofar as it became evident that it was the philosophy that he himself wished to provide. However, since I have nothing to go by except my own opinion, it is not feasible to pursue this subject further.

** Constantin Constantius has called attention to this by pointing out that immanence runs aground upon "interest." With this concept, actuality for the first time properly comes into view.

IV
293

with which it can occupy itself is not that sin comes into existence [*bliver til*], but how it can come into existence. Psychology can bring its concern to the point where it seems as if sin were there, but the next thing, that sin is there, is qualitatively different from the first. The manner in which this presupposition for scrupulous psychological contemplation and observation appears to be more and more comprehensive is the interest of psychology. Psychology may abandon itself, so to speak, to the disappointment that sin is there as an actuality. But this last disappointment reveals the impotence of psychology and merely shows that its service has come to an end.

That human nature is so constituted that it makes sin possible is, psychologically speaking, quite correct, but wanting to make the possibility of sin its actuality is revolting to ethics, and to dogmatics it sounds like blasphemy, because freedom is never possible; as soon as it is, it is actual, in the same sense as it was said in an older philosophy that if God's existence [*Tilværelse*] is possible, it is necessary.[52]

As soon as sin is actually posited, ethics is immediately on the spot, and now ethics follows every move sin makes. How sin came into the world is not the concern of ethics, apart from the fact that it is certain that sin came into the world as sin. But still less than the concern of ethics with sin's coming into existence is its concern with the still-life of sin's possibility.

If one asks more specifically in what sense and to what extent psychology pursues the observation of its object, it is obvious in itself and from the preceding that every observation of the actuality of sin as an object of thought is irrelevant to it and that as observation it does not belong to ethics, for ethics is never observing but always accusing, judging, and acting. Furthermore, it is obvious in itself as well as from the preceding that psychology has nothing to do with the detail of the empirically actual except insofar as this lies outside of sin. Indeed, as a science psychology can never deal empirically with the detail that belongs to its domain, but the more concrete psychology becomes, the more the detail attains a scientific representation. In our day, this science, which indeed more than any other is allowed almost to intoxicate itself in the foaming multifariousness of life, has become as abstemious and ascetic as a flagellant. However, this is not the fault of science but of its devotees. On the other hand, when it comes to sin, the whole content of actuality is denied to psychology. Only the possibility of sin still belongs to it. But for ethics the possibility of sin never occurs.[53] Ethics never allows itself to be fooled and does not waste time on such deliberations. Psychology, on the other hand, loves these, and as it sits and traces the contours and calculates the angles of possibility, it does not allow itself to be disturbed any more than did Archimedes.

As psychology now becomes deeply absorbed in the possibility of sin, it is unwittingly in the service of another science that only waits for it to finish so that it can begin and assist psychology to the explanation. This science is not ethics, for ethics has nothing at all to do with this possibility. This science is dogmatics, and here in turn the issue of hereditary sin appears. While psychology thoroughly explores the real possibility of sin, dogmatics explains hereditary sin, that is, the ideal possibility of sin. The second ethics, however, has nothing to do with the possibility of sin or with hereditary sin. The first ethics ignores sin. The second ethics has the actuality of sin within its scope, and here psychology can intrude only through a misunderstanding.

If what has been developed here is correct, it is easily seen that the author is quite justified in calling the present work a psychological deliberation, and also how this deliberation, insofar as it becomes conscious of its relation to science, belongs to the domain of psychology and in turn tends toward dogmatics.[54] Psychology has been called the doctrine of the subjective spirit.[55] If this is pursued more accurately,[56] it will become apparent how psychology, when it comes to the issue of sin, must first pass over [*slaa over*] into the doctrine of the absolute spirit. Here lies the place of dogmatics. The first

IV
296

ethics presupposes metaphysics; the second ethics presupposes dogmatics but completes it also in such a way that here, as everywhere, the presupposition is brought out.

This was the task of the introduction. The introduction may be correct, while the deliberation itself concerning the concept of anxiety may be entirely incorrect. Whether this is the case remains to be seen.

I

Anxiety as the Presupposition of Hereditary Sin and as Explaining Hereditary Sin Retrogressively in Terms of Its Origin

§1.[1]
HISTORICAL INTIMATIONS REGARDING THE CONCEPT OF HEREDITARY SIN

Is the concept of hereditary sin identical with the concept of the first sin, Adam's sin, the fall of man? At times it has been understood so, and then the task of explaining hereditary sin has become identical with explaining Adam's sin. When thought met with difficulties, an expedient was seized upon. In order to explain at least something, a fantastic presupposition was introduced, the loss of which constituted the fall as the consequence. The advantage gained thereby was that everyone willingly admitted that a condition such as the one described was not found anywhere in the world, but that they forgot that as a result the doubt became a different one, namely, whether such a condition ever had existed, something that was quite necessary in order to lose it. The history of the human race acquired a fantastic beginning. Adam was fantastically placed outside this history. Pious feeling and fantasy got what they demanded, a godly prelude, but thought got nothing. In a double sense, Adam was held fantastically outside. The presupposition was dialectical-fantastic, especially in Catholicism (Adam lost *donum divinitus datum supra-naturale et admirable* [a supernatural and wonderful gift bestowed by God]).[2] It was historical-fantastic, especially in the federal theology,[3] which lost itself dramatically in a fantasy view of Adam's appearance as a plenipotentiary for the whole race. Obviously neither explanation explains anything. The one merely explains away what it has fictitiously composed; the other merely composes fiction that explains nothing.

Does the concept of hereditary sin differ from the concept of the first sin in such a way that the particular individual participates in inherited sin only through his relation to Adam and not through his primitive relation to sin? In that case Adam is placed fantastically outside history. Adam's sin is then more than something past (*plus quam perfectum* [pluperfect]). Hereditary sin is something present; it is sinfulness, and Adam is the only one in whom it was not found, since it came into being through him. Hence one would not try to explain Adam's sin but instead would explain hereditary sin in terms of its consequences. However, the explanation is not suitable for thought. One can therefore readily understand that one of the symbolical books declares the impossibility of an explanation, and that this declaration without contradiction gives the explanation. The *Smalcald Articles*[4] teach distinctly: *peccatum haereditarium tam profunda et tetra est corruptio naturae, ut nullius hominis ratione intelligi possit, sed ex scripturae patefactione agnoscenda et credenda sit* [hereditary sin is so profound and detestable a corruption in human nature that it cannot be comprehended by human understanding, but must be known and believed from the revelation of the Scriptures]. This statement is easily reconciled with the explanations, for in these it is not so much rational definitions as such that are brought forth, but a pious feeling (with an ethical tone) that gives vent to its indignation over hereditary sin. This feeling assumes the role of an accuser, who with an almost feminine passion and with the fanaticism of a girl in love is now concerned only with making sinfulness and his own participation in it more and more detestable, and in such a manner that no word can be severe enough to describe the single individual's participation in it. If with this in mind one reviews the different confessions, a gradation appears in which the profound Protestant piety is victorious. The Greek Church speaks of hereditary sin as the sin of the ἁμάρτημα πρωτοπατορικόν [first father].[5] It does not even have a concept, for the term is only an historical designation, which does not, like the concept, designate what is present, but only what is historically concluded. *Vitium originis* [vice of origin] (Tertullian)[6] is indeed a concept; nevertheless, its linguistic form allows for the conception of the historical as the predominant factor. *Peccatum originale* [original sin], because it has been *quia originaliter tradatur* [transmitted from the origin] (Augustine), designates the concept, which is still more clearly defined by the distinction between *peccatum originans* and *originatum* [sin as a cause and as caused]. Protestantism rejects the Scholastic definitions, *carentia imaginis dei, defectus justitiae originalis* [the absence of the image of God, the loss of original righteousness],[7] as well as the view that hereditary sin is *poena* [punishment]. *Concupiscentiam poenam esse non peccatum, disputant adversarii* [our adversaries contend that concupiscence is punishment and not a sin] (*Apologia A.C.*).[8] And now begins the enthusiastic climax: *vitium, peccatum, reatus, culpa* [vice, sin, guilt, transgression].[9] Because the only concern is the eloquence of the contrite soul, a quite contradictory thought (*nunc quoque afferens iram dei iis, qui secundum exemplum Adami peccarunt* [which now brings the wrath of God upon them that have sinned after the example of Adam]) can occasionally be introduced into the discussion of hereditary sin. Or a rhetorical concern, with no consideration whatever for thought, makes the most terrifying pronouncement about hereditary sin: *quo fit, ut omnes propter inobedientiam Adae et Hevae in odio apud deum simus* [from which it follows that all of us, because of the disobedience of Adam and Eve, are hated by God]—*Formula of Concord*.[10] The *Formula* is nevertheless circumspect enough to protest against thinking this, for if one were to think it, sin would become man's substance.* As soon as the enthusiasm of faith and contrition disappear, one can no longer be helped by such determinations, which only make it easy for cunning prudence to escape the recognition of sin. But to need other determinations is after all a dubious proof of the perfection of our age, quite in the same sense as that of needing other than Draconian laws.[11]

IV
300

---

* The fact that the *Formula of Concord* forbade thinking this concept must nonetheless be commended as proof of the energetic passion by which it knows how to let thought collide with the unthinkable, an energy that is very admirable in contrast to modern thought, which is all too slack.

IV
299

The fantastic presentation that is evident here repeats itself consistently at another point in dogmatics, namely, in the Atonement. It is taught that Christ has made satisfaction for hereditary sin. But what then happens to Adam? Was not he the one who brought hereditary sin into the world? Was not hereditary sin an actual sin in him? Or does hereditary sin signify the same for Adam as for everyone in the race? In that case, the concept is canceled. Or was Adam's whole life hereditary sin? Did not the first sin beget other sins in him, i.e., actual sins? The error in the preceding is here more evident, for as a result of this Adam is now so fantastically placed outside of history that he is the only one who is excluded from the Atonement.

No matter how the problem is raised, as soon as Adam is placed fantastically on the outside, everything is confused. To explain Adam's sin is therefore to explain hereditary sin. And no explanation that explains Adam but not hereditary sin, or explains hereditary sin but not Adam, is of any help. The most profound reason for this is what is essential to human existence: that man is *individuum* and as such simultaneously himself and the whole race, and in such a way that the whole race participates in the individual and the individual in the whole race.* If this is not held fast, one will fall either into the Pelagian, Socinian, and philanthropic singular[12] or into the fantastic. The matter-of-factness of the understanding is that the race is numerically resolved into an *einmal ein* [one times one]. What is fantastical is that Adam enjoys the well-meant honor of being more than the whole race or the ambiguous honor of standing outside the race.

At every moment, the individual is both himself and the race. This[13] is man's perfection viewed as a state. It is also a contradiction, but a contradiction is always the expression of a task, and a task is movement, but a movement that as a task is the same as that to which the task is directed is an historical

IV
301

IV
300
* If a particular individual could fall away entirely from the race, his falling away would require a different qualification of the race. Whereas if an animal should fall away from the species, the species would remain entirely unaffected.

movement.[14] Hence the individual has a history. But i
individual has a history, then the race also has a history.
individual has the same perfection, and precisely because of
this individuals do not fall apart from one another numerically any more than the concept of race is a phantom. Every
individual is essentially interested in the history of all other
individuals, and just as essentially as in his own. Perfection in
oneself is therefore the perfect participation in the whole. No
individual is indifferent to the history of the race any more
than the race is indifferent to the history of the individual. As
the history of the race moves on, the individual begins constantly anew, because he is both himself and the race, and by
this, in turn, the history of the race.

Adam is the first man. He is at once himself and the race. It
is not by virtue of the esthetically beautiful that we hold on to
him, nor is it by virtue of a magnanimous feeling that we join
ourselves to him in order, as it were, not to leave him in the
lurch as the one who was responsible for everything. It is not
by virtue of a zealous sympathy and the persuasion of piety
that we resolve to share his guilt with him the way a child
wishes to be guilty along with the father. It is not by virtue of
a forced compassion that teaches us to put up with that
which, after all, cannot be otherwise, but it is by virtue of
thought that we hold fast to him. Consequently, every attempt to explain Adam's significance for the race as *caput
generis humani naturale, seminale, foederale* [head of the human
race by nature, by generation, by covenant],[15] to recall the
expression of dogmatics, confuses everything. He is not essentially different from the race, for in that case there is no
race at all; he is not the race, for in that case also there would
be no race. He is himself and the race. Therefore that which
explains Adam also explains the race and vice versa.

§2.
THE CONCEPT OF THE FIRST SIN

According to traditional concepts, the difference between
Adam's first sin and the first sin of every other man is this:

Adam's sin conditions sinfulness as a consequence, the other first sin presupposes sinfulness as a state. Were this so, Adam would actually stand outside the race, and the race would not have begun with him but would have had a beginning outside itself, something that is contrary to every concept.

That the *first* sin signifies something different from *a* sin (i.e., a sin like many others), something different from *one* sin (i.e., no. 1 in relation to no. 2), is quite obvious. The first sin constitutes the nature of the quality:[16] the first sin is the sin. This is the secret of the first, and is an offense to abstract common sense, which maintains that one time amounts to nothing but that many times amounts to something, which is preposterous, since many times signifies either that each particular time is just as much as the first or that all of the times, when added together, are not nearly as much. It is therefore a superstition when it is maintained in logic that through a continued quantification a new quality is brought forth. It is an unforgivable reticence when one makes no secret of the fact that things indeed do not happen quite that way in the world and yet conceals the consequence of this for the whole of logical immanence by permitting it to drift into logical movement as does Hegel.* The new quality appears with the first, with the leap, with the suddeness of the enigmatic.

If the first sin means *one* sin in the numerical sense, no history can result from it, and sin will have no history, either in the individual or in the race. For the conditionality is the same

IV
303 (margin)

IV
302 (margin)

* After all, this proposition about the relation between a quantitative determination and a new quality has a long history. Strictly speaking, all of Greek sophistry merely consisted in affirming a quantitative determination; consequently its highest diversity was that of likeness and unlikeness. In recent philosophy, Schelling[17] was the first to make use of a quantitative determination to account for all diversity. Later he reproved Eschenmayer for doing the same (in his doctoral disputation). Hegel made use of the leap, but in logic. Rosenkranz (in his *Psychology*) admires Hegel for this. In his latest publication (dealing with Schelling), Rosenkranz[18] reproves Schelling and praises Hegel. However, Hegel's misfortune is exactly that he wants to maintain the new quality and yet does not want to do it, since he wants to do it in logic, which, as soon as this is recognized, must acquire a different consciousness of itself and of its significance.

IV
303 (margin)

for both, although the history of the race is not that of the individual any more than the history of the individual is that of the race, except insofar as the contradiction continually expresses the task.

Through the first sin, sin came into the world.[19] Precisely in the same way it is true of every subsequent man's first sin, that through it sin comes into the world. That it was not in the world before Adam's first sin is, in relation to sin itself, something entirely accidental and irrelevant. It is of no significance at all and cannot justify making Adam's sin greater or the first sin of every other man lesser. It is indeed a logical and ethical heresy to wish to give the appearance that sinfulness[20] in a man determines itself quantitatively until at last, through a *generatio aequivoca* [descent without mating], it brings forth the first sin in a man. But this does not take place any more than Trop,[21] who by being a master in the service of quantitative determination, could thereby attain a degree in jurisprudence. Let mathematicians and astronomers save themselves if they can with infinitely disappearing minute magnitudes, but in life itself this does not help a man to obtain his examination papers, and much less to explain spirit. If every subsequent man's first sin were thus brought about by sinfulness, his first sin would only in a nonessential way be qualified as the first, and be essentially qualified—if this is thinkable—by its serial number in the universal sinking fund of the race. But this is not the case. It is equally foolish, illogical, unethical, and un-Christian to court the honor of being the first inventor and then to shirk one's responsibility by being unwilling to think something, by saying that one has done nothing more than what everyone else has done. The presence of sinfulness in a man, the power of the example, etc.—these are only quantitative determinations that explain nothing,* unless it be assumed that one individual is the race, whereas every individual is both himself and the race.

The Genesis story of the first sin, especially in our day, has

---

* What significance they have otherwise in the history of the race or as preliminary runs to the leap, without being able to explain the leap, is something else.

been regarded somewhat carelessly as a myth.[22] There is a good reason why it has, because what was substituted in its place was precisely a myth, and a poor one at that. When the understanding takes to the mythical, the outcome is seldom more than small talk. The Genesis story presents the only dialectically consistent view. Its whole content is really concentrated in one statement: *Sin came into the world by a sin.* Were this not so, sin would have come into the world as something accidental, which one would do well not to explain. The difficulty for the understanding is precisely the triumph of the explanation and its profound consequence, namely, that sin presupposes itself, that sin comes into the world in such a way that by the fact that it is, it is presupposed. Thus sin comes into the world as the sudden, i.e., by a leap; but this leap also posits the quality, and since the quality is posited, the leap in that very moment is turned into the quality and is presupposed by the quality and the quality by the leap. To the understanding, this is an offense; *ergo* it is a myth. As a compensation, the understanding invents its own myth, which denies the leap and explains the circle as a straight line, and now everything proceeds quite naturally. The understanding talks fantastically about man's state prior to the fall, and, in the course of the small talk, the projected innocence is changed little by little into sinfulness, and so there it is. The lecture of the understanding may on this occasion be compared with the counting rhyme in which children delight:[23] one-nis-ball, two-nis-balls, three-nis-balls, etc., up to nine-nis-balls and tennis balls. Here it is, brought about quite naturally by the preceding. Insofar as the myth of the understanding is supposed to contain anything, it would be that sinfulness precedes sin. But if this were true in the sense that sinfulness has come in by something other than sin, the concept would be canceled. But if it comes in by sin, then sin is prior to sinfulness. This contradiction is the only dialectical consequence that accommodates both the leap and the immanence (i.e., the subsequent immanence).

IV
305   By Adam's first sin, *sin came into the world*. This statement, which is the common one, nevertheless contains an altogether

outward reflection that doubtless has contributed greatly to the rise of vague misunderstanding. That sin came into the world is quite true. But this does not really concern Adam. To express this precisely and accurately, one must say that by the first sin, sinfulness came into Adam. It could not occur to anyone to say about any subsequent man that by his first sin sinfulness came into the world; and yet it comes into the world by him in a similar way (i.e., in a way not essentially different), because, expressed precisely and accurately, sinfulness is in the world only insofar as it comes into the world by sin.

That this has been expressed differently in the case of Adam is only because the consequence of his fantastic relation to the race should become evident everywhere. His sin is hereditary sin. Apart from this, nothing is known about him. But hereditary sin, as seen in Adam, is only that first sin. Is Adam, then, the only individual who has no history? If so, the race has its beginning with an individual who is not an individual, and thereby the concepts of race and individual are both canceled. If any other individual in the race can by its history have significance in the history of the race, then Adam has it also. If Adam has it only by virtue of that first sin, the concept of history[24] is canceled, i.e., history has come to an end in the very moment it began.*

Since the race does not begin anew with every individual,** the sinfulness of the race does indeed acquire a history. Meanwhile, this proceeds in quantitative determinations while the individual participates in it by the qualitative leap. For this reason the race does not begin anew with every indi-

* The problem is always that of getting Adam included as a member of the race, and precisely in the same sense in which every other individual is included. This is something to which dogmatics should pay attention, especially for the sake of the Atonement. The doctrine that Adam and Christ correspond to each other[25] explains nothing at all but confuses everything. It may be an analogy, but the analogy is conceptually imperfect. Christ alone is an individual who is more than an individual. For this reason he does not come in the beginning but in the fullness of time.

** The contrary is expressed in §1. As the history of the race moves on, the individual continually begins anew.

vidual, in which case there would be no race at all, but every individual begins anew with the race.

In saying that Adam's sin brought the sin of the race into the world, one may understand this fantastically, in which case every concept is canceled, or one may be equally justified in saying this about every individual who by his own first sin brings sinfulness into the world. To let the race begin with an individual who stands outside the race is as much a myth of the understanding as is that of letting sinfulness begin in any other way than with sin. What is accomplished is merely to delay the problem, which naturally turns now to man no. 2 for the explanation or, more correctly, to man no. 1, since no. 1 has now become no. 0.

What often misleads and brings people to all kinds of fantastic imaginings is the problem of the relation of generations, as though the subsequent man were essentially different from the first by virtue of descent. Descent, however, is only the expression for the continuity in the history of the race, which always moves by quantitative determinations and therefore is incapable of bringing forth an individual. A species of animals, although it has preserved itself through thousands of generations, never brings forth an individual. If the second human being were not descended from Adam, he would never have been the second but only an empty repetition from which could have been derived neither race nor individual. Every particular Adam would have become a statue by himself, and hence qualified only by an indifferent determination, i.e., number, and in a much more imperfect sense than the "blue boys"[26] who are named by number. At most, every particular man would have been himself, not himself and the race, and would never have acquired a history, just as an angel has no history but is only himself without participating in any history.

It hardly needs to be said that this view is not guilty of Pelagianism, which permits every individual to play his little history in his own private theater unconcerned about the race. For the history of the race proceeds quietly on its course, and in this no individual begins at the same place as another, but

every individual begins anew, and in the same moment he is
at the place where he should begin in history.

§3.

THE CONCEPT OF INNOCENCE

IV
306

Here, as everywhere, it is true that if one wants to maintain a
dogmatic definition in our day, one must begin by forgetting
what Hegel has discovered in order to help dogmatics. One
gets a queer feeling when at this point one finds in works on
dogmatics,[27] which otherwise propose to be somewhat or-
thodox, a reference to Hegel's favored remark[28] that the nature of the immediate is to be annulled, as though immediacy
and innocence were exactly identical. Hegel[29] has quite consistently volatilized every dogmatic concept just enough to
appeal to a man of reduced existence as a clever expression for
the logical. That the immediate must be annulled, we do not
need Hegel to tell us, nor does he deserve immortal merit for
having said it, since it is not even logically correct, for the
immediate is not to be annulled, because it at no time exists
[*er til*]. The concept of immediacy belongs in logic; the concept of innocence, on the other hand, belongs in ethics. Every
concept must be dealt with by the science to which it belongs,
whether the concept belongs to the science in such a way that
it is developed there or is developed by being presupposed.

IV
307

It is indeed unethical to say that innocence must be annulled, for even if it were annulled at the moment this is uttered, ethics forbids us to forget that it is annulled only by
guilt. Therefore, if one speaks of innocence as immediacy and
is logically offensive and rude enough to have let this fleeting
thing vanish, or if one is esthetically sensitive about what it
was and the fact that it has vanished, he is merely *geistreich*
[clever] and forgets the point.

Just as Adam lost innocence by guilt, so every man loses it
in the same way. If it was not by guilt that he lost it, then it
was not innocence that he lost; and if he was not innocent before becoming guilty, he never became guilty.

As for Adam's innocence, there has been no lack of fantastic notions, whether these attained symbolic dignity in times when the velvet on the church pulpit as well as on the origin of the race was less threadbare than now or whether they floated about more romantically like the suspicious inventions of fiction. The more fantastically Adam was arrayed, the more inexplicable became the fact that he could sin and the more appalling became his sin. As it was, he had once and for all forfeited all the glory, and about that, whenever it suited them, men became sentimental or witty, melancholy or frivolous, historically contrite or fantastically cheerful, but the point of it they did not grasp ethically.

IV
308

As for the innocence of subsequent men (i.e., all with the exception of Adam and Eve), there has been only a faint conception. Ethical rigor overlooked the limit of the ethical and was honest enough to believe that men would not avail themselves of the opportunity to slip away from the whole thing when escape was made so easy. Light-mindedness grasped nothing at all. But innocence is lost only by guilt. Every man loses innocence essentially in the same way that Adam lost it. It is not in the interest of ethics to make all men except Adam into concerned and interested spectators of guiltiness but not participants in guiltiness, nor is it in the interest of dogmatics to make all men into interested and sympathetic spectators of the Atonement [*Forsoning*] but not participants in the Atonement.

That the time of dogmatics and ethics, as well as one's own time, has often been wasted by pondering what might have happened had Adam not sinned merely proves that one brings along an incorrect mood, and consequently an incorrect concept. It would never occur to the innocent person to ask such a question, and when the guilty asks it, he sins, for in his esthetic curiosity he ignores that he himself brought guiltiness into the world and that he himself lost innocence by guilt.

Innocence, unlike immediacy, is not something that must be annulled, something whose quality is to be annulled, something that properly does not exist [*er til*], but rather, when it is annulled, and as a result of being annulled, it for the first time comes into existence [*bliver til*] as that which it was before being annulled and which now is annulled. Immediacy is not annulled by mediacy, but when mediacy appears, in that same moment it has annulled immediacy.[30] The annulment of immediacy is therefore an immanent movement within immediacy, or it is an immanent movement in the opposite direction within mediacy, by which mediacy presupposes immediacy. Innocence is something that is canceled by a transcendence, precisely because innocence is *something* (whereas the most correct expression for immediacy is that which Hegel uses about pure being:[31] it is nothing). The reason is that when innocence is canceled by transcendence, something entirely different comes out of it, whereas mediacy is just immediacy. Innocence is a quality, it is a *state* that may very well endure, and therefore the logical haste to have it annulled is meaningless, whereas in logic it should try to hurry a little more,[32] for in logic it always comes too late, even when it hurries. Innocence is not a perfection that one should wish to regain, for as soon as one wishes for it, it is lost, and then it is a new guilt to waste one's time on wishes. Innocence is not an imperfection in which one cannot remain, for it is always sufficient unto itself, and he who has lost it, that is, not in a manner in which it might have pleased him to have lost it but in the only way in which it can be lost, that is, by guilt—to him it could never occur to boast of his perfection at the expense of innocence.

The narrative in Genesis[33] also gives the correct explanation of innocence. Innocence is ignorance. It is by no means the pure being of the immediate, but it *is* ignorance. The fact that ignorance when viewed from without is regarded as something defined in the direction of knowledge is of no concern whatever to ignorance.

Obviously this view is in no way guilty of any Pelagianism. The race has its history, within which sinfulness continues to have its quantitative determinability, but innocence is always lost only by the qualitative leap of the individual. It is no doubt true that this sinfulness, which is the progression of the race, may express itself as a greater or lesser disposition in the particular individual who by his act assumes it, but this

IV
309

is a more or less, a quantitative determination, which does not constitute the concept of guilt.

§4.
THE CONCEPT OF THE FALL

If innocence is ignorance, it might appear that, inasmuch as the quantitative determinability of the guiltiness of the race is present in the ignorance of the single individual and by his act manifests itself as his guiltiness, there will be a difference between Adam's innocence and that of every subsequent person. The answer is already given: a "more" does not constitute a quality. It might also appear that it would be easier to explain how a subsequent person lost innocence. But this is only apparent. The greatest degree of quantitative determinability no more explains the leap than does the least degree; if I can explain guilt in a subsequent person, I can explain it in Adam as well. By habit, and especially by thoughtlessness and ethical stupidity, it has been made to appear that the first is easier than the last. We want so badly to sneak away from the sunstroke of the consequence that aims at the top of our heads. We would put up with sinfulness, go along with it, etc., etc. One need not trouble oneself; sinfulness is not an epidemic that spreads like cowpox, "and every mouth shall be stopped."[34] It is true that a person can say in profound earnestness that he was born in misery and that his mother conceived him in sin,[35] but he can truly sorrow over this only if he himself brought guilt into the world and brought all this upon himself, for it is a contradiction to sorrow *esthetically* over *sinfulness*. The only one who sorrowed innocently over sinfulness was Christ, but he did not sorrow over it as a fate he had to put up with. He sorrowed as the one who freely chose to carry all the sin of the world[36] and to suffer its punishment. This is no esthetic qualification, for Christ was more than an individual.

Innocence is ignorance, but how is it lost? I do not intend to repeat all the ingenious and stupid hypotheses with which thinkers and speculators have encumbered the beginning of history, men who only out of curiosity were interested in the great human concern called sin, partly because I do not wish to waste the time of others in telling what I myself wasted time in learning, and partly because the whole thing lies outside of history, in the twilight where witches and speculators race on broomsticks and sausage-pegs.

The science that deals with the explanation is psychology, but it can explain only up to the explanation and above all must guard against leaving the impression of explaining that which no science can explain and that which ethics explains further only by presupposing it by way of dogmatics. If one were to take the psychological explanation and repeat it a number of times and thereby arrive at the opinion that it is not improbable that sin came into the world in this way, everything would be confused. Psychology must remain within its boundary; only then can its explanation have significance. IV 311

A psychological explanation of the fall is clearly and well set forth in Usteri's development of the Pauline doctrines.[37] Now theology has become so speculative that it makes light of such things, because, after all, it is much easier to explain that the immediate must be annulled, and theology sometimes does what is still more convenient: it becomes invisible to the speculative devotees at the decisive moment of the explanation. Usteri's explanation is to the effect that it was the prohibition itself not to eat of the tree of knowledge that gave birth to the sin of Adam. This does not at all ignore the ethical, but it admits that somehow the prohibition only predisposes that which breaks forth in Adam's qualitative leap. It is not my intention to continue this account any further. Everyone has read it or can read it in this author's work.*

* Everyone who reflects upon the present subject is of course familiar with what Franz Baader[38] has set forth with his usual vigor and authority in several works concerning the significance of temptation for the consolidation of freedom, and the misunderstanding of conceiving temptation one-sidedly as temptation to evil or as something with the purpose of bringing man to the fall, when temptation should rather be viewed as freedom's "necessary other." To repeat this is not necessary here. Franz Baader's works are obtainable. To pursue his thought any further is not feasible, for it seems to me that Franz Baader has overlooked the intermediate terms. The transition from in-

IV
312

Where this explanation falters is in its wish not to be altogether psychological, and for this it cannot be blamed, because it did not wish to be that but set itself another task, that of developing the doctrines of St. Paul and of attaching itself to the Bible. But in this respect the Bible has often had a harmful effect. In beginning a deliberation, a person has certain classical passages fixed in his mind, and now his explanation and knowledge consist in an arrangement of these passages, as if the whole matter were something foreign. The more natural the better, even if he is willing with all deference to refer the explanation to the verdict of the Bible, and, if it is not in accord with the Bible, to try over again. Thus a person does not bring himself into the awkward position of having to understand the explanation before he has understood what it should explain,[39] nor into the subtle position of using Scripture passages as the Persian king[40] in the war against the Egyptians used their sacred animals, that is, in order to shield himself.

If the prohibition is regarded as conditioning the fall, it is also regarded as conditioning *concupiscentia* [inordinate desire]. At this point psychology has already gone beyond its competence. *Concupiscentia* is a determinant of guilt and sin antecedent to guilt and sin, and yet still is not guilt and sin, that is, introduced by it. The qualitative leap is enervated; the fall becomes something successive. Nor can it be discerned how the prohibition awakens *concupiscentia*, even though it is certain from pagan as well as from Christian experience that man's desire is for the forbidden. But a person cannot appeal to experience as a matter of course, for it could be asked more particularly in which period of life this is experienced. This intermediate term, *concupiscentia*, is not ambiguous either,

---

IV
311

nocence to guilt merely through the concept of temptation easily brings God into an almost imaginatively constructed [*experimenterende*] relation to man and ignores the intermediate psychological observation, because the intermediate term still is *concupiscentia* [inordinate desire]. Finally, Baader's account is a rather dialectical deliberation of the concept of temptation instead of a psychological explanation of the more specific.

from which it can be seen immediately that it is no psychological explanation. The strongest, indeed, the most positive expression the Protestant Church uses for the presence of hereditary sin in man is precisely that he is born with *concupiscentia* (*Omnes homines secundum naturam propagati nascuntur cum peccato h.e. sine metu dei, sine fiducia erga deum et cum concupiscentia* [all men begotten in a natural way are born with sin, i.e., without the fear of God, without trust in God, and with concupiscence]).[41] Nevertheless, the Protestant doctrine makes an essential distinction between the innocence of the subsequent person (if such a one can be spoken of) and that of Adam.[42]

The psychological explanation must not talk around the point but remain in its elastic ambiguity, from which guilt breaks forth in the qualitative leap.

§5.

THE CONCEPT OF ANXIETY

Innocence is ignorance. In innocence, man is not qualified as spirit but is psychically qualified in immediate unity with his natural condition. The spirit in man is dreaming. This view is in full accord with that of the Bible,[43] which by denying that man in his innocence has knowledge of the difference between good and evil denounces all the phantasmagoria of Catholic meritoriousness.

In this state there is peace and repose,[44] but there is simultaneously something else that is not contention and strife, for there is indeed nothing against which to strive. What, then, is it? Nothing. But what effect does nothing have? It begets anxiety. This is the profound secret of innocence, that it is at the same time anxiety. Dreamily the spirit projects its own actuality, but this actuality is nothing, and innocence always sees this nothing outside itself.

Anxiety is a qualification of dreaming spirit, and as such it has its place in psychology. Awake, the difference between myself and my other is posited; sleeping, it is suspended;

dreaming, it is an intimated nothing.[45] The actuality of the spirit constantly shows itself as a form that tempts its possibility but disappears as soon as it seeks to grasp for it, and it is a nothing that can only bring anxiety. More it cannot do as long as it merely shows itself. The concept of anxiety is almost never treated in psychology. Therefore, I must point out that it is altogether different from fear and similar concepts that refer to something definite, whereas anxiety is freedom's actuality as the possibility of possibility.[46] For this reason, anxiety is not found in the beast, precisely because by nature the beast is not qualified as spirit.

When we consider the dialectical determinations of anxiety, it appears that exactly these have psychological ambiguity. Anxiety is *a sympathetic antipathy* and *an antipathetic sympathy*.[47] One easily sees, I think, that this is a psychological determination in a sense entirely different from the *concupiscentia* [inordinate desire] of which we spoke. Linguistic usage confirms this perfectly. One speaks of a pleasing anxiety, a pleasing anxiousness [*Beængstelse*], and of a strange anxiety, a bashful anxiety, etc.

The anxiety that is posited in innocence is in the first place no guilt, and in the second place it is no troublesome burden, no suffering that cannot be brought into harmony with the blessedness of innocence. In observing children, one will discover this anxiety intimated more particularly as a seeking for the adventurous, the monstrous, and the enigmatic. That there are children in whom this anxiety is not found proves nothing at all, for neither is it found in the beast, and the less spirit, the less anxiety. This anxiety belongs so essentially to the child that he cannot do without it. Though it causes him anxiety, it captivates him by its pleasing anxiousness [*Beængstelse*]. In all cultures where the childlike is preserved as the dreaming of the spirit, this anxiety is found. The more profound the anxiety, the more profound the culture. Only a prosaic stupidity maintains that this is a disorganization. Anxiety has here the same meaning as melancholy at a much later point, when freedom, having passed through the imperfect forms of its history, in the profoundest sense will come to itself.*

Just as the relation of anxiety to its object, to something that is nothing (linguistic usage also says pregnantly: to be anxious about nothing), is altogether ambiguous, so also the transition that is to be made from innocence to guilt will be so dialectical that it can be seen that the explanation is what it must be, psychological. The qualitative leap stands outside of all ambiguity. But he who becomes guilty through anxiety is indeed innocent, for it was not he himself but anxiety, a foreign power, that laid hold of him, a power that he did not love but about which he was anxious. And yet he is guilty, for he sank in anxiety, which he nevertheless loved even as he feared it. There is nothing in the world more ambiguous; therefore this is the only psychological explanation. But, to repeat once more, it could never occur to the explanation that it should explain the qualitative leap. Every notion that suggests that the prohibition tempted him, or that the seducer deceived him, has sufficient ambiguity only for a superficial observation, but it perverts ethics, introduces a quantitative determination, and will by the help of psychology pay man a compliment at the sacrifice of the ethical, a compliment that everyone who is ethically developed must reject as a new and more profound seduction.

That anxiety makes its appearance is the pivot upon which everything turns. Man is a synthesis of the psychical and the physical; however, a synthesis is unthinkable if the two are not united in a third. This third is spirit.[48] In innocence, man is not merely animal, for if he were at any moment of his life merely animal, he would never become man. So spirit is present, but as immediate, as dreaming. Inasmuch as it is now present, it is in a sense a hostile power, for it constantly disturbs the relation between soul and body, a relation that in- IV
315

* Concerning this, one should consult *Either/Or* (Copenhagen: 1843), especially if one is aware that the first part expresses the melancholy in its anguished [*angestfulde*] sympathy and egotism, which is explained in the second part. IV
314

deed has persistence and yet does not have endurance, inasmuch as it first receives the latter by the spirit. On the other hand, spirit is a friendly power, since it is precisely that which constitutes the relation. What, then, is man's relation to this ambiguous power? How does spirit relate itself to itself and to its conditionality? It relates itself as anxiety. Do away with itself, the spirit cannot; lay hold of itself, it cannot, as long as it has itself outside of itself. Nor can man sink down into the vegetative, for he is qualified as spirit; flee away from anxiety, he cannot, for he loves it; really love it, he cannot, for he flees from it. Innocence has now reached its uttermost point. It is ignorance; however, it is not an animal brutality but an ignorance qualified by spirit, and as such innocence is precisely anxiety, because its ignorance is about nothing. Here there is no knowledge of good and evil etc., but the whole actuality of knowledge projects itself in anxiety as the enormous nothing of ignorance.

Innocence still is, but only a word is required and then ignorance is concentrated. Innocence naturally cannot understand this word, but at that moment anxiety has, as it were, caught its first prey. Instead of nothing, it now has an enigmatic word. When it is stated in Genesis that God said to Adam, "Only from the tree of the knowledge of good and evil you must not eat," it follows as a matter of course that Adam really has not understood this word, for how could he understand the difference between good and evil when this distinction would follow as a consequence of the enjoyment of the fruit?

When it is assumed that the prohibition awakens the desire, one acquires knowledge instead of ignorance, and in that case Adam must have had a knowledge of freedom, because the desire was to use it. The explanation is therefore subsequent. The prohibition induces in him anxiety, for the prohibition awakens in him freedom's possibility. What passed by innocence as the nothing of anxiety has now entered into Adam, and here again it is a nothing—the anxious possibility of *being able*. He has no conception of what he is able to do; otherwise—and this is what usually happens—that which comes later, the difference between good and evil, would have to be presupposed. Only the possibility of being able is present as a higher form of ignorance, as a higher expression of anxiety, because in a higher sense it both is and is not, because in a higher sense he both loves it and flees from it.

After the word of prohibition follows the word of judgment: "You shall certainly die."[49] Naturally, Adam does not know what it means to die. On the other hand, there is nothing to prevent him from having acquired a notion of the terrifying, for even animals can understand the mimic expression and movement in the voice of a speaker without understanding the word. If the prohibition is regarded as awakening the desire, the punishment must also be regarded as awakening the notion of the deterrent. This, however, will only confuse things. In this case, the terror is simply anxiety. Because Adam has not understood what was spoken, there is nothing but the ambiguity of anxiety. The infinite possibility of being able that was awakened by the prohibition now draws closer, because this possibility points to a possibility as its sequence.

In this way, innocence is brought to its uttermost. In anxiety it is related to the forbidden and to the punishment. Innocence is not guilty, yet there is anxiety as though it were lost.

Further than this, psychology cannot go, but so far it can go, and above all, in its observation of human life, it can point to this again and again.

Here, in the conclusion, I have adhered to the Biblical narrative. I have assumed the prohibition and the voice of punishment as coming from without. Of course, this is something that has troubled many thinkers. But the difficulty is merely one to smile at. Innocence can indeed speak, inasmuch as in language it possesses the expression for everything spiritual. Accordingly, one need merely assume that Adam talked to himself. The imperfection in the story, namely, that another spoke to Adam about what he did not understand, is thus eliminated. From the fact that Adam was able to talk, it does not follow in a deeper sense that he was able to understand what was said. This applies above all to the difference between good and evil, which indeed can be expressed in language but nevertheless *is* only for freedom, because for innocence it can have only the meaning we have indicated in the preceding account. Innocence can indeed express this difference, but the difference is not for innocence, and for innocence it can only have the meaning that was indicated in the preceding account.

§6.

ANXIETY AS THE PRESUPPOSITION OF HEREDITARY SIN AND AS EXPLAINING HEREDITARY SIN RETROGRESSIVELY IN TERMS OF ITS ORIGIN

Let us now examine the narrative in Genesis more carefully as we attempt to dismiss the fixed idea that it is a myth, and as we remind ourselves that no age has been more skillful than our own in producing myths of the understanding, an age that produces myths and at the same time wants to eradicate all myths.

Adam was created; he had given names to the animals (here there is language, though in an imperfect way similar to that of children who learn by identifying animals on an A B C board)[50] but had not found company for himself. Eve was created, formed from his rib. She stood in as intimate a relation to him as possible, yet it was still an external relation. Adam and Eve are merely a numerical repetition. In this respect, a thousand Adams signify no more than one. So much with regard to the descent of the race from one pair. Nature does not favor a meaningless superfluity. Therefore, if we assume that the race descended from several pairs, there would be a moment when nature had a meaningless superfluity. As soon as the relationship of generation is posited, no man is superfluous, because every individual is himself and the race.[51]

Now follows the prohibition and the judgment. But the serpent was more cunning[52] than all the animals of the field. He seduced the woman. Even though one may call this a myth, it neither disturbs thought nor confuses the concept, as does a myth of the understanding. The myth allows something that is inward to take place outwardly.

First we must note that the woman was the first to be seduced, and that therefore she in turn seduced the man. In what sense woman is the weaker sex, as it is commonly said of her, and also that anxiety belongs to her more than to man,* I shall try to develop in another chapter.

In the foregoing, it has been said several times that the view presented in this work does not deny the propagation of sinfulness through generation, or, in other words, that sinfulness has its history through generation. Yet it is said only that sinfulness moves in quantitative categories, whereas sin constantly enters by the qualitative leap of the individual. Here already one can see one significant aspect of the quantitation that takes place in generation. Eve is a derived creature. To be sure, she is created like Adam, but she is created out of a previous creature. To be sure, she is innocent like Adam, but there is, as it were, a presentiment of a disposition that indeed is not sinfulness but may seem like a hint of the sinfulness that is posited by propagation. It is the fact of being derived that predisposes the particular individual, yet without making him guilty.

Here we must remember what was said about the prohibition and the word of judgment in §5. The imperfection in the narrative—how it could have occurred to anyone to say to Adam what he essentially could not understand—is eliminated if we bear in mind that the speaker is language, and also that it is Adam himself who speaks.**

IV
318

* Nothing is hereby determined about woman's imperfection in relation to man. Although anxiety belongs to her more than to man, anxiety is by no means a sign of imperfection. If one is to speak of imperfection, this must be found in something else, namely, that in anxiety she moves beyond herself to another human being, to man.

IV
317

** If one were to say further that it then becomes a question of how the first man learned to speak, I would answer that this is very true, but also that the question lies beyond the scope of the present investigation. However, this must not be understood in the manner of modern philosophy as though my reply were evasive, suggesting that I *could* answer the question in another place. But this much is certain, that it will not do to represent man himself as the inventor of language.[53]

IV
318

There remains the serpent. I am no friend of cleverness and shall, *volente deo* [God willing], resist the temptations of the serpent, who, as at the dawn of time when he tempted Adam and Eve, has in the course of time tempted writers to be clever. Instead, I freely admit my inability to connect any definite thought with the serpent.[54] Furthermore, the difficulty with the serpent is something quite different, namely, that of regarding the temptation as coming from without. This is simply contrary to the teaching of the Bible, contrary to the well-known classical passage in James,[55] which says that God tempts no man and is not tempted by anyone, but each person is tempted by himself. If one indeed believes that he has rescued God by regarding man as tempted by the serpent and believes that in this way one is in accord with James, "that God tempts no one," he is confronted with the second statement, that God is not tempted by anyone. For the serpent's assault upon man is also an indirect temptation of God, since it interferes in the relation between God and man, and one is confronted by the third statement, that every man is tempted by himself.

IV
319

Now follows the fall. This is something that psychology is unable to explain, because the fall is the qualitative leap. However, let us for a moment consider the consequence as it is presented in the narrative in order to fix our attention once more on anxiety as the presupposition for hereditary sin.

The consequence is a double one, that sin came into the world and that sexuality was posited; the one is to be inseparable from the other. This is of utmost importance in order to show man's original state. If he were not a synthesis that reposed in a third, one thing could not have two consequences. If he were not a synthesis of psyche and body that is sustained by spirit, the sexual could never have come into the world with sinfulness.

We shall leave project makers[56] out of consideration and simply assume the presence of the sexual difference before the fall, except that as yet it was not, because in ignorance it is not. In this respect we have support in the Scriptures.[57]

In innocence, Adam as spirit was a dreaming spirit. Thus

the synthesis is not actual, for the combining factor is precisely the spirit, and as yet this is not posited as spirit. In animals the sexual difference can be developed instinctively, but this cannot be the case with a human being precisely because he is a synthesis. In the moment the spirit posits itself, it posits the synthesis, but in order to posit the synthesis it must first pervade it differentiatingly, and the ultimate point of the sensuous is precisely the sexual. Man can attain this ultimate point only in the moment the spirit becomes actual. Before that time he is not animal, but neither is he really man. The moment he becomes man, he becomes so by being animal as well.

So sinfulness is by no means sensuousness, but without sin there is no sexuality, and without sexuality, no history. A perfect spirit has neither the one nor the other, and therefore the sexual difference is canceled in the resurrection, and therefore an angel has no history. Even if Michael had made a record of all the errands he had been sent on and performed, this is nevertheless not his history. First in sexuality is the synthesis posited as a contradiction, but like every contradiction it is also a task, the history of which begins at that same moment. This is the actuality that is preceded by freedom's possibility. However, freedom's possibility is not the ability to choose the good or the evil. Such thoughtlessness is no more in the interest of Scriptures than in the interest of thought. The possibility is to *be able*. In a logical system, it is convenient to say that possibility passes over into actuality. However, in actuality it is not so convenient, and an intermediate term is required. The intermediate term is anxiety, but it no more explains the qualitative leap than it can justify it ethically. Anxiety is neither a category of necessity nor a category of freedom; it is entangled freedom, where freedom is not free in itself but entangled, not by necessity, but in itself. If sin has come into the world by necessity (which is a contradiction), there can be no anxiety. Nor can there be any anxiety if sin came into the world by an act of an abstract *liberum arbitrium*[58] (which no more existed in the world in the beginning than in a late period, because it is a nuisance for thought). To want to give a logical explanation of the coming of sin into the world is a stupidity that can occur only to people who are comically worried about finding an explanation.[59]

Were I allowed to make a wish, then I would wish that no reader would be so profound as to ask: What if Adam had not sinned? In the moment actuality is posited, possibility walks by its side as a nothing that entices every thoughtless man. If only science could make up its mind to keep men under discipline and to bridle itself! When someone asks a stupid question, care should be taken not to answer him, lest he who answers becomes just as stupid as the questioner. The foolishness of the above question consists not so much in the question itself as in the fact that it is directed to science. If one stays at home with it, and, like Clever Elsie[60] with her projects, calls together like-minded friends, then he has tolerably understood his own stupidity. Science, on the contrary, cannot explain such things. Every science lies either in a logical immanence or in an immanence within a transcendence that it is unable to explain. Now sin is precisely that transcendence, that *discrimen rerum* [crisis] in which sin enters into the single individual as the single individual. Sin never enters into the world differently and has never entered differently. So when the single individual is stupid enough to inquire about sin as if it were something foreign to him, he only asks as a fool, for either he does not know at all what the question is about, and thus cannot come to know it, or he knows it and understands it, and also knows that no science can explain it to him. However, science at times has been adequately accommodating in responding to wishes with weighty hypotheses that it at last admits are inadequate as explanations. This, of course, is entirely true, yet the confusion is that science did not energetically dismiss foolish questions but instead confirmed superstitious men in their notion that one day there would come a project maker who is smart enough to come up with the right answer. That sin came into the world six thousand years ago is said in the same way that one would say about Nebuchadnezzar that it was four thousand years ago that he became an ox.[61] When the case is understood in this way, it is

IV
321

no wonder that the explanation accords with it. What in one respect is the simplest thing in the world has been made the most difficult. What the most ordinary man understands in his own way, and quite correctly so—because he understands that it is not just six thousand years since sin came into the world—science with the art of speculators has announced as a prize subject that as yet has not been answered satisfactorily. How sin came into the world, each man understands solely by himself. If he would learn it from another, he would *eo ipso* misunderstand it. The only science that can help a little is psychology, yet it admits that it explains nothing, and also that it *cannot* and *will not* explain more. If any science could explain it, everything would be confused. That the man of science ought to forget himself is entirely true; nevertheless, it is therefore also very fortunate that sin is no scientific problem, and thus no man of science has an obligation (and the project maker just as little) to forget how sin came into the world. If this is what he wants to do, if he magnanimously wants to forget himself in the zeal to explain all of humanity, he will become as comical as that privy councilor who was so conscientious about leaving his calling card with every Tom, Dick, and Harry that in so doing he at last forgot his own name. Or his philosophical enthusiasm will make him so absent-minded that he needs a good-natured, level-headed wife whom he can ask, as Soldin asked Rebecca when in enthusiastic absent-mindedness he also lost himself in the objectivity of the chatter: "Rebecca, is it I who is speaking?"[62]

IV
322

That the admired men of science in my most honored contemporary age, men whose concern in their search after the system is known to the whole congregation and who are concerned also to find a place for sin within it, may find the above position highly unscientific is entirely in order. But let the congregation join in the search, or at least include these profound seekers in their pious intercessions; they will find the place as surely as he who hunts for the burning tow finds it when he is unaware that it is burning in his own hand.

II

Anxiety as Explaining Hereditary Sin Progressively

With sinfulness, sexuality was posited. In that same moment the history of the race begins. Just as the sinfulness of the race moves in quantitative determinations, so also does anxiety. The consequence of hereditary sin or the presence of hereditary sin in the single individual is anxiety, which differs only quantitatively from that of Adam. In the state of innocence—and of such a state one might also speak in the case of subsequent man—inherited sin must also have the same dialectical ambiguity out of which guilt breaks forth by a qualitative leap. On the other hand, anxiety will be more reflective in a subsequent individual than in Adam, because the quantitative accumulation left behind by the race now makes itself felt in that individual. Anxiety becomes no more an imperfection in man than before. On the contrary, the more primitive a man is, the more profound is his anxiety, because the presupposition of sinfulness, which his individual life must assume when indeed he enters into the history of the race, must be appropriated. Thus sinfulness has now attained a greater power, and hereditary sin is growing. That there may be men who never experience any anxiety must be understood in the sense that Adam would have perceived no anxiety had he been merely animal.

The subsequent individual, like Adam, is a synthesis that is sustained by spirit, but the synthesis is derived, and accordingly, the history of the race is posited in it. Herein lies the more or less of anxiety in the subsequent individual. Nevertheless, his anxiety is not anxiety about sin, for as yet the distinction between good and evil is not, because this distinction first comes about with the actuality of freedom. This distinction, if present, is only a foreboding presentiment that through the history of the race may signify a more or a less.

Anxiety in a later individual is more reflective as a consequence of his participation in the history of the race—something that can be compared with habit, which is something of a second nature, not a new quality but simply a quantitative progression—because anxiety has now entered into the world with a new significance. Sin entered in anxiety, but sin in turn brought anxiety along with it. To be sure, the actuality of sin is an actuality that has no endurance. On the one hand, the continuity of sin is the possibility that brings anxiety. On the other hand, the possibility of salvation is again a nothing, which the individual both loves and fears, because this is always possibility's relation to individuality. Only in the moment that salvation is actually posited is this anxiety overcome. Man's and creation's eager longing[1] is not, as has been sentimentally expressed, a sweet longing; in order for longing to be such, sin would have to be disarmed. He who will truly acquaint himself with the state of sin, and with what the expectation of salvation might be, will no doubt acknowledge this and be a little embarrassed by the esthetic unembarrassment. As long as it is only a question of expectation, sin continues to be in control and naturally conceives of the expectation in a hostile manner. (This will be dealt with later.) When salvation is posited, anxiety, together with possibility, is left behind. This does not mean that anxiety is annihilated, but that when rightly used it plays another role (see Chapter V).

Strictly speaking, the anxiety that sin brings with it is only when the individual himself posits sin, and yet this anxiety is obscurely present as a more or a less in the quantitative history of the race. Hence one will even encounter the phenomenon that a person seems to become guilty merely through anxiety about himself, something that could not have happened in the case of Adam. It is nevertheless true that every individual becomes guilty only through himself; yet what is quantitative in his relation to the race in this case reaches its maximum here and will have the power to confuse every

view so long as one does not hold fast to the distinction
specified earlier between the quantitative accumulation and
the qualitative leap. This phenomenon[2] will be considered
later. Usually it is ignored, which of course is easiest. Or it is
construed sentimentally and movingly with a cowardly sympathy that thanks God for not being like such a person,[3]
without understanding that such a thanksgiving is treason
against both God and oneself, and without considering that
life always holds in store analogous phenomena that one
probably will not escape. One must have sympathy. However, this sympathy is true only when one admits rightly and
profoundly to oneself that what has happened to one human
being can happen to all. Only then can one benefit both oneself and others. The physician at an insane asylum who is
foolish enough to believe that he is eternally right and that his
bit of reason is ensured against all injury in this life is in a
sense wiser than the demented, but he is also more foolish,
and surely he will not heal many.

Consequently, anxiety means two things: the anxiety in
which the individual posits sin by the qualitative leap, and the
anxiety that entered in and enters in with sin, and that also,
accordingly, enters quantitatively into the world every time
an individual posits sin.

It is not my intention to write a learned work or to waste
time in search of literary proof texts. Often the examples
mentioned in psychologies lack true psychological-poetic authority. They stand as isolated *notarialiter* [notarized facts],
and as a result one does not know whether to laugh or to
weep at the attempts of such lonely and obstinate persons to
form some sort of a rule. One who has properly occupied
himself with psychology and psychological observation acquires a general human flexibility that enables him at once to
construct his example which even though it lacks factual authority nevertheless has an authority of a different kind. The
psychological observer ought to be more nimble than a tight-
rope dancer in order to incline and bend himself to other

IV
325

people and imitate their attitudes, and his silence in the moment of confidence should be seductive and voluptuous, so that what is hidden may find satisfaction in slipping out to chat with itself in the artificially constructed nonobservance and silence. Hence he ought also to have a poetic originality in his soul so as to be able at once to create both the totality and the invariable from what in the individual is always partially and variably present. Then, when he has perfected himself, he will have no need to take his examples from literary repertoires and serve up half-dead reminiscences, but will bring his observations entirely fresh from the water, wriggling and sparkling in the play of their colors. Nor will he have to run himself to death to become aware of something. On the contrary, he should sit entirely composed in his room, like a police agent who nevertheless knows everything that takes place. What he needs he can fashion at once; what he needs he has at hand at once by virtue of his general practice, just as in a well-equipped house one need not carry water from the street but has it on his level by high pressure. If he were to become doubtful, he is so well-oriented in human life and his eyes are so inquisitorially sharp that he knows where to look to discover easily a suitable individuality who can be useful to the imaginary construction [*Experimentet*]. His observation will be more reliable than that of others, even though he does not support it by references to names and learned quotations— such as, that in Saxony there once lived a peasant girl in whom a physician observed, that in Rome there was once an emperor of whom a historian relates, etc.—as if such things happen only once in a thousand years. What interest could psychology have in that? No, such things happen every day, if only the observer is present. His observation will have the quality of freshness and the interest of actuality if he is prudent enough to control his observations. To that end he imitates in himself every mood, every psychic state that he discovers in another. Thereupon he sees whether he can delude the other by the imitation and carry him along into the subsequent development, which is his own creation by virtue of the idea. Thus if someone wants to observe a passion, he must

IV
326

choose his individual. At that point, what counts is stillness, quietness, and obscurity, so that he may discover the individual's secret. Then he must practice what he has learned until he is able to delude the individual. Thereupon he fictitiously invents the passion and appears before the individual in a preternatural magnitude of the passion. If it is done correctly, the individual will feel an indescribable relief and satisfaction, such as an insane person will feel when someone has uncovered and poetically grasped his fixation and then proceeds to develop it further. If it does not succeed, it may be because of a defect in the operation, but it may also be because the individual is a poor example.

§1.
OBJECTIVE ANXIETY

When we use the expression objective anxiety, it might seem natural to think of the anxiety belonging to innocence, the anxiety that is freedom's reflection within itself in its possibility. To object to this by saying that we now find ourselves at a different place in the inquiry would be an unsatisfactory claim. It might be more useful to remember that what distinguishes objective anxiety lies in its difference from subjective anxiety, a distinction that does not pertain to Adam's state of innocence. In the strictest sense, subjective anxiety is the anxiety that is posited in the individual and is the consequence of his sin. Anxiety in this sense will be dealt with in a later chapter. If the term "anxiety" is to be understood in this sense, the contrast of an objective anxiety is removed, and anxiety appears precisely as what it is, namely, as the subjective. The distinction between objective and subjective anxiety belongs in the contemplation of the world and the subsequent individual's state of innocence. The distinction made here is that subjective anxiety signifies the anxiety that is present in the individual's state of innocence and corresponds to that of Adam, but it is nevertheless quantitatively different from that of Adam because of the quantitative determination of the generation. By objective anxiety we understand, on the other hand, the reflection of the sinfulness of the generation in the whole world.

The purpose of §2 of the previous chapter was to call to mind that the expression "by Adam's sin, sinfulness came *into the world*" contains an external reflection. Therefore we shall return to that expression to discover the truth that may be found in it. The moment Adam has posited sin, our consideration leaves him in order to consider the beginning of every subsequent individual's sin, for as a result generation is introduced. If by Adam's sin[4] the sinfulness of the race is posited in the same sense as his erect walking etc., the concept of the individual is canceled. This was developed previously, where objection also was made against the imaginatively constructing inquisitiveness that wants to treat sin as a curiosity. The dilemma was also raised that one would have to imagine either a questioner who did not even know what he was asking about or a questioner who knew and whose pretended ignorance became a new sin.

If all this is kept in mind, the above expression will have a limited truth. The first posits the quality. Adam, then, posits sin in himself, but also for the race. However, the concept of race is too abstract to allow the positing of so concrete a category as sin, which is posited precisely in that the single individual himself, as the single individual, posits it. Thus sinfulness in the race becomes only a quantitative approximation. Still this has its beginning with Adam. Herein lies the great significance of Adam[5] above that of every other individual in the race, and herein lies the truth of the above expression. Even orthodoxy, if it is to understand itself, must admit this, because it teaches that by the sin of Adam nature as well as the race was brought under sin. However, in the case of nature it certainly will not do to maintain that sin entered in as the quality of sin.

IV
328

By coming into the world, sin acquired significance for the whole creation. This effect of sin in nonhuman existence [*Tilværelse*] I have called objective anxiety.

The meaning of this I can indicate by calling attention to the Scriptural expression ἀποκαραδοκία[6] τῆς κτίσεως [the eager longing of creation] (Romans 8:19). Inasmuch as one can speak of an eager longing, it follows as a matter of course that the creation is in a state of imperfection. One often fails to see that expressions and concepts such as longing, eager longing, expectation, etc. imply a preceding state, and that this state is present and makes itself felt at the same time that longing is developing. A person is not in this state of expectation by accident etc., so that he finds himself a total stranger to it, but he himself is at the same time producing it. The expression for such a longing is anxiety, for the state out of which he longs to be proclaims itself in anxiety, and it proclaims itself because the longing alone is not sufficient to save him.

The sense in which creation sank into corruption through Adam's sin, how freedom was posited by the fact that its misuse was posited and thus cast a reflection of possibility and a trembling of complicity over creation, the sense in which this had to take place because man is a synthesis whose most extreme opposites were posited and whose one opposite, precisely on account of man's sin, became a far more extreme opposite than it was before—all this has no place in a psychological deliberation but belongs in dogmatics, in the Atonement, in the explanation by which this science explains the presupposition of sinfulness.*

IV
329
This anxiety in creation may rightly be called objective anxiety. It is not brought forth by creation but by the fact that creation is placed in an entirely different light because of Adam's sin, and insofar as it continues to come into the world, sensuousness is constantly degraded to mean sinfulness. One can easily see that this interpretation also has its eyes open in the sense that it parries the rationalistic view according to which sensuousness as such is sinfulness. After sin came into the world, and every time sin comes into the world, sensuousness becomes sinfulness. But what it be-

---

* Dogmatics must be designed in this way. Above all, every science must vigorously lay hold of its own beginning and not live in complicated relations with other sciences. If dogmatics begins by wanting to explain sinfulness or by wanting to prove its actuality, no dogmatics will come out of it, but the entire existence of dogmatics will become problematic and vague.[7]

comes is not what it first was. Franz Baader has often protested against the proposition that finitude[8] and sensuousness
as such are sinfulness. If care is not taken at this point, Pelagianism emerges from an entirely different side. Franz Baader,
however, did not take into account the history of the race. In
the quantitation of the race (i.e., nonessentially), sensuousness is sinfulness, but, in relation to the individual, this is not
the case until he himself, by positing sin, again makes sensuousness sinfulness.

Some men of Schelling's school*[9] have been especially
aware of the alteration** that has taken place in nature because

IV
330

---

* Schelling himself has often spoken of anxiety, anger, anguish, suffering,
etc. But one ought always to be a little suspicious of such expressions, so as
not to confuse the consequence of sin in creation with what Schelling also
characterizes as states and moods in God. By these expressions, he characterizes, if I may say so, the creative birth pangs of the deity. By such figurative expressions he signifies what in some cases he has called the negative and
what in Hegel became: the negative more strictly defined as the dialectical (τὸ
ἕτερον).[10] The ambiguity is also found in Schelling because he speaks of a
melancholy that is spread over nature, as well as of a depression in the deity.[11] Yet, above all, Schelling's main thought is that anxiety, etc., characterize especially the suffering of the deity in his endeavor to create. In Berlin,
he expressed the same thought[12] more definitely by comparing God with
Goethe and Joh. von Müller, both of whom felt well only when producing,
and also by calling attention to the fact that such a bliss, when it cannot
communicate itself, is unhappiness. I mention this here because his remark
has already found its way into print in a pamphlet by Marheineke,[13] who
treats it with irony. This, however, one ought not to do, for a vigorous and
full-blooded anthropomorphism has considerable merit. The mistake, however, is a different one, and here is an example of how strange everything
becomes when metaphysics and dogmatics are distorted by treating dogmatics metaphysically and metaphysics dogmatically.

** The word "alteration"[14] in Danish expresses the ambiguity very well.
The word "alterate" is used in the sense of changing, distorting, or bringing
out of its original state (the thing becomes something else). But one also
speaks of "becoming alterated" [*altereret*] in the sense of becoming
frightened, for this is fundamentally the first unavoidable consequence. To
my knowledge, the word is not used at all in Latin, which instead, strangely
enough, uses the word *adulterare* [to seduce to adultery, to falsify, to distort].
The Frenchman says *altérer les monnaies* [to counterfeit money] and *être altéré*
[to be frightened]. In Danish, the word is used in everyday speech almost
only in the sense of being frightened, and so one may hear an ordinary person
say, "I am quite *altereret*." At least I have heard a peddler use it in that way.

IV
329

IV
330

of sin. Mention has been made also of the anxiety that is supposed to be in inanimate nature. The effect, however, is
weakened when at one moment one is to believe that he is
dealing with a subject in natural philosophy that is treated
cleverly with the help of dogmatics, and in another moment a
dogmatic definition that glories in the borrowed reflection of
the magical marvels of the contemplation of nature.

However, at this point I break off the digression, which for
a moment I permitted to go beyond the boundary of this investigation. Anxiety as it appeared in Adam will never again
return, for by him sinfulness came into the world. Because of
this, Adam's anxiety has two analogies, the objective anxiety
in nature and the subjective anxiety in the individual, of
which the latter contains a more and the first a less than the
anxiety in Adam.

§2.
SUBJECTIVE ANXIETY

The more reflective one dares to posit anxiety, the easier it
may seem for anxiety to pass over into guilt. But here it is
important not to allow oneself to be deluded by determinants
of approximation: a "more" cannot bring forth the leap, and
no "easier" can in truth make the explanation easier. If this is
not held fast, one runs the risk of suddenly meeting a phenomenon in which everything takes place so easily that the
transition becomes a simple transition, or the other risk of
never daring to bring one's thought to a conclusion, since a
purely empirical observation can never be finished.[15] Therefore, although anxiety becomes more and more reflective, the
guilt that breaks forth in anxiety by the qualitative leap retains
the same accountability as that of Adam, and the anxiety the
same ambiguity.

To want to deny that every subsequent individual has and
must be assumed to have had a state of innocence analogous
to that of Adam would be shocking to everyone and would
also annul all thought, because there would then be an individual who is not an individual and who relates himself

merely as a specimen [*Exemplar*] to his species, although he would at the same time be regarded as guilty under the category of the individual.

Anxiety may be compared with dizziness. He whose eye happens to look down into the yawning abyss becomes dizzy. But what is the reason for this? It is just as much in his own eye as in the abyss, for suppose he had not looked down. Hence anxiety is the dizziness of freedom, which emerges when the spirit wants to posit the synthesis and freedom looks down into its own possibility, laying hold of finiteness to support itself. Freedom succumbs in this dizziness. Further than this, psychology cannot and will not go. In that very moment everything is changed, and freedom, when it again rises, sees that it is guilty. Between these two moments lies the leap, which no science has explained and which no science can explain. He who becomes guilty in anxiety becomes as ambiguously guilty as it is possible to become. Anxiety is a feminine weakness in which freedom faints. Psychologically speaking, the fall into sin always takes place in weakness.[16] But anxiety is of all things the most selfish, and no concrete expression of freedom is as selfish as the possibility of every conciction. This again is the overwhelming factor that determines the individual's ambiguous relation, sympathetic and antipathetic.[17] In anxiety there is the selfish infinity of possibility, which does not tempt like a choice but ensnaringly disquiets [*ængster*] with its sweet anxiousness [*Beængstelse*].

In each subsequent individual, anxiety is more reflective. This may be expressed by saying that the nothing that is the object of anxiety becomes, as it were, more and more a something. We do not say that it actually becomes a something or actually signifies something; we do not say that instead of a nothing we shall now substitute sin or something else, for what holds true of the innocence of the subsequent individual also holds true of Adam. All of this *is* only for freedom, and it *is* only as the single individual himself posits sin by the qualitative leap. Here the nothing of anxiety is a complex of presentiments, which, reflecting themselves in themselves, come

IV
332

nearer and nearer to the individual, even though again, when viewed essentially in anxiety, they signify a nothing—yet, mark well, not a nothing with which the individual has nothing to do, but a nothing that communicates vigorously with the ignorance of innocence. This reflectiveness is a predisposition that, before the individual becomes guilty, signifies essentially nothing; whereas when by the qualitative leap he becomes guilty, it is the presupposition by which he goes beyond himself, because sin presupposes itself, obviously not before it is posited (which is predestination), but in that it is posited.

We shall now consider more particularly the something that the nothing of anxiety may signify in the subsequent individual. In the psychological deliberation, it truly counts as something. But the psychological deliberation does not forget that if an individual becomes guilty as a matter of course by this something, then all consideration is annulled. This something, which hereditary sin signifies *stricte sic dicta* [in the strict sense of the word], is:

A. The Consequence of the Relationship of Generation

It is obvious that our subject is not one that may occupy physicians, such as whether one is born deformed etc., nor is the subject that of arriving at results by tabulated surveys. Here, as elsewhere, it is important that the mood be the correct one. When a person has been taught that hail and crop failures are to be ascribed to the devil, this may be very well meant, but such a teaching is essentially a cleverness that weakens the concept of evil and introduces into it an almost jesting note, just as, esthetically, it is jest to speak of a stupid devil. So when in dealing with the concept of faith the historical is made so one-sidedly significant that the primitive originality of faith in the individual is overlooked, faith becomes a finite pettiness instead of a free infinite. The consequence is that faith may come to be regarded in the manner of Hieronymus in Holberg's play,[18] when he says about Erasmus Montanus that he has heretical views of faith because he believes that the earth is round and not flat, as one generation after another in the village had believed. Thus a person might become a heretic in his faith by wearing wide pants when everyone else in the village wears tight pants. When someone offers statistical surveys of the proportions of sinfulness, draws a map of it in color and relief, so as to guide the eye quickly in its perspicuity, he makes an attempt at treating sin as a peculiarity of nature that is not to be annulled but is to be calculated just as atmospheric pressure and rainfall are. The mean and the arithmetical average that result are nonsense of a kind that has no comparison in the purely empirical sciences. It would be a very ridiculous abracadabra if anyone should seriously suggest that sinfulness averages 3⅜ inches in every man or that in Languedoc the average is merely 2¼ inches, while in Bretagne it is 3⅞. Examples such as these are no more superfluous than those in the introduction, because they are drawn from the sphere within which the following discussion moves.

By sin, sensuousness became sinfulness. This proposition has a double significance: by sin sensuousness becomes sinfulness, and by Adam sin entered into the world. These two determinations must constantly counterbalance each other; otherwise what is said becomes something untrue. That sensuousness at one time became sinfulness is the history of the generation, but that sensuousness becomes sinfulness is the qualitative leap of the individual.

Attention has been called to the fact (Chapter I §6) that the creation of Eve outwardly prefigures the consequence of the relationship of generation. In a sense, she signifies that which is derived. What is derived is never as perfect as the original.* However, here the difference is merely quantitative. Each subsequent individual is essentially as original as the first. The difference *in pleno* [common] to all subsequent individuals is derivation, but for the single individual derivation may again signify a more or a less.

IV
334

IV
333

---

* This, of course, pertains only to the human race, because the individual is qualified as spirit. In animal species, on the other hand, every subsequent specimen [*Exemplar*] is just as good as the first, or, more correctly, to be the first in such a case signifies nothing at all.

The derivation of woman also contains an explanation of the sense in which she is weaker than man, something that in all times has been assumed, whether it is a pasha speaking or a romantic knight. Nevertheless, the difference is not such that man and woman are not essentially alike despite the dissimilarity. The expression for the difference is that anxiety is reflected more in Eve than in Adam. This is because woman is more sensuous than man. Obviously, the point here is not an empirical state or an average, but the dissimilarity in the synthesis. If in one part of the synthesis there is a "more," a consequence will be that when the spirit posits itself the cleft becomes deeper and that in freedom's possibility anxiety will find a greater scope. In the Genesis account, it is Eve who seduces Adam. But from this it in no way follows that her guilt is greater than Adam's, and still less that anxiety is an imperfection;[19] on the contrary, the greatness of anxiety is a prophecy of the greatness of the perfection.

At this point, the investigation already shows that the proportion of sensuousness corresponds to that of anxiety. Therefore, as soon as the relationship of generation appears, whatever was said of Eve becomes an intimation of every subsequent individual's relation to Adam, namely, that as sensuousness is increased in the generation, anxiety is also increased. The consequence of the relationship of generation signifies a "more" in such a way that no individual can escape this "more," which is a "more" to all subsequent individuals in their relation to Adam. But this "more" is never of such a kind that one becomes essentially different from Adam.

However, before we proceed to this, I shall first shed some light on the proposition that woman is more sensuous than man and has more anxiety.

That woman is more sensuous than man appears at once in her physical structure. To deal more particularly with this is not my concern but is a task for physiology. However, I shall present my proposition in a different way. First I shall introduce her esthetically under her ideal aspect, which is beauty. To call attention to the circumstance that this is her ideal as-

pect indicates precisely that she is more sensuous than man.
Then I shall introduce her ethically under her ideal aspect,
which is procreation, and point out that the circumstance that
this is her ideal aspect indicates precisely that she is more
sensuous than man.

When beauty must reign, a synthesis results, from which
spirit is excluded.[20] This is the secret of all of Greek culture.
Because of this, there is a repose, a quiet solemnity about
Greek beauty, but precisely for this reason there is also an
anxiety of which the Greek was scarcely aware, although his
plastic beauty trembled with this anxiety. Therefore there is
light-heartedness in Greek beauty, because the spirit is
excluded, and also a profound, unexplained sorrow. Thus
sensuousness is not sinfulness but an unexplained riddle that
causes anxiety. Hence this naiveté is accompanied by an inexplicable nothing, which is the nothing of anxiety.

It is true that Greek beauty conceives of man and of woman
in the same way, as nonspiritual. Nevertheless, there is a distinction within this likeness. The spiritual has its expression in
the face. In the beauty of the man, the face and its expression
are more essential than in the beauty of the woman, although
the eternal youthfulness of plastic art constantly prevents the
more deeply spiritual from appearing. To develop this further
is not my task, but I shall indicate the dissimilarity with a
single suggestion. Venus is essentially just as beautiful when
she is represented as sleeping, possibly more so, yet the sleeping state is the expression for the absence of spirit. For this
reason, the older and the more spiritually developed the individuality is, the less beautiful it is in sleep, whereas the child is
more beautiful in sleep. Venus arises from the sea and is represented in a position of repose, a position that reduces the
expression of the face to the nonessential. If, on the other
hand, Apollo is to be represented, it would no more be appropriate to have him sleep than it would be to have Jupiter
do so. Apollo would thereby become ugly and Jupiter ridiculous. One might make an exception of Bacchus, because in
Greek art he represents the similarity between manly and

womanly beauty, as a consequence of which his forms are also feminine. In the case of a Ganymede, however, the expression of the face is already more essential.

As the conception of beauty becomes different in romanticism, the dissimilarity is again repeated within the essential likeness. While the history of spirit (and it is precisely the secret of spirit that it has a history) ventures to stamp itself upon the countenance of the man in such a way that everything is forgotten if only the imprint is distinct and noble, the woman on the other hand will make her effect as a whole in another way, even though her face has acquired a greater significance than in classical art. The expression must be that of a totality with no history. Therefore silence is not only woman's greatest wisdom but also her highest beauty.

IV
336

Viewed ethically, woman culminates in procreation. Therefore the Scriptures[21] say that her desire shall be for her husband. Although it is also true that the husband's desire is for her, his life does not culminate in this desire, unless his life is wretched or lost. But the fact that woman's life culminates in procreation indicates precisely that she is more sensuous.[22]

Woman is more anxious than man. This is not because of her lesser physical strength etc., for that kind of anxiety is not the issue here, but because she is more sensuous than man and yet, like him, is essentially qualified as spirit. What has often been said about her, that she is the weaker sex, is something entirely indifferent to me, because she therefore could very well be less anxious than man. In this investigation, anxiety is always conceived in the direction of freedom. So when the Genesis story,[23] contrary to all analogy, represents the woman as seducing the man, this is on further reflection quite correct, for this seduction is precisely a feminine seduction, because only through Eve could Adam be seduced by the serpent. In every other place where there is a question of seduction, linguistic usage (delude, persuade, etc.) always attributes superiority to man.

What is assumed to be recognized in all experience, I shall merely point out by an imaginatively constructed observation. Picture an innocent young girl; let a man fasten his desirous glance upon her, and she becomes anxious. In addition, she might become indignant etc., but first she will be in anxiety. On the other hand, if I picture a young woman fastening her desirous look upon an innocent young man, his mood will not be anxiety but disgust mingled with modesty, precisely because he is more qualified as spirit.

By Adam's sin, sinfulness entered into the world, and for Adam, sexuality came to signify sinfulness. The sexual was posited. There has been a great deal of idle talk both spoken and written in the world about naiveté. However, although innocence alone is naive, it is also ignorant. As soon as the sexual is brought to consciousness, to speak of naiveté is thoughtlessness, affectation, and, what is worse, a disguise for lust.[24] But from the fact that man is no longer naive, it by no means follows that he sins. Such dull flatteries only allure men precisely by diverting their attention from the true and the moral.[25]

IV
337

The whole question of the significance of the sexual, as well as its significance in the particular spheres, has undeniably been answered poorly until now;[26] moreover, it has seldom been answered in the correct mood. To offer witticisms about the sexual is a paltry art, to admonish is not difficult, to preach about it in such a way that the difficulty is omitted is not hard, but to speak humanly about it is an art. To leave it to the stage and the pulpit to undertake the answer in such a way that the one is embarrassed by what the other says, with the result that the explanation of the one is revoltingly different from that of the other, is really to surrender all and to place upon men the heavy burden,[27] which one does not oneself lift a finger to relieve, finding meaning in both explanations while the respective teachers continually expound the one or the other. This inconsistency would long since have been recognized if in our day men had not perfected themselves thoughtlessly to waste lives so beautifully designed, and thoughtlessly to participate noisily whenever there is talk about one or another imposing, prodigious idea, in the fulfillment of which they unite in an unshakable faith that in union there is strength, a faith as marvelous as that of the alehouse keeper who sold his beer for a penny less than he paid for it and still counted on a profit, "for it is the *quantity* that does it." Since this is the case, it is not surprising that in these days no one pays attention to such a deliberation. But this I know: had Socrates lived now, he would have reflected on such things and would have done it better and, if I may say so, more divinely than I can do. I am convinced that he would have said to me: "My dear fellow, you act correctly in considering such things, which are well worth pondering; indeed, one could converse whole nights and never finish fathoming the wonders of human nature." And this assurance is worth infinitely more to me than the loud praises of all my contemporaries, for this assurance makes my soul unshakable; the applause would make it doubtful.

The sexual as such is not the sinful. Real ignorance of it, when it nevertheless is essentially present, is reserved for the beast, which therefore is a slave of blind instinct and acts blindly. An ignorance that is also an ignorance of that which is not is the ignorance of the child. Innocence is a knowledge that denotes ignorance. Its distinction from moral ignorance is easily recognized by the fact that innocence is qualified in the direction of knowledge. With innocence, a knowledge begins that has ignorance as its first qualification. This is the concept of modesty (*Scham*). In modesty there is an anxiety, because spirit is found at the extreme point of the difference of the synthesis in such a way that spirit is not merely qualified as body but as body with a generic difference. Nevertheless, modesty is a knowledge of the generic difference, but not as a relation to a generic difference, which is to say, the sexual urge as such is not present. The real significance of modesty is that spirit, so to speak, cannot acknowledge itself at the extreme point of the synthesis. Therefore the anxiety found in modesty is prodigiously ambiguous. There is no trace of sensuous lust, and yet there is a sense of shame. Shame of what? Of nothing. And yet the individual may die of shame. A wounded modesty is the deepest pain, because it is the most inexplicable of all. For this reason, the anxiety in modesty can awaken by itself.[28] Here, of course, it is important that it is not lust that plays this role. An example of the latter is found in one of Friedrich Schlegel's tales (*Sämmtliche Werke*, vol. 7, p. 15, the story of Merlin).

In modesty, the generic difference is posited, but not in relation to its other. That takes place in the sexual drive. But since the drive is not instinct or instinct only, it *eo ipso* has a τέλος [end], which is propagation, while the reposing is love, the purely erotic. As yet spirit is not posited. As soon as it is posited not merely as that which constitutes the synthesis but as spirit, the erotic comes to an end. The highest pagan expression for this is that the erotic is the comic. Of course, this must not be understood in the sense in which a sensualist might take the erotic to be comical and material for his lascivious wit; but it is the power of intelligence and its preponderance that in the indifference of the spirit neutralize both the erotic and the moral relation to the erotic. This power has a very deep source. The anxiety in modesty arose from the spirit's feeling that it was a foreigner; now spirit has conquered completely and perceives the sexual as the foreign and as the comic. Modesty naturally could not have this freedom of the spirit. The sexual is the expression for the prodigious *Widerspruch* [contradiction] that the immortal spirit is determined as *genus*. This contradiction expresses itself in the profound *Scham* that conceals this contradiction and does not dare to understand it. In the erotic, the contradiction is understood as the beautiful, for beauty is precisely the unity of the psychic and the somatic. But this contradiction, which the erotic transfigures in beauty, is for spirit at once both the beautiful and the comic. The expression of spirit for the erotic is, therefore, that it is simultaneously the beautiful and the comic. Here there is no sensuous reflection upon the erotic, for that would be sensuality, in which case the individual would lie far below the beauty of the erotic; rather it is the maturity of spirit. Obviously, very few have understood this in its purity. Socrates did. Therefore when Xenophon represents Socrates as having said that one ought to love ugly women,[29] this expression, like everything else by Xenophon, becomes a repulsive, narrow-minded philistinism, which is

IV
339

most unlike Socrates. The meaning is that Socrates has reduced the erotic to indifference, and the contradiction that underlies the comic he expresses correctly by the corresponding ironic contradiction that one should love the ugly.*[30]

IV
340

However, such a view rarely occurs in its lofty purity. It requires an unusual interplay of a fortunate historical development and primitive talent. If such an objection is even remotely possible, the view is repulsive and an affectation.

In Christianity, the religious has suspended the erotic,[31] not merely as sinful, through an *ethical* misunderstanding, but as indifferent, because in spirit there is no difference between man and woman.[32] Here the erotic is not neutralized by irony, but it is suspended because the tendency of Christianity is to bring the spirit further. When in modesty the spirit becomes anxious of and shy of putting on the generic difference,

IV
339

* What Socrates said to Critobulus about the kiss[33] must be understood in this way. I believe it must be obvious to everyone that it would have been impossible for Socrates to have spoken in all seriousness with such pathos about the danger of the kiss, and also that he was no timid ninny who did not dare to look at a woman. In southern countries and among more passionate peoples, the kiss no doubt means more than in the north (concerning this one may refer to Puteanus's letter to John Bapt. Saccum: *nesciunt nostrae virgines ullum libidinis rudimentum oculis aut osculis inesse, ideoque fruuntur. Vestrae sciunt* [our Belgian maidens do not know that a kiss or a glance of the eye can be the beginning of lust, and therefore abandon themselves to it. Your Italian maidens know it]. Cf. Kempius, *Dissertatio de osculis*, in Bayle).[34] Nevertheless, it is unlike Socrates both as an ironist and as a moralist to speak in this way. When one is too zealous a moralist, one awakens desire and tempts the pupil almost against his will to become ironical toward the teacher. Socrates' relation to Aspasia points to the same thing. He associated with her, quite unconcerned about her ambiguous life. He only wanted to learn from her (Athenaeus),[35] and as a teacher she seems to have had talents, because it is

IV
340

told that husbands brought their wives with them to Aspasia[36] so that they might learn from her. However, as soon as Aspasia wanted to impress Socrates by her loveliness, he presumably explained to her that one ought to love the ugly women, and that she should not exert her charms any further, because for the attainment of his purpose he had enough in Xantippe (cf. Xenophon's account[37] of Socrates' view of his relation to Xantippe). Unfortunately, because again and again men approach the reading of everything with preconceived opinions, it is no wonder that everyone has the opinion that a Cynic is a profligate. Yet it might be possible precisely among the Cynics to find an example of the interpretation of the erotic as the comic.

the individuality suddenly leaps off and, instead of pervading the generic difference ethically, seizes an explanation from the highest sphere of the spirit. This is one side of the monastic view, whether it is more particularly determined as ethical rigor or as predominantly contemplation.*

As anxiety is posited in modesty, so it is present in all erotic enjoyment, and by no means because it is sinful. This is the case even though the minister blesses the couple ten times. Even when the erotic expresses itself as beautifully, purely, and, morally as possible, undisturbed in its joy by any lascivious reflection, anxiety is nevertheless present, not as a disturbing but as an accompanying factor.   IV 341

In these matters, it is extremely difficult to make observations. The observer must especially exercise the caution of physicians who when they take the pulse make sure that it is not their own they feel but that of the patient. In the same manner, the observer must take care that the movement he discovers is not his own restlessness in carrying out his observation. It is indeed certain that all poets describe love, but however pure and innocent, it is presented in such a way that anxiety is also posited with it. To pursue this further is a matter for an esthetician. But why this anxiety? It is because spirit cannot participate in the culmination of the erotic. Let me express myself in the manner of the Greeks. The spirit is indeed present, because it is spirit that establishes the synthesis, but it cannot express itself in the erotic. It feels itself a stranger. It says, as it were, to the erotic: My dear, in this I cannot be a third party; therefore I shall hide myself for the time being. But this precisely is anxiety, and modesty as well. For it is a great stupidity to assume that the marriage ceremony of the church or the faithfulness of the husband in keeping himself to his wife alone is all that is needed. Many a marriage has been profaned, and not by a stranger. However, when the

---

* However strange it may seem to one who is unaccustomed to view phenomena intrepidly, there is nevertheless a perfect analogy between Socrates' ironic view of the erotic as comical and the relation of a monk to *mulieres subintroductae* [women who were secretly brought in].[38] The abuse naturally concerns only those who have a liking for abuse.   IV 340

erotic is pure, innocent, and beautiful, this anxiety is friendly and gentle. Therefore the poets are correct in speaking of a sweet anxiousness.[39] Yet it is quite obvious that anxiety is greater in woman than in man.

We shall now return to the subject with which we were dealing, namely, the consequence of the relationship of generation in the individual, which is the "more" that every subsequent individual has in his relation to Adam. In the moment of conception, spirit is furthest away, and therefore the anxiety is the greatest. In this anxiety the new individual comes into being. In the moment of birth, anxiety culminates a second time in the woman, and in this moment the new individual comes into the world. It is well-known that a woman in childbirth is in anxiety. Physiology has its explanation, and psychology must also have its explanation. In childbirth the woman is again at the furthest point of one extreme of the synthesis. Therefore the spirit trembles, for in this moment it does not have its task, it is as if it were suspended. Anxiety, however, is an expression of the perfection of human nature; therefore it is only among aboriginal peoples that one finds the analogy to the easy delivery of animals.

The more anxiety, the more sensuousness. The procreated individual is more sensuous than the original, and this "more" is the universal "more" of the generation for every subsequent individual in relation to Adam.

But this "more" of anxiety and sensuousness for every subsequent man in relation to Adam may, of course, signify a more or a less in the particular individual. Here lie differences that in truth are so appalling that surely no one would dare to think about them in a deeper sense, i.e., with true human sympathy, unless he was firmly and unshakably convinced that never in the world has there been or ever will be a "more" such that by a simple transition it transforms the quantitative into the qualitative. What Scripture teaches,[40] that God avenges the iniquity of the fathers upon the children to the third and fourth generation, life proclaims loudly enough. To want to talk oneself out of this dreadful fact by explaining that this saying is a Jewish teaching is of no help.

Christianity has never assented to giving each particular individual the privilege of starting from the beginning in an external sense. Each individual begins in an historical nexus, and the consequences of nature still hold true. The difference, however, consists in that Christianity teaches him to lift himself above this "more," and it judges him who does not do so as being unwilling.

Precisely because sensuousness is here determined as a "more," the spirit's anxiety in assuming responsibility for sensuousness becomes a greater anxiety. At the maximum we find here the dreadful fact that *anxiety about sin produces sin*. If evil desire, concupiscence, etc. are regarded as innate in the individual, there is not the ambiguity in which the individual becomes both guilty and innocent. In the impotence of anxiety, the individual succumbs, and precisely for that reason he is both guilty and innocent.

I shall not cite detailed examples of this infinitely fluctuating more or less. To have any significance, such examples would require extensive and careful esthetic-psychological treatment.

B. The Consequence of the Historical Relationship

If I should express in a single sentence the "more" that every subsequent individual has in his relation to Adam, I would say: It is that sensuousness may signify sinfulness, that is, signify the obscure knowledge of it, in addition to an obscure knowledge of whatever else sin might signify, as well as a misunderstood appropriation of the historical *de te fabula narratur* [the story is told about you], in which the point, the originality of the individual, is excluded, and the individual forthwith confounds himself with the race and its history. We do not say that sensuousness is sinfulness, but that sin makes it sinfulness. Now if we consider the subsequent individual, every such individual has an historical environment in which it may become apparent that sensuousness can signify sinfulness. For the individual himself, sensuousness does not signify this, but this knowledge gives anxiety a "more." So spirit is posited not only in relation to the opposite of sensu-

IV
343

ousness, but also to that of sinfulness. It follows as a matter of course that the innocent individual does not as yet understand this knowledge, for it can only be understood qualitatively. However, this knowledge is again a new possibility, so that freedom in its possibility, as it relates itself to the sensuous, comes into still greater anxiety.

That this universal "more" may indicate a more and a less for the particular individual follows as a matter of course. Attention is at once called to an imposing difference. After Christianity had come into the world and redemption was posited, sensuousness was placed in a light of opposition such as was not found in paganism, which serves to confirm the proposition that sensuousness is sinfulness.

Within the Christian difference, this "more" may again signify a more and a less. This is owing to the relation of the particular innocent individual to his historical environment. In this respect, the most dissimilar things may produce the same effect. Freedom's possibility announces itself in anxiety. Consequently, a warning may bring an individual to succumb to anxiety (it should be remembered that, as always, I only speak psychologically and never annul the qualitative leap), although of course the warning was intended to do the opposite. The sight of the sinful may save one individual and bring another to fall. A jest may have the effect of seriousness, but also the opposite. Speech and silence can produce an effect opposite to what was intended. In this respect there are no limits. So here again one observes the correctness of the determination that this is a quantitative more or less, for the quantitative is precisely the infinite limit.[41]

I shall not pursue this any further by means of imaginatively constructed observations, because to do so would cause a delay. However, life is rich enough, if only one understands how to see. One need not travel to Paris and London; besides, this would be of no help if one is unable to see.

Moreover, anxiety has the same ambiguity here as it always has. At this point a maximum may appear that corresponds to the aforementioned—that the individual in anxiety about sin brings forth sin—namely, *the individual, in anxiety not about becoming guilty but about being regarded as guilty, becomes guilty*.

Furthermore, the ultimate more in this respect is that an individual from his earliest awakening is placed and influenced in such a way that sensuousness for him has become identical with sinfulness,[42] and this ultimate more will appear in the most painful form of collision if in the whole surrounding world he finds nothing that can give him support. If to this ultimate more is added the confusion that the individual confounds himself with his historical knowledge of sinfulness, and in the pallor of anxiety at once subsumes himself *qua* individual under the same category while forgetting the pronouncement of freedom, "If you do likewise"—then the ultimate more is present.

What has here been briefly indicated, namely, that it requires a very rich experience to understand and that much has been said both clearly and definitely, has often enough been the object of deliberation. This deliberation is usually called: concerning the power of the example. It cannot be denied— although this has not been the case in recent superphilosophical times—that fine things have been said about this subject; however, a psychological intermediate term is frequently lacking, namely, the explanation of how it happens that the example has such power. Moreover, in these spheres the matter is often treated a little too carelessly and without the awareness that a single little mistake in the smallest detail is capable of confusing the prodigious balance sheet of life. The attention of psychology is fixed exclusively upon the particular phenomenon, but at the same time it does not have its eternal categories ready and does not lay adequate emphasis upon saving mankind, which can be done only by saving each particular individual into the race, whatever the cost may be. The example is supposed to have had an influence upon the child. The child is represented as just a little angel, but the corrupt environment plunged it into corruption. Accounts are given again and again of how bad the environment was— and so, so the child became depraved. But if this takes place

through a simple quantitative process, every concept is canceled. This is something that is overlooked. The child is represented as being basically wicked, as having not had the advantage of the good example. However, care must be taken
that the child does not become so wicked that it acquires the
power to make fools not only of its parents but of all human
speech and thought, just as the *rana paradoxa* [paradoxical
frog][43] mocks and defies the naturalists' classification of
frogs. There are many men who well understand how to
view the particular, but who at the same time are unable to
keep the totality *in mente* [in mind]. Every such view, although otherwise meritorious, can only bring about confusion. Or, the child was, like most children, neither good nor
bad. But then it came into good company and became good
or into bad company and became evil. Intermediate terms! Intermediate terms! An intermediate term is provided that has
the ambiguity that rescues thought (without which the salvation of the child becomes an illusion), namely, that the child,
whatever its circumstance was, can become both guilty and
innocent. If one does not have the intermediate terms
promptly and clearly at hand, the concepts of hereditary sin,
of sin, of race, and of the individual are lost, and with these
the child also.

Sensuousness, then, is not sinfulness, but since sin was posited and continues to be posited, it makes sensuousness sinfulness. That sinfulness consequently signifies something else
as well goes without saying. But what sin further signifies is
not within the scope of our investigation, the task of which is
to immerse oneself psychologically in the state that precedes
sin and, psychologically speaking, predisposes more or less to
sin.

By the eating of the fruit of the tree of knowledge, the distinction between good and evil came into the world, but also
the sexual difference as a drive. How this came about, no science can explain. Psychology comes closest and explains the
last approximation, which is freedom's showing-itself-for-

IV
345

itself in the anxiety of possibility, or in the nothing of possibility, or in the nothing of anxiety. If the object of anxiety is a something, we have no leap but a quantitative transition. The subsequent individual has a "more" in relation to Adam, and again a more or a less in relation to other individuals. Nevertheless, it remains true that the object of anxiety is a nothing. If the object of anxiety is such a something that when viewed essentially, i.e., in the direction of freedom, it signifies something, then we do not have a leap but a quantitative transition that confuses every concept. Even when I say that for an individual sensuousness is posited as sinfulness before the leap, it remains true nevertheless that it is not essentially posited as such, for essentially the individual does not posit it or understand it. Even when I say that there is posited a "more" of sensuousness in the procreated individual with respect to the leap, this "more" is nevertheless an invalid "more."

IV
346

Consequently, if science has any other psychological intermediate term that has the dogmatic, the ethical, and the psychological advantages that anxiety possesses, then that should be preferred.

Moreover, it is easily seen that what has been presented here can very well be brought into conformity with the explanation commonly given of sin, namely, that it is selfishness. But when someone becomes absorbed in this qualification, he does not undertake at all to explain the preceding psychological difficulty. Furthermore, this also defines sin too pneumatically, and it is not adequately observed that by being introduced, sin posits just as much a sensuous as a spiritual consequence.

Although in the newer science[44] sin has so often been explained as selfishness, it is incomprehensible that it has not been recognized that precisely here lies the difficulty of finding a place for its explanation in any science. For selfishness is precisely the particular, and what this signifies only the single individual can know as the single individual, because when it is viewed under universal categories it may signify everything in such a way that it signifies nothing at all. The definition of sin as selfishness may therefore be quite correct, especially

when at the same time it is held that scientifically it is so
empty of content that it signifies nothing at all. Finally, in the
definition of sin as selfishness, no account is taken of the distinction between sin and hereditary sin, nor of the sense in
which the one explains the other, sin explaining hereditary sin
and hereditary sin explaining sin.

As soon as one wants to speak scientifically about this
selfishness, everything is dissolved into tautology, or one becomes clever and everything becomes confused. Who can
forget that natural philosophy found selfishness in all creation, found it in the movement of the stars that nevertheless
are bound in obedience to the laws of the universe, found that
the centrifugal force in nature is selfishness. If a concept is
brought that far, it might just as well lie down and, if possible, sleep off its drunkenness and become sober again. In this
respect, our age has been untiring in its efforts to make everything signify all things. Has it not often been seen how cleverly and doggedly some clever mystagogue[45] prostituted a
whole mythology so that by his falcon eye every particular
myth might become a whim for his jew's-harp? Cannot at
times an entire Christian terminology be seen to degenerate
into ruin by some pretentious speculator's treatment?

If a person does not first make clear to himself the meaning
of "self," it is of no use to say of sin that it is selfishness. But
"self" signifies precisely the contradiction of positing the
universal as the particular. Only when the concept of the particular is given can there be any talk of selfishness; however,
although there have lived countless millions of such "selves,"
no science can say what the self is without again stating it
quite generally.* And this is the wonder of life, that each man

---

* This is well worth further consideration, for precisely at this point it
must become apparent to what extent the recent principle that thought and
being are one is adequate, if on the one hand a person does not impair it with
untimely and partly foolish misunderstandings, and if on the other hand he
does not wish to have a highest principle that commits him to thoughtlessness. Only the universal is by the fact that it is thought and can be thought
(not merely in imaginative constructing, for what cannot be thought!) and is
as that which can be thought. The point about the particular is precisely its
negative relation to the universal and its repellent relation to it. But as soon as

who is mindful of himself knows what no science knows, since he knows who he himself is, and this is the profundity of the Greek saying γνῶθι σεαυτόν [know yourself],* which too long has been understood in the German way as pure self-consciousness, the airiness of idealism.[46] It is about time to seek to understand it in the Greek way, and then again as the Greeks would have understood it if they had possessed Christian presuppositions. However, the real "self" is posited only by the qualitative leap. In the prior state there can be no question about it. Therefore, when sin is explained by selfishness, one becomes entangled in indistinctness, because, on the contrary, it is by sin and in sin that selfishness comes into being. If selfishness is supposed to have been the occasion for Adam's sin, the explanation becomes a game in which the interpreter finds what he himself first has hidden. If it is to be said that selfishness brought about Adam's sin, one has leaped over the intermediate state and the explanation has acquired a suspicious ease. Moreover, it gives us no knowledge of the significance of the sexual. Here I am back to my old point. Sexuality is not sinfulness. However, to speak foolishly for a moment and by way of accommodation, let us suppose that Adam had not sinned: then the sexual would never have come into being as a drive. A perfect spirit cannot be conceived as sexually qualified. This is also in accord with the teaching of the Church about the nature of the Resurrection,[47] in accord with its representation of angels,[48] and in accord with the dogmatic definitions with respect to the person of Christ.[49] Just by way of suggestion, while it is said that Christ was

---

a person thinks the particular away it is canceled, and as soon as it is thought, it is altered. Therefore, either he does not think the particular but only imagines that he thinks it, or he thinks it and merely imagines that it is included in thought.

* The Latin saying *unum noris omnes* [if you know one, you know all][50] light-mindedly expresses the same and actually expresses the same, if by *unum* is understood the observer himself, and one does not inquisitively look for an *omnes* but earnestly holds fast to the one that actually is all. Men generally do not believe this and even think that it is too proud; the reason is that they are rather too cowardly and comfortably inclined to venture to understand and to acquire understanding of true pride.

tried in all human ordeals, there is no mention of a temptation in this respect, which has its explanation precisely in that he withstood all temptations.

Sensuousness is not sinfulness. Sensuousness in innocence is not sinfulness; nevertheless, sensuousness is there. Adam of course needed food, drink, etc. The generic difference is posited in innocence, but it is not posited as such. Only at the moment that sin is posited is the generic difference posited as a drive.

IV
349

Here, as everywhere, I must decline every misunderstood conclusion, as if, for instance, the true task should now be to abstract from the sexual, i.e., in an outward sense to annihilate it. When the sexual is once posited as the extreme point of the synthesis, all abstraction is of no avail. The task, of course, is to bring it under the qualification of the spirit (here lie all the moral problems of the erotic). The realization of this is the victory of love in a person in whom the spirit is so victorious that the sexual is forgotten, and recollected only in forgetfulness. When this has come about, sensuousness is transfigured in spirit and anxiety is driven out.

If this view, whether called Christian or called by any other name, is compared with the Greek view, then I believe that more has been gained than lost. Doubtless something of the plaintive, erotic *Heiterkeit* [cheerfulness][51] has been lost. But something has also been gained, namely, a qualification of spirit unknown to Greek culture. The only ones who truly lose are the many who constantly live on as if it were 6,000 years since sin entered into the world, as if it were a curiosity that did not concern them. They do not gain the Greek *Heiterkeit*, which precisely cannot be *won* but can only be lost, nor do they gain the eternal qualification of spirit.[52]

III

Anxiety as the Consequence of that Sin which Is Absence of the Consciousness of Sin

In the two previous chapters, it was maintained continually that man is a synthesis of psyche and body that is constituted and sustained by spirit. In the individual life, anxiety is the moment—to use a new expression that says the same as was said in the previous discussion, but that also points toward that which follows.

In recent philosophy there is a category that is continually used in logical no less than in historical-philosophical inquiries. It is the category of transition.[1] However, no further explanation is given. The term is freely used without any ado, and while Hegel and the Hegelian school startled the world with the great insight of the presuppositionless beginning of philosophy, or the thought that before philosophy there must be nothing but the most complete absence of presuppositions, there is no embarrassment at all over the use in Hegelian thought of the terms "transition," "negation," "mediation," i.e., the principles of motion, in such a way that they do not find their place in the systematic progression. If this is not a presupposition, I do not know what a presupposition is. For to use something that is nowhere explained is indeed to presuppose it. The system is supposed to have such marvelous transparency and inner vision that in the manner of the *omphalopsychoi* [navel souls][2] it would gaze immovably at the central nothing[3] until at last everything would explain itself and its whole content would come into being by itself. Such introverted openness to the public was to characterize the system. Nevertheless, this is not the case, because systematic thought seems to pay homage to secretiveness with respect to its innermost movements. Negation, transition, mediation are three disguised, suspicious, and secret agents (*agentia* [main springs]) that bring about all movements. Hegel would hardly call them presumptuous, because it is with his gracious permission that they carry on their ploy so unembarrassedly that even logic uses terms and phrases borrowed from transition in time: "thereupon," "when," "as being it is this," "as becoming it is this," etc.

Let this be as it may. Let logic take care to help itself. The term "transition" is and remains a clever turn in logic. Transition belongs in the sphere of historical freedom, for transition is a *state* and it is actual.* Plato fully recognized the difficulty of placing transition in the realm of the purely metaphysical, and for that reason the category of *the moment*** cost him so much effort. To ignore the difficulty certainly is not to "go

---

* Therefore, when Aristotle says that the transition from possibility to actuality is a κίνησις [movement],[4] it is not to be understood logically but with reference to historical freedom.

** Plato conceives of the moment as purely abstract. In order to become acquainted with its dialectic, one should keep in mind that the moment is non-being under the category of time. Non-being (τὸ μὴ ὄν; τὸ κενόν [that which is not; the empty][5] of the Pythagoreans) occupied the interest of ancient philosophers more than it does modern philosophers. Among the Eleatics, non-being was conceived ontologically in such a way that what was affirmed about it could be stated only in the contradictory proposition that only being is. If one pursues this further, he will see that it reappears in all the spheres. In metaphysical propaedeutics, the proposition was expressed thus: He who expresses non-being says nothing at all (this misunderstanding is refuted in *The Sophist*,[6] and in a more mimical way it was refuted in an earlier dialogue, *Gorgias*).[7] Finally, in the practical spheres the Sophists used non-being as a means to do away with all moral concepts; non-being is not, *ergo* everything is true, *ergo* everything is good, *ergo* deceit etc. are not. This position is refuted by Socrates in several dialogues. Plato dealt with it especially in *The Sophist*, which like all of his dialogues at the same time artistically illustrates what it also teaches, for the Sophist, whose concept and definition the dialogue seeks while it deals principally with non-being, is himself a non-being. Thus the concept and the example come into being at the same time in the warfare in which the Sophist is attacked, and which ends not with his annihilation but with his coming into being [*bliver til*], which is the worst thing that can happen to him, for despite his sophistry, which like the armor of Mars[8] enables him to become invisible, he must come forth into the light. Recent philosophy has not essentially come any further in its conception of

further" than Plato. To ignore it, and thus piously to deceive thought in order to get speculation afloat and the movement in logic going, is to treat speculation as a rather finite affair. However, I remember once having heard a speculator[9] say that one must not give undue thought to the difficulties before-

IV
353

IV
354

---

non-being, even though it presumes to be Christian. Greek philosophy and the modern alike maintain that everything turns on bringing non-being into being, for to do away with it or to make it vanish seems extremely easy. The Christian view takes the position that non-being is present everywhere as the nothing from which things were created, as semblance and vanity, as sin, as sensuousness removed from spirit, as the temporal forgotten by the eternal; consequently, the task is to do away with it in order to bring forth being. Only with this orientation in mind can the concept of Atonement be correctly understood historically, that is, in the sense in which Christianity brought it into the world. If the term is understood in the opposite sense (the movement proceeding from the assumption that non-being is not), the Atonement is volatilized and turned inside out.

It is in *Parmenides* that Plato sets forth "the moment." This dialogue is engaged in pointing out contradictions within the concepts themselves, something that Socrates expressed in so decisive a way, that while it does not serve to put to shame the beautiful old Greek philosophy, it may well put to shame a more recent boastful philosophy, which unlike the Greek does not make great demands upon itself but upon men and their admiration. Socrates points out that there is nothing wonderful about being able to demonstrate contrariety (τὸ ἐναντίον) of a particular thing participating in diversity, but if anyone were able to show contradictions in the concepts themselves, that would be something to admire (ἀλλ' εἰ ὃ ἔστιν ἕν, αὐτὸ τοῦτο πολλὰ ἀποδείξει καὶ αὖ τὰ πολλὰ δὴ ἕν, τοῦτο ἤδη θαυμάσομαι. καὶ περὶ τῶν ἄλλων ἁπάντων ὡσαύτως [But if anyone can prove that what is simply unity itself is many or that plurality itself is one, then I shall begin to be surprised] 129 B C).

IV
353

The procedure is that of an imaginatively constructing dialectic.[10] It is assumed both that the one (τὸ ἕν) is and that is not, and then the consequences for it and for the rest are pointed out. As a result, the moment appears to be this strange entity (ἄτοπον [that which has no place],[11] the Greek word is especially appropriate) that lies between motion and rest without occupying any time, and into this and out from this that which is in motion changes into rest, and that which is at rest changes into motion. Thus the moment becomes the category of transition (μεταβολή), for Plato shows in the same way that the moment is related to the transition of the one to the many, of the many to the one, of likeness to unlikeness, etc., and that it is the moment in which there is neither ἕν [one] nor πολλά [many], neither a being determined nor a being combined (οὔτε διακρίνεται οὔτε ξυγκρίνεται,[12]

hand, because then one never arrives at the point where he can speculate. If the important thing is to get to the point where one can begin to speculate, and not that one's speculation in fact becomes true speculation, it is indeed resolutely said that the important thing is to get the point of speculating, just as it is praiseworthy for a man who has no means of riding to Deer Park in his own carriage to say: One must not trouble himself about such things, because he can just as well ride a coffee grinder.[13] This, of course, is the case. Both riders hope to arrive at Deer Park. On the other hand, the man who firmly resolves not to trouble himself about the means of con-

---

IV
353

§157 A). Plato deserves credit for having clarified the difficulty; yet the moment remains a silent atomistic abstraction, which, however, is not explained by ignoring it. Now if logic would be willing to state that it does not have the category of transition (and if it does have this category, it must find a place for it within the system itself, although in fact it also operates in the system), it will become clearer that the historical spheres and all the knowledge that rests on a historical presupposition have the moment. This category is of utmost importance in maintaining the distinction between Christianity and pagan philosophy, as well as the equally pagan speculation in Christianity. Another passage in the dialogue *Parmenides* points out the consequence of treating the moment as such an abstraction. It shows how, if the one is assumed to have the determination of time, the contradiction appears that the one (τὸ ἕν) becomes older and younger than itself and the many (τὰ πολλά), and then again neither younger nor older than itself or the many (§151 E). The one must nevertheless be, so it is said, and then "to be" is defined as fol-

IV
354

lows: Participation in an essence or a nature in the present time[14] (τὸ δὲ εἶναι ἄλλο τί ἐστι ἢ μέθεξις οὐσίας μετὰ χρόνου τοῦ παρόντος, §151 E). In the further development of the contradictions [§152 B C], it appears that the present (τὸ νῦν) vacillates between meaning the present, the eternal, and the moment. This "now" (τὸ νῦν) lies between "was" and "will become," and naturally "the one" cannot, in passing from the past to the future, bypass this "now." It comes to a halt in the now, does not become older but is older. In the most recent philosophy,[15] abstraction culminates in pure being, but pure being is the most abstract expression for eternity, and again as "nothing" it is precisely the moment. Here again the importance of the moment becomes apparent, because only with this category is it possible to give eternity its proper significance, for eternity and the moment become the extreme opposites, whereas dialectical sorcery, on the other hand, makes eternity and the moment signify the same thing. It is only with Christianity that sensuousness, temporality, and the moment can be properly understood, because only with Christianity does eternity become essential.

veyance, just as long as he can get to the point where he can speculate, will hardly reach speculation.

In the sphere of historical freedom, transition is a state. However, in order to understand this correctly, one must not forget that the new is brought about through the leap. If this is not maintained, the transition will have a quantitative preponderance over the elasticity of the leap.

Man, then, is a synthesis of psyche and body, but he is also a *synthesis of the temporal and the eternal*. That this often has been stated, I do not object to at all, for it is not my wish to discover something new, but rather it is my joy and dearest occupation to ponder over that which is quite simple.[16]

As for the latter synthesis, it is immediately striking that it is formed differently from the former. In the former, the two factors are psyche and body, and spirit is the third, yet in such a way that one can speak of a synthesis only when spirit is posited. The latter synthesis has only two factors, the temporal and the eternal. Where is the third factor? And if there is no third factor, there really is no synthesis, for a synthesis that is a contradiction cannot be completed as a synthesis without a third factor, because the fact that the synthesis is a contradiction asserts that it is not. What, then, is the temporal?

If time is correctly defined as an infinite succession,[17] it most likely is also defined as the present, the past, and the future. This distinction, however, is incorrect if it is considered to be implicit in time itself, because the distinction appears only through the relation of time to eternity and through the reflection of eternity in time. If in the infinite succession of time a foothold could be found, i.e., a present, which was the dividing point, the division would be quite correct. However, precisely because every moment, as well as the sum of the moments, is a process (a passing by), no moment is a present, and accordingly there is in time neither present, nor past, nor future. If it is claimed that this division can be maintained, it is because the moment is *spatialized*, but thereby the infinite succession comes to a halt, it is because representation is introduced that allows time to be represented instead of being thought. Even so, this is not correct procedure, for

IV
355

even as representation, the infinite succession of time is an infinitely contentless present (this is the parody of the eternal). The Hindus[18] speak of a line of kings that has ruled for 70,000 years. Nothing is known about the kings, not even their names (this I assume). If we take this as an example of time, the 70,000 years are for thought an infinite vanishing; in representation it is expanded and is spatialized into an illusionary view of an infinite, contentless nothing.* As soon as the one is regarded as succeeding the other, the present is posited.

IV
356

The present, however, is not a concept of time, except precisely as something infinitely contentless, which again is the infinite vanishing. If this is not kept in mind, no matter how quickly it may disappear, the present is posited, and being posited it again appears in the categories: the past and the future.

The eternal, on the contrary, is the present. For thought, the eternal is the present in terms of an annulled succession (time is the succession that passes by). For representation, it is a going forth that nevertheless does not get off the spot, because the eternal is for representation the infinitely contentful present. So also in the eternal there is no division into the past and the future, because the present is posited as the annulled succession.

Time is, then, infinite succession; the life that is in time and is only of time has no present. In order to define the sensuous life, it is usually said that it is in the moment[19] and only in the moment. By the moment, then, is understood that abstraction from the eternal that, if it is to be the present, is a parody of it. The present is the eternal, or rather, the eternal is the present, and the present is full. In this sense the Latin said of the deity that he is *praesens* (*praesentes dii* [the presence of the gods]),[20] by which expression, when used about the deity, he also signified the powerful assistance of the deity.

* Incidentally, this is space. The skillful reader will no doubt see herein the proof of the correctness of my presentation, because for abstract thought, time and space are entirely identical (*nacheinander, nebeneinander*), and become so for representation, and are truly so in the definition of God as *omnipresent*.

The moment signifies the present as that which has no past and no future, and precisely in this lies the imperfection of the sensuous life. The eternal also signifies the present as that which has no past and no future, and this is the perfection of the eternal.

IV
357

If at this point one wants to use the moment to define time and let the moment signify the purely abstract exclusion of the past and the future and as such the present, then the moment is precisely not the present, because the intermediary between the past and the future, purely abstractly conceived, is not at all. Thus it is seen that the moment is not a determination of time, because the determination of time is that it "passes by." For this reason time, if it is to be defined by any of the determinations revealed in time itself, is time past. If, on the contrary, time and eternity touch each other, then it must be in time, and now we have come to the moment.

"The moment" is a figurative expression,[21] and therefore it is not easy to deal with. However, it is a beautiful word to consider. Nothing is as swift as a blink of the eye, and yet it is commensurable with the content of the eternal. Thus when Ingeborg[22] looks out over the sea after Frithiof, this is a picture of what is expressed in the figurative word. An outburst of her emotion, a sigh or a word, already has as a sound more of the determination of time and is more present as something that is vanishing and does not have in it so much of the presence of the eternal. For this reason a sigh, a word, etc. have power to relieve the soul of the burdensome weight, precisely because the burden, when merely expressed, already begins to become something of the past. A blink is therefore a designation of time, but mark well, of time in the fateful conflict when it is touched by eternity.* What we call the moment,

---

* It is remarkable that Greek art culminates in the plastic, which precisely lacks the glance. This, however, has its deep source in the fact that the Greeks did not in the profoundest sense grasp the concept of spirit and therefore did not in the deepest sense comprehend sensuousness and temporality. What a striking contrast to Christianity, in which God is pictorially represented as an eye.

Plato calls τὸ ἐξαίφνης [the sudden]. Whatever its etymological explanation, it is related to the category of the invisible, because time and eternity were conceived equally abstractly, because the concept of temporality was lacking, and this again was due to the lack of the concept of spirit. The Latin term is *momentum* (from *movere* [to move]), which by derivation expresses the merely vanishing.*

Thus understood, the moment is not properly an atom of time but an atom of eternity. It is the first reflection of eternity in time, its first attempt, as it were, at stopping time. For this reason, Greek culture did not comprehend the moment, and even if it had comprehended the atom of eternity, it did not comprehend that it was the moment, did not define it with a forward direction but with a backward direction. Because for Greek culture the atom of eternity was essentially eternity, neither time nor eternity received what was properly its due.

The synthesis of the temporal and the eternal is not another synthesis but is the expression for the first synthesis, according to which man is a synthesis of psyche and body that is sustained by spirit. As soon as the spirit is posited, the moment is present. Therefore one may rightly say reproachfully of man that he lives only in the moment, because that comes

---

* In the New Testament there is a poetic paraphrase of the moment. Paul[23] says the world will pass away in a moment, ἐν ἀτόμῳ καὶ ἐν ῥιπῇ ὀφθαλμοῦ [in the twinkling of an eye]. By this he also expresses that the moment is commensurable with eternity, precisely because the moment of destruction expresses eternity at the same moment. Permit me to illustrate what I mean, and forgive me if anyone should find the analogy offensive. Once here in Copenhagen there were two actors who probably never thought that their performance could have a deeper significance. They stepped forth onto the stage, placed themselves opposite each other, and then began the mimical representation of one or another passionate conflict. When the mimical act was in full swing and the spectators' eyes followed the story with expectation of what was to follow, they suddenly stopped and remained motionless as though petrified in the mimical expression of the moment. The effect of this can be exceedingly comical, for the moment in an accidental way becomes commensurable with the eternal. The plastic effect is due to the fact that the eternal expression is expressed eternally; the comic effect, on the other hand, consists in the eternalization of the accidental expression.

to pass by an arbitrary abstraction. Nature does not lie in the moment.

It is with temporality as it is with sensuousness, for temporality seems still more imperfect and the moment still more insignificant than nature's apparently secure endurance in time. However, the contrary is the case. Nature's security has its source in the fact that time has no significance at all for nature.[24] Only with the moment does history begin. By sin, man's sensuousness is posited as sinfulness and is therefore lower than that of the beast, and yet this is because it is here that the higher begins, for at this point spirit begins.

The moment is that ambiguity in which time and eternity touch each other, and with this the concept of *temporality* is posited, whereby time constantly intersects eternity and eternity constantly pervades time. As a result, the above-mentioned division acquires its significance: the present time, the past time, the future time.

By this division, attention is immediately drawn to the fact that the future in a certain sense signifies more than the present and the past, because in a certain sense the future is the whole of which the past is a part, and the future can in a certain sense signify the whole. This is because the eternal first signifies the future or because the future is the incognito in which the eternal, even though it is incommensurable with time, nevertheless preserves its association with time. Linguistic usage at times also takes the future as identical with the eternal (the future life—the eternal life). In a deeper sense, the Greeks did not have the concept of the eternal; so neither did they have the concept of the future. Therefore Greek life cannot be reproached for being lost in the moment, or more correctly, it cannot even be said that it was lost, for temporality was conceived by the Greeks just as naively as sensuousness, because they lacked the category of spirit.

The moment and the future in turn posit the past. If Greek life in any way denotes any qualification of time, it is past time. However, past time is not defined in its relation to the present and the future but as a qualification of time in general, as a passing by. Here the significance of the Platonic "recol-

IV
360

lection"[25] is obvious. For the Greeks, the eternal lies behind as
the past that can only be entered backwards.* However, the
eternal thought of as the past is an altogether abstract concept,
whether the eternal is further defined philosophically (a philosophical dying away)[26] or historically.

On the whole, in defining the concepts of the past, the future, and the eternal, it can be seen how the moment is defined. If there is no moment, the eternal appears behind as the
past. It is as when I imagine a man walking along a road but
do not posit the step, and so the road appears behind him as
the distance covered. If the moment is posited but merely as a
discrimen [division], then the future is the eternal. If the moment is posited, so is the eternal, but also the future, which
reappears as the past. This is clearly seen in the Greek, the
Jewish, and the Christian views. The pivotal concept in
Christianity, that which made all things new, is the fullness of
time,[27] but the fullness of time is the moment as the eternal,
and yet this eternal is also the future and the past. If attention
is not paid to this, not a single concept can be saved from a
heretical and treasonable admixture that annihilates the concept. One does not get the past by itself but in a simple continuity with the future (with this the concepts of conversion,
atonement, and redemption are lost in the world-historical
significance and lost in the individual historical development).
The future is not by itself but in a simple continuity with the
present (thereby the concepts of resurrection and judgment
are destroyed).

Let us now consider Adam and also remember that every
subsequent individual begins in the very same way, but
within the quantitative difference that is the consequence of
the relationship of generation and the historical relationship.
Thus the moment is there for Adam as well as for every subsequent individual. The synthesis of the psychical and the
physical[28] is to be posited by spirit; but spirit is eternal, and
the synthesis is, therefore, only when spirit posits the first
synthesis along with the second synthesis of the temporal and

IV
361

IV
360

* Here the category that I maintain should be kept in mind, namely, repetition, by which eternity is entered forwards.

the eternal. As long as the eternal is not introduced, the moment is not, or is only a *discrimen* [boundary]. Because in innocence spirit is qualified only as dreaming spirit, the eternal appears as the future, for this is, as has been said, the first expression of the eternal, and its incognito. Just as (in the previous chapter) the spirit, when it is about to be posited in the synthesis, or, more correctly, when it is about to posit the synthesis as the spirit's (freedom's) possibility in the individuality, expresses itself as anxiety, so here the future in turn is the eternal's (freedom's) possibility in the individuality expressed as anxiety. As freedom's possibility manifests itself for freedom, freedom succumbs, and temporality emerges in the same way as sensuousness in its significance as sinfulness. Here again I repeat that this is only the final psychological expression for the final psychological approximation to the qualitative leap. The difference between Adam and the subsequent individual is that for the latter the future is reflected more than for Adam. Psychologically speaking, this more may signify what is appalling, but in terms of the qualitative leap it signifies the nonessential. The highest difference in relation to Adam is that the future seems to be anticipated by the past or by the anxiety that the possibility is lost before it has been.

The possible corresponds exactly to the future. For freedom, the possible is the future, and the future is for time the possible. To both of these corresponds anxiety in the individual life. An accurate and correct linguistic usage[29] therefore associates anxiety and the future. When it is sometimes said that one is anxious about the past, this seems to be a contradiction of this usage. However, to a more careful examination, it appears that this is only a manner of speaking and that the future in one way or another manifests itself. The past about which I am supposed to be anxious must stand in a relation of possibility to me. If I am anxious about a past misfortune, then this is not because it is in the past but because it may be repeated, i.e., become future. If I am anxious because of a past offense, it is because I have not placed it in an essential relation to myself as past and have in some deceitful way or another prevented it from being past. If indeed it is actually past, then I cannot be anxious but only repentant. If I do not repent, I have allowed myself to make my relation to the offense dialectical, and by this the offense itself has become a possibility and not something past. If I am anxious about the punishment, it is only because this has been placed in a dialectical relation to the offense (otherwise I suffer my punishment), and then I am anxious for the possible and the future.

IV
362

Thus we have returned to where we were in Chapter I. Anxiety is the psychological state that precedes sin. It approaches sin as closely as possible, as anxiously as possible, but without explaining sin, which breaks forth only in the qualitative leap.

The moment sin is posited, temporality is sinfulness.* We

---

* From the determination of the temporal as sinfulness, death in turn follows as punishment. This is a progression, with the analogue, *si placet* [if one wishes], that even in relation to the external phenomenon, death declares itself more terrible the more perfect the organism is. Thus while the death and decay of a plant spread a fragrance almost more pleasing than its spring breath, the decay of an animal infects the air. It is true in a deeper sense that the higher man is valued, the more terrifying is death. The beast does not really die, but when the spirit is posited as spirit, death shows itself as the terrifying. The anxiety of death therefore corresponds to the anxiety of birth, yet I do not wish to repeat here what has been said, partly truly and partly cleverly, partly enthusiastically and partly frivolously, that death is a metamorphosis. At the moment of death, man finds himself at the uttermost point of the synthesis. It is as though spirit cannot be present, for it cannot die, and yet it must wait, because the body must die. Because the pagan view of sensuousness was more naive, its temporality more carefree, so the pagan view of death was milder and more attractive, but it lacked the ultimate. In reading the beautiful essay of Lessing[30] on the representation of death in classical art, one cannot deny being sadly and pleasurably moved by the picture of this sleeping genius or by seeing the beautiful solemnity with which the genius of death bows his head and extinguishes the torch. There is, if you will, something indescribably persuasive and alluring in trusting oneself to such a guide who is as conciliatory as a recollection in which nothing is recollected. On the other hand, there is something sinister in following this silent guide, because he does not conceal anything. His form is no incognito. Just as he is, so is death,[31] and with that, everything is over. There is an incomprehensible sadness in seeing this genius with his friendly figure bend down over the dying and with the breath of his last kiss extinguish the last spark of life, while all that was experienced has already vanished little by little, and

IV
363

do not say that temporality is sinfulness any more than that sensuousness is sinfulness, but rather that when sin is posited, temporality signifies sinfulness. Therefore he sins who lives only in the moment as abstracted from the eternal. But to speak foolishly and by way of accommodation, had Adam not sinned, he would in the same moment have passed over into eternity. On the other hand, as soon as sin is posited, it is of no help to wish to abstract from the temporal any more than from the sensuous.*[32]

§1.

THE ANXIETY OF SPIRITLESSNESS

A person who observes life will soon convince himself that what has been set forth here is correct, namely, that anxiety is the final psychological state from which sin breaks forth in the qualitative leap. Nevertheless, the whole of paganism and its repetition within Christianity lie in a merely quantitative determination from which the qualitative leap of sin does not break forth. This state, however, is not the state of innocence; rather, viewed from the standpoint of spirit, it is precisely that of sinfulness.

It is quite remarkable that Christian orthodoxy has always taught that paganism lay in sin, while the consciousness of sin was first posited by Christianity. Orthodoxy, however, is correct when it explains itself more precisely. By quantitative determinations, paganism stretches out time, as it were, and never arrives at sin in the deepest sense, yet this is precisely sin.

It is easy to show that this is the case in paganism.[33] But in

---

death remains as that which, itself unexplained, explains that the whole of life was a game that came to an end, and in which everyone, the greatest and well as the least, made their departures like school children,[34] extinguished like sparks of burning paper, and last of all the soul itself as the schoolmaster. And so there is also a muteness of annihilation found in the fact that the whole was merely a children's game, and now the game is over.

* What has been set forth here could just as well have been dealt with in Chapter I. However, I wished to deal with it here because it leads to what follows.

the case of paganism within Christianity, it is a different matter. The life of Christian paganism is neither guilty nor not guilty. It really knows no distinction between the present, the past, the future, and the eternal. Its life and its history go on crabbedly like the writing in ancient manuscripts, without any punctuation marks, one word, one sentence after the other. From an esthetic point of view, this is very comical, for while it is beautiful to listen to a brook running murmuring through life, it is nevertheless comical that a sum of rational creatures is transformed into a perpetual muttering without meaning. Whether philosophy can use this *plebs* [multitude] as a category by making it a substratum for the greater, just as vegetative sludge gradually becomes solid earth, first peat and so on, I do not know. Viewed from the standpoint of spirit, such an existence is sin, and the least one can do is to state this and demand spirit from it.

What has been set forth here does not apply to paganism. Such an existence can be found only within Christianity. The reason for this is that the higher that spirit is posited, the more profound the exclusion appears, and the higher that is which is lost, the more wretched in their contentment are οἱ ἀπηλγηκότες [those who are past feeling] (Eph. 4:19). If the bliss of this spiritlessness is compared with the state of slaves in paganism, then there is after all some sense in slavery, because it is nothing in itself. On the other hand, the lostness of spiritlessness is the most terrible of all, because the misfortune is precisely that spiritlessness has a relation to spirit, which is nothing. To a certain degree, spiritlessness may therefore possess the whole content of spirit, but mark well, not as spirit but as the haunting of ghosts, as gibberish, as a slogan, etc. It may possess the truth, but mark well, not as truth but as rumor and old wives' tales. Esthetically viewed, this is the profoundly comical in spiritlessness, something that is not generally noticed, because the actor himself is more or less insecure with regard to spirit. So when spiritlessness is to be represented, mere twaddle is simply put into the mouth of the actor, because no one has the courage to put into the mouth of spiritlessness the same words one uses oneself. This is insecurity. Spiritlessness can say exactly the same thing that the richest spirit has said, but it does not say it by virtue of spirit. Man qualified as spiritless has become a talking machine, and there is nothing to prevent him from repeating by rote a philosophical rigmarole, a confession of faith, or a political recitative. Is it not remarkable that the only ironist and the greatest humorist[35] joined forces in saying what seems the simplest of all, namely, that a person must distinguish between what he understands and what he does not understand? And what can prevent the most spiritless man from repeating the same thing verbatim? There is only one proof of spirit,[36] and that is the spirit's proof within oneself. Whoever demands something else may get proofs in superabundance, but he is already characterized as spiritless.

In spiritlessness there is no anxiety, because it is too happy, too content, and too spiritless for that. But this is a very lamentable reason, and paganism differs from spiritlessness in that the former is qualified *toward* spirit and the latter *away from* spirit. Paganism is, if I may say so, the absence of spirit, and thus quite different from spiritlessness. To that extent, paganism is much to be preferred. Spiritlessness is the stagnation of spirit and the caricature of ideality. Spiritlessness, therefore, is not dumb when it comes to repetition by rote, but it is dumb in the sense in which salt is said to be so. If the salt becomes dumb, with what shall it be salted?[37] The lostness of spiritlessness, as well as its security, consists in its understanding nothing spiritually and comprehending nothing as a task, even if it is able to fumble after everything with its limp clamminess. If on a particular occasion spiritlessness is touched by spirit and for a moment begins to twitch like a galvanized frog, a phenomenon occurs that corresponds perfectly to pagan fetishism. For spiritlessness there is no authority, because it knows indeed that for spirit there is no authority; however, since it unfortunately is not spirit, despite its knowledge, it is a perfect idol worshipper. It worships a dunce and a hero[38] with equal veneration, but above anything else its real fetish is a charlatan.

Even though there is no anxiety in spiritlessness, because it

IV
366 is excluded as is spirit, anxiety is nevertheless present, except that it is waiting. It is conceivable that a debtor may be fortunate enough to slip away from a creditor and hold him off with talk, but there is a creditor who never came off badly, namely, spirit. Viewed from the standpoint of spirit, anxiety is also present in spiritlessness, but it is hidden and disguised. Even observation shudders at the sight of it, because just as the figure of anxiety—if the imagination is allowed to form such a figure—is appalling and terrifying to look at, so the figure will terrify still more when it finds it necessary to disguise itself in order not to appear as what it is, even though it nevertheless is what it is. When death appears in its true form as the lean and dismal reaper, one does not look at it without terror; however, when it appears disguised in order to mock the men who fancy they can mock death, when the observer sees that the unknown figure who captivates all by his courtesy and causes all to exult in the wild gaiety of desires is death, then he is seized by a profound terror.

IV
366

§2.
ANXIETY DEFINED DIALECTICALLY AS FATE

It is usually said of paganism that it lies in sin; perhaps it might be more correct to say that it lies in anxiety. Paganism on the whole is sensuousness, but it is a sensuousness that has a relation to spirit, although spirit is not in the deepest sense posited as spirit. Yet this possibility is precisely anxiety.

If we ask more particularly what the object of anxiety is, then the answer, here as elsewhere, must be that it is nothing. Anxiety and nothing always correspond to each other. As soon as the actuality of freedom and of spirit is posited, anxiety is canceled. But what then does the nothing of anxiety signify more particularly in paganism? This is fate.

Fate is a relation to spirit as external. It is a relation between spirit and something else that is not spirit and to which fate nevertheless stands in a spiritual relation. Fate may also signify exactly the opposite, because it is the unity of necessity and the accidental. This is something to which we have not always paid attention. People have talked about the pagan *fatum*[39] (which is characterized differently in the Oriental conception and in the Greek) as if it were necessity. A vestige of this necessity has been permitted to remain in the Christian view, in which it came to signify fate, i.e., the accidental, that which is incommensurable with providence. However, this is not the case, for fate is precisely the unity of necessity and the accidental. This is ingeniously expressed in the saying, fate is blind, for he who walks forward blindly walks as much by necessity as by accident. A necessity that is not conscious of itself is *eo ipso* the accidental in relation to the next moment. Fate, then, is the nothing of anxiety. It is nothing because as soon as spirit is posited, anxiety is canceled, but so also is fate, for thereby providence is also posited. Therefore what Paul said about the idol[40] may be said of fate: there is no idol in the world; nevertheless, the idol is the object of the pagan's religiousness.

IV
367

Thus in fate the anxiety of the pagan has its object, its nothing. He cannot come into a relation to fate, because in the one moment it is the necessary and in the next it is the accidental. And yet he stands related to it, and this relation is anxiety.[41] Nearer to fate than this, the pagan cannot come. The attempt of paganism to do so was profound enough to shed a new light upon fate. Whoever wants to explain fate must be just as ambiguous as fate. And this the *oracle* was. However, the oracle in turn might signify the exact opposite. So the pagan's relation to the oracle is again anxiety. Herein lies the profound and inexplicable tragicalness of paganism. However, what is tragic does not lie in the ambiguity of the utterance of the oracle but in the pagan's not daring to forbear taking counsel with it. He stands in relation to it; he dares not fail to consult it. Even in the moment of consultation, he stands in an ambiguous relation to it (sympathetic and antipathetic). And at this point he reflects on the oracle's explanations!

The concepts of guilt and sin in their deepest sense do not emerge in paganism. If they had emerged, paganism would have perished upon the contradiction that one became guilty by fate. Precisely this is the greatest contradiction, and out of this contradiction Christianity breaks forth. Paganism does not comprehend it because it is too light-minded in its determination of the concept of sin.

The concepts of sin and guilt posit precisely the single individual as the single individual. There is no question about his relation to the whole world or to all the past. The point is only that he is guilty, and yet he is supposed to have become guilty by fate, consequently by all that of which there is no question, and thereby he is supposed to have become something that precisely cancels the concept of fate, and this he is supposed to have become by fate.

A misunderstanding of this contradiction will result in a misunderstanding of the concept of hereditary sin; rightly understood, it gives the true concept, in the sense that every individual is both himself and the race, and the subsequent individual is not essentially different from the first. In the possibility of anxiety, freedom collapses, overcome by fate, and as a result, freedom's actuality rises up with the explanation that it became guilty. Anxiety at its most extreme point, where it seems as if the individual has become guilty, is not as yet guilt. So sin comes neither as a necessity nor as an accident, and therefore providence corresponds to the concept of sin.

Within Christianity, the anxiety of paganism in relation to sin is found wherever spirit is indeed present but is not essentially posited as spirit. The phenomenon appears most clearly in a genius. Immediately considered, the genius is predominantly subjectivity.[42] At that point, he is not yet posited as spirit, for as such he can be posited only by spirit. As "immediate," he can be spirit (herein lies the deception that gives the appearance that his extraordinary talent is spirit posited by spirit), but then spirit has something else outside itself that is not spirit and is itself in an external relation to spirit. Therefore the genius continually discovers fate, and the more profound the genius, the more profound the discovery of fate. To spiritlessness, this is naturally foolishness, but in actuality it is greatness, because no man is born with the idea of providence, and those who think that one acquires it gradually through education are greatly mistaken, although I do not thereby deny the significance of education. The genius shows his primitive strength precisely by his discovery of fate, but in turn he also shows his impotence. To the immediate spirit, which the genius always is, except that he is an immediate spirit *sensu eminentiori* [in the eminent sense], fate is the limit. Not until sin is reached is providence posited. Therefore the genius has an enormous struggle to reach providence. If he does not reach it, truly he becomes a subject for the study of fate.

The genius is an omnipotent *Ansich* [in-itself][43] which as such would rock the whole world. For the sake of order, another figure appears along with him, namely, fate. Fate is nothing. It is the genius himself who discovers it, and the more profound the genius, the more profoundly he discovers fate, because that figure is merely the anticipation of providence. If he continues to be merely a genius and turns outward, he will accomplish astonishing things; nevertheless, he will always succumb to fate, if not outwardly, so that it is tangible and visible to all, then inwardly. Therefore a genius-existence is always like a fairy tale if in the deepest sense the genius does not turn inward into himself. The genius is able to do all things, and yet he is dependent upon an insignificance that no one comprehends, an insignificance upon which the genius himself by his omnipotence bestows omnipotent significance. Therefore a second lieutenant, if he is a genius, is able to become an emperor and change the world, so that there becomes one empire and one emperor. But therefore, too, the army may be drawn up for battle, the conditions for the battle be absolutely favorable, and yet in the next moment wasted; a kingdom of heroes may plead that the order for battle be given—but he cannot: he must wait for the fourteenth of June. And why? Because that was the date of the battle of Marengo. So all things may be in readiness, he himself stands before the legions, waiting only for the sun to rise in order to announce the time for the oration that will electrify the soldiers, and the sun may rise more glorious than ever, an inspiring and inflaming sight for all, only not for him, because the sun did not rise as glorious as this at Auster-

IV
369

litz, and only the sun of Austerlitz[44] gives victory and inspira-
tion. Thus the inexplicable passion with which such a one
may often rage against an entirely insignificant man, when
otherwise he may show humanity and kindness even toward
his enemies. Yes, woe unto the man, woe unto the woman,
woe unto the innocent child, woe unto the beast of the field,
woe unto the bird whose flight, woe unto the tree whose
branch comes in his way at the moment he is to interpret his
omen.[45]

The outward as such has no significance for the genius, and
therefore no one can understand him. Everything depends
upon how he himself understands it in the presence of his secret friend (fate). All may be lost; both the simplest and the
wisest men unite in admonishing him not to undertake the
fruitless venture. But the genius knows he is stronger than the
whole world, provided that at this point there is found no
doubtful commentary to the invisible writing by which he
reads the will of fate. If he reads it according to his wish, he
says with his omnipotent voice to the captain of the ship,
"Sail on, you carry Caesar and his fortune."[46] All may be
won, and in the very moment he receives the intelligence,
perhaps there is uttered a word along with it, the significance
of which no creature, not even God in heaven, understands
(for in a certain sense God in heaven does not understand the
genius), and with that the genius collapses in impotence.

Thus the genius is placed outside the universal. He is great
by reason of his belief in fate whether he conquers or falls, for
he conquers by himself and falls by himself, or rather, both
are by fate. Usually his greatness is admired only when he
conquers, and yet he is never greater than when he falls by his
own hand. This, of course, must be understood in the sense
that fate does not proclaim itself outwardly. When, however,
at the very moment that, humanly speaking, all is won, he
discovers the doubtful writing and then collapses, one might
well exclaim, "What a giant it would take to overthrow
him." Therefore no one was capable of doing this except
himself. The belief that subdued the kingdoms and countries
of the world under his mighty hand, while men believed they

envisioned a legend, is the same belief that overthrew him, and his fall was an even more unfathomable legend.

Therefore the timing of the genius's anxiety is quite different from that of ordinary men who first discover the danger in the moment of danger. Until then they feel secure, and when the danger is past, they are again secure. In the moment of danger, the genius is stronger than ever. His anxiety, on the other hand, lies in the moment before and after the danger, that trembling moment when he must converse with the great unknown, which is fate. His anxiety is perhaps greatest precisely in the moment after, because the impatience of certitude always increases in inverse ratio to the brevity of the distance to victory, since there is more and more to lose the nearer one comes to victory, and most of all in the moment of victory, because the consistency of fate is precisely its inconsistency.

The genius as such cannot apprehend himself religiously, and therefore he reaches neither sin nor providence, and for this reason the genius is found in the relation of anxiety to fate. There has never existed a genius without this anxiety unless he was also religious.

IV
371

If the genius remains thus immediately determined and turned outward, he will indeed become great and his accomplishment astounding, but he will never come to himself and never become great to himself. All his activity is turned outward, and if I may so speak, the planetarean core that radiates everything never comes into existence [*bliver til*]. The significance of the genius to himself is *nil*, or as dubiously melancholy as the sympathy with which the inhabitants of one of the Faroe Islands would rejoice if on this island there lived a native Faroese who astounded all of Europe by his writings in various European languages and transformed the sciences by his immortal contributions, but at the same time never wrote a single line in Faroese, and then at last also forgot how to speak it. In the deepest sense, the genius does not become significant to himself. His compass cannot be determined higher than that of fate in relation to fortune, misfortune, esteem, honor, power, immortal fame—all of which are temporal determinations. Every deeper dialectical determination of sin is excluded. The ultimate would be that of being regarded as guilty in such a way that anxiety is not directed toward guilt but toward the appearance of guilt, which is the category of honor. Such a state of the soul would be very appropriate for poetic treatment. What has been described can happen to every man, but the genius would at once lay hold of it so profoundly that he would not be striving with men but with the profoundest mysteries of existence [*Tilværelsen*].

That such a genius-existence is sin, despite its splendor, glory, and significance, is something that requires courage to understand, and it can hardly be understood before one has learned to satisfy the hunger of the wishing soul. It is true nonetheless. That such an existence may nevertheless be happy to a certain degree proves nothing. Talent may be conceived of as a means of diversion, and in so doing one realizes that at no moment is it possible to raise oneself above the categories in which the temporal lies. Only through a religious reflection can genius and talent in the deepest sense be justified. Take a genius like Talleyrand.[47] There was in him the possibility of a much deeper reflection upon life. This he shunned. He followed that constituent in him that turned outward. As intriguer, his admired genius was gloriously demonstrated; his resilience, the power of his genius to saturate (to use a term used by the chemists of corrosive acids) is admired, but he belongs to the temporal. If such a genius had disdained the temporal as immediate and turned toward himself and toward the divine, what a religious genius[48] would have emerged! But what agonies he would have had to endure. To follow immediate qualifications is a relief in life, whether one is great or small, but the reward is also in proportion to it, whether one is great or small. And he who is not so spiritually mature as to apprehend that even immortal honor throughout all generations is merely a qualification of the temporal, he who does not apprehend that this for which men strive and which keeps them sleepless with wishes and desire is exceedingly imperfect in comparison with the im-

IV
372

mortality that is for every man and that rightly would arouse the justifiable envy of all the world if it were reserved for only one man—he will not get far in his explanation of spirit and immortality.

§3.

ANXIETY DEFINED DIALECTICALLY AS GUILT

IV
372

It is usually said that Judaism is the standpoint of the law. However, this could also be expressed by saying that Judaism lies in anxiety. But here the nothing of anxiety signifies something other than fate. It is in this sphere that the phrase "to be anxious—nothing" appears most paradoxical, for guilt is indeed something. Nevertheless, it is true that as long as guilt is the object of anxiety, it is nothing. The ambiguity lies in the relation, for as soon as guilt is posited, anxiety is gone, and repentance is there. The relation, as always with the relation of anxiety, is sympathetic and antipathetic. This in turn seems paradoxical, yet such is not the case, because while anxiety fears, it maintains a subtle communication with its object, cannot look away from it, indeed will not, for if the individual wills it, repentance is there. That someone or other will find this statement difficult is something I cannot help. He who has the required firmness to be, if I dare say so, a divine prosecutor, not in relation to others but in relation to himself, will not find it difficult. Furthermore, life offers sufficient phenomena in which the individual in anxiety gazes almost desirously at guilt and yet fears it. Guilt has for the eye of the spirit the fascinating power of the serpent's glance. The truth in the Carpocratian view[49] of attaining perfection through sin lies at this point. It has its truth in the moment of decision when the immediate spirit posits itself as spirit by spirit; contrariwise, it is blasphemy to hold that this view is to be realized *in concreto*.

IV
373

It is precisely by the anxiety of guilt that Judaism is further advanced than Greek culture, and the sympathetic factor in its anxiety-relation to guilt may be recognized by the fact that it would not at any price forego this relation in order to acquire the more rash expressions of Greek culture: fate, fortune, misfortune.

The anxiety found in Judaism is anxiety about guilt. Guilt is a power that spreads itself everywhere, and although it broods over existence [*Tilværelsen*], no one can understand it in a deeper sense. Whatever is to explain it must therefore be of the same nature, just as the oracle corresponds to fate. To the oracle in paganism corresponds the sacrifice in Judaism. But for that reason no one can understand the sacrifice. Herein lies the profound tragedy of Judaism, analogous to the relation of the oracle in paganism. The Jew has his recourse to the sacrifice, but this does not help him, for that which properly would help him would be the cancellation of the relation of anxiety to guilt and the positing of an actual relation. Since this does not come to pass, the sacrifice becomes ambiguous, which is expressed by its repetition, the further consequence of which would be a pure skepticism in the form of reflection upon the sacrificial act itself.

Thus what held true in the preceding, that only with sin is providence posited, again holds true here: only with sin is atonement posited, and its sacrifice is not repeated. The reason for this, if I may so speak, is not the outward perfection of the sacrifice; on the contrary, the perfection of the sacrifice corresponds to the fact that the actual relation of sin is posited. Whenever the actual relation of sin is not posited, the sacrifice must be repeated[50] (thus the sacrifice is repeated in Catholicism, although the absolute perfection of the sacrifice is still recognized).

What has been indicated briefly here about the relation of the world-historical is repeated within Christianity in the individualities. Here again the genius exhibits most clearly what in less original men is present in such a way that it cannot easily be categorized. On the whole, the genius differs from every other man only in that he consciously begins within his historical presupposition just as primitively as Adam did. Every time a genius is born, existence is, as it were, put to a test, because he traverses and experiences all that is past, until he catches up with himself. Therefore the knowledge the genius has of the past is entirely different from that offered in world-historical surveys.[51]

It has been indicated already that the genius may remain in his immediate determination, and the explanation that this is sin also implies true courtesy toward the genius. Every human life is religiously designed. To want to deny this confuses everything and cancels the concepts of individuality, race, and immortality. Herein lie very difficult problems, for which reason one could wish that more people would exercise discernment at this point. To say that someone with a mind for intrigue ought to be a diplomat or a detective, that someone with a mimic talent for the comical ought to be an actor, and that someone with no talent at all ought to be a stoker in the courthouse is an altogether meaningless view of life, or it is rather no view at all, for it merely states what is obvious. However, to explain how my religious existence comes into relation with and expresses itself in my outward existence, that is the task. But in our time who would trouble himself to think about such things, although now more than ever the present life appears as a fleeting, transitory moment? Yet instead of learning from this how to lay hold of the eternal, we only learn how to drive ourselves, our neighbors, and the moment to death—in the pursuit of the moment. If a person could have a part just once, could lead the waltz of the moment just once—then he has lived, then he becomes the envy of the less fortunate, those who are not born but rush headlong into life, and headlong continue to rush forward, never reaching it. Then one has lived, for what is more valuable in human life than a young woman's brief loveliness, which indeed already has held up unusually well if for one night it has enchanted the lives of dancers and faded for the first time in the early morning. There is no time to consider how a religious existence pervades and interweaves the outward existence. Although one does not rush with the haste of despair, one still lays hold of what is closest at hand. In that way, a person may even become something great in the world, and furthermore, if he also attends church once in awhile, every thing will be extremely well with him. This seems to indicate that while for some individuals the religious is the absolute, for others it is not,* and then goodnight to all meaning in life. Naturally the deliberation becomes more difficult the more remote the outward task is from the religious as such. What profound religious reflection would be required to reach such an outward task, for example, that of becoming a comic actor! That it can be done, I do not deny, for whoever has some understanding of the religious knows that it is more pliant than gold, and absolutely commensurable. The fault of the Middle Ages[53] was not religious reflection, but that it broke off too soon. Here the question about repetition reappears: to what extent can an individuality, after having begun religious reflection, succeed in returning to himself again, whole in every respect? In the Middle Ages, a break was made. Therefore, when an individuality was to return to himself, having encountered, for example, the fact that he possessed wit, a sense for the comic, etc., he annihilated all of this as something imperfect. Nowadays, this is all too readily regarded as foolishness. For if someone has wit and a sense for the comic, he is a Pamphilius of fortune.[54] What more can he wish? Naturally such explanations have not the faintest presentiment of the problem, for although nowadays men are born more worldly-wise than in the old days, the greater number of them are born blind in relation to the religious. Nevertheless, in the Middle Ages there were also examples of carrying this deliberation further. For example, when a painter apprehended his talent religiously, but this talent could not express itself in achievements that lie closest to the religious, such an artist might have been seen piously concentrating all

* Among the Greeks the question about the religious could not arise in this manner. However, it is beautiful to read what Plato recounts[52] in one place and applies. After Epimetheus had equipped man with all sorts of gifts, he asked Zeus whether he should distribute the ability to choose between good and evil in the same way that he had distributed the other gifts, so that one man received this ability while another got the gift of eloquence, and another that of poetry, and a third that of art. But Zeus replied that this ability should be distributed equally among all, because it belongs essentially to every man alike.

his ability in the painting of a Venus, and apprehending his artistic calling with all the piety of an artist who came to the aid of the church and captivated the eyes of the congregation with a vision of the heavenly beauty. However, in regard to all this, one has to wait for the appearance of individuals who, despite outward gifts, do not choose the broad way but rather the pain, the distress, and the anxiety in which they religiously call to mind what meanwhile they lose, as it were, namely, what is too seductive to possess. Such a struggle is indubitably very exhausting, because there will come moments when they almost regret having begun it and recall with melancholy, at times possibly unto despair, the smiling life that would have opened before them had they pursued the immediate inclination of their talent. Nevertheless, in the extreme terror of distress, when it is as though all were lost because the way along which he would advance is impassable, and the smiling way of talent is cut off from him by his own act, the person who is aware will indubitably hear a voice saying: Well done, my son! Just keep on, for he who loses all, gains all.[55]

IV
376

We will now consider a genius who is religious, that is, one who does not remain in his immediacy. Whether he at any time turns himself outward remains for him a subsequent question. The first thing he does is to turn toward himself. Just as the immediate genius has fate as the figure that follows him, so he has guilt. In turning toward himself, he *eo ipso* turns toward God, and there is a ceremonial rule that says that when the finite spirit would see God, it must begin as guilty. As he turns toward himself, he discovers guilt. The greater the genius, the more profoundly he discovers guilt. To me it is a joy and a gratifying sign that to spiritlessness this is foolishness. The genius is not like most people and would not be satisfied to be so. This is not because he disdains men, but because he is primitively concerned with himself, whereas other men and their explanations are of no help to him.

The fact that he discovers guilt so profoundly indicates that this concept is present to him *sensu eminentiori* [in the eminent sense], just as its opposite, innocence, is also. So it was in the case of the relation of the immediate genius to fate, for every man has a little relation to fate, but there it ends in talk that does not notice what Talleyrand[56] (and Young before him expressed) discovered and expressed, although not as fully as empty talk does, that the purpose of language is to conceal thought—namely, to conceal that one has none.

In turning inward, he discovers freedom. He does not fear fate, for he lays hold of no outward task, and freedom is for him his bliss, not freedom to do this or that in the world, to become king and emperor or an abusive street corner orator, but freedom to know of himself that he is freedom. Yet the higher an individual rises, the greater is the price he must pay for everything; and for the sake of order, another figure comes into being with the *Ansich* [in-itself] of freedom, namely, guilt. Guilt in turn is what fate was, the only thing he fears, and yet his fear is not of what was the maximum in the former case, namely, fear of being thought guilty, but fear of being guilty.

To the degree he discovers freedom, to that same degree the anxiety of sin is upon him in the state of possibility. He fears only guilt, for guilt alone can deprive him of freedom. Here it is readily seen that freedom is by no means defiance, nor is it selfish freedom in a finite sense. By such an assumption, attempts often have been made to explain the origin of sin, but such efforts are only wasted labor, because the acceptance of such an assumption presents a greater difficulty than the explanation. When freedom is apprehended in this way, it has necessity as its opposite, which shows that it has been conceived as a category of reflection. No, the opposite of freedom is guilt, and it is the greatness of freedom that it always has to do only with itself, that in its possibility it projects guilt and accordingly posits it by itself. And if guilt is posited actually, freedom posits it by itself. If this is not kept in mind, freedom is confused in a clever way with something entirely different, with *force*.

Now when freedom fears guilt, what it fears is not to recognize itself as guilty, if it is, but rather it fears to become guilty, for which reason freedom, as soon as guilt is posited, returns as repentance. For the time being, freedom's relation to guilt is a possibility. Here again genius manifests itself by not side-stepping the primitive decision, by not seeking the decision outside itself with Tom, Dick, and Harry, and by not being content with the usual bargaining. Only by itself can freedom come to know whether it is freedom or whether guilt is posited. Therefore nothing is more ridiculous than to assume that the question of whether one is a sinner or guilty belongs under the rubric: lesson to be memorized.

The relation of freedom to guilt is anxiety, because freedom and guilt are still only possibilities. However, as freedom with all its passion wishfully stares at itself and would keep guilt at a distance so that not a single particle of it might be found in freedom, it cannot refrain from staring at guilt, and this staring is the ambiguous staring of anxiety, just as renunciation within the possibility is itself a coveting.

IV
378

Here it clearly appears in what sense there is a more in the anxiety of the subsequent individual than in Adam's anxiety.* Guilt is a more concrete conception, which becomes more and more possible in the relation of possibility to freedom. At last it is as if the guilt of the whole world united to make him guilty, and, what is the same, as if in becoming guilty he became guilty of the guilt of the whole world. Guilt has the dialectical character that it does not allow itself to be transferred, but whoever becomes guilty also becomes guilty of that which occasioned the guilt. For guilt never has an external occasion, and whoever yields to temptation is himself guilty of the temptation.

In the relation of possibility, this appears as an illusion. However, as soon as repentance breaks forth with the actual sin,[57] then it has the actual sin as its object. In freedom's possibility, it holds true that the more profoundly guilt is discovered, the greater the genius, because the greatness of a man

---

* Yet it must not be forgotten that here the analogy is inaccurate, inasmuch as we are not dealing with innocence in the subsequent individual but with a repressed sin-consciousness.

depends simply and solely on the energy of the God-relation in him, even though the God-relation finds an altogether wrong expression as fate.

Just as fate at last captures the immediate genius, and this is indeed his moment of culmination, not the glittering outward realization that amazes men and even calls the artisan from his daily work to stop and take notice, but the moment when by himself he collapses for himself by fate, guilt likewise captures the genius who is religious,[58] and this is the moment of culmination, the moment when he is greatest, not the moment when the sight of his piety is like the festivity of a special holiday, but when by himself he sinks before himself in the depth of sin-consciousness.

Anxiety of Sin or
Anxiety as the Consequence of Sin in
the Single Individual

By a qualitative leap sin entered into the world, and it continually enters into the world in that way. As soon as the leap is posited, one would think that anxiety would be canceled, because anxiety is defined as freedom's disclosure to itself in possibility. The qualitative leap is clearly actuality, and so it would seem that possibility is annulled along with anxiety. However, this is not the case. First of all, actuality is not one factor; second, the actuality posited is an unwarranted actuality. So anxiety again comes into relation with what is posited as well as with the future. Yet this time the object of anxiety is a determinate something and its nothing is an actual something, because the distinction between good and evil* is pos-

---

* The question "What is the good?" is one issue that comes closer and closer to our age, because it has decisive significance for the question of the relationship between church, state, and morality. In attempting an answer, one must be cautious. Hitherto, the true has in a strange way had the priority, because the trilogy—the beautiful, the good, the true—has been conceived and represented in the sphere of the true (namely, as knowledge). The good cannot be defined at all. The good is freedom. The difference between good and evil is only for freedom and in freedom, and this difference is never *in abstracto* but only *in concreto*. Therefore, for one not experienced in the Socratic method it is disturbing when Socrates instantly draws what is apparently infinitely abstract, the good, back to the most concrete. The method is entirely correct, except that he was mistaken (according to Greek thought, he acted correctly) in conceiving the good from its external side (the useful, the finitely teleological). The difference between good and evil is indeed for freedom, but not *in abstracto*. This misunderstanding arises because freedom is changed into something else, into an object of thought. But freedom is never *in abstracto*. If freedom is given a moment to choose between good and evil, a moment when freedom itself is in neither the one nor the other, then in that

IV
380
ited *in concreto*—and anxiety therefore loses its dialectical ambiguity. This is true of Adam as well as of every subsequent individual, for in the qualitative leap they are completely alike.

When sin is posited in the particular individual by the qualitative leap, the difference between good and evil is also posited. We have nowhere been guilty of the foolishness that holds that man *must* sin; on the contrary, we have always protested against all merely imaginatively constructed knowledge. We have said what we again repeat, that sin presupposes itself, just as freedom presupposes itself, and sin cannot be explained by anything antecedent to it, anymore than can freedom. To maintain that freedom begins as *liberum arbitrium*

IV
381
(which is found nowhere, cf. Leibniz)[1] that can choose good just as well as evil inevitably makes every explanation impossible. To speak of good and evil as the objects of freedom finitizes both freedom and the concepts of good and evil. Freedom is infinite and arises out of nothing. Therefore, to want to say that man sins by necessity makes the circle of the leap into a straight line. Such a procedure seems highly plausible to many, because to a great many thoughtlessness is the most natural thing, and in all ages their number is legion who re-

---

very moment freedom is not freedom, but a meaningless reflection. So for what purpose is the imaginary construction except to confuse? If (*sit venia verbo* [pardon the expression]) freedom remains in the good, then it knows nothing at all of evil. In this sense one may say about God (if anyone misunderstands this, it is not my fault) that he knows nothing of evil. By this I by no means say that evil is merely the negative, *das Aufzuhebende* [that which is to be annulled]; on the contrary, that God knows nothing of evil, that he neither can nor will know of it, is the absolute punishment of evil. In this sense the preposition ἀπό [away from] is used in the New Testament to signify removal from God or, if I dare put it this way, God's ignoring of evil. If one conceives of God finitely, it is indeed convenient for evil if God ignores it, but because God is the infinite, his ignoring is the living annihilation, for evil cannot dispense with God, even merely in order to be evil. Here I shall quote a passage from Scripture, II Thessalonians 1:9, where it is said of those who do not know God and do not obey the gospel: οἵτινες δίκην τίσουσιν ὄλεθρον αἰώνιον ἀπὸ προσώπου τοῦ κυρίου, καὶ ἀπὸ τῆς δόξης τῆς ἰσχύος αὐτοῦ [they shall suffer the punishment of eternal destruction and exclusion from the presence of the Lord and from the glory of his might].

gard as praiseworthy that way of thinking that through all centuries has in vain been labeled λόγος ἀργός [lazy reasoning][2] (Chrysippus), *ignava ratio* (Cicero), *sophisma pigrum, la raison paresseuse* (Leibniz).

Now psychology again has anxiety as its object, but it must be cautious. The history of the individual life proceeds in a movement from state to state. Every state is posited by a leap. As sin entered into the world, so it continues to enter into the world if it is not halted. Nevertheless, every such repetition is not a simple consequence but a new leap. Every such leap is preceded by a state as the closest psychological approximation. This state is the object of psychology. To the extent that in every state possibility is present, anxiety is also present. Such is the case after sin is posited, for only in the good is there a unity of state and transition.

§1.[3]

ANXIETY ABOUT EVIL

IV
381

(a) The posited sin is indeed an annulled possibility, but it is also an unwarranted actuality, and as such, anxiety can relate itself to it. Since sin is an unwarranted actuality, it is also to be negated. This work anxiety will undertake. Here is the playground of the ingenious sophistry of anxiety. While the actuality of sin holds one hand of freedom in its icy right hand just as the Commandant[4] held Don Giovanni, the left hand gesticulates with delusion, deception, and the eloquence of illusion.*

IV
382

(b) The posited sin is in itself also a consequence, even though it is a consequence foreign to freedom. This consequence announces itself, and anxiety relates itself to the future appearance of this consequence, which is the possibility of a new state. No matter how deep an individual has sunk, he can sink still deeper, and this "can" is the object of anxiety. The more relaxed anxiety becomes at this point, the more it sig-

---

* Because of the form of the investigation, I can indicate the particular state only very briefly, almost algebraically. This is not the place for a thorough description.

nifies that the consequence of sin has entered the individual *in succum et sanguinem* [in flesh and blood] and that sin has obtained a domicile in individuality.

Here sin, of course, signifies the concrete, for one never sins on the average or in general.[5] Even that sin of wishing to go back to the time before the actuality of sin* is not a sin on the average, for such a sin has never occurred. Whoever has some understanding of men knows very well that sophistry always fixes upon one particular point and continually skirts the point. Anxiety wants to have the actuality of sin removed, not entirely but to a certain degree, or to put it more exactly, to a certain degree it wants to have the actuality of sin continue—but note, only to a certain degree. Therefore anxiety is not disinclined to flirt a little with quantitative determinants. The more developed anxiety is, the further it dares to pursue the flirtation. But as soon as the jest and the diversion of quantitative determinants are about to capture the individual in the qualitative leap, which lies in wait like the larva of the ant-lion[6] in the funnel formed in the loose sand, anxiety cautiously withdraws; then it has a little point that must be saved and that is without sin, and in the next moment another point. A consciousness of sin profoundly and seriously formed in the expression of repentance is a great rarity. However, for my own sake, as well as for the sake of thought and neighbor, I shall take care not to express it as Schelling[7] probably would, who speaks somewhere of a genius for action in the same sense as for music etc. Thus, without being aware of it, one can at times annihilate everything with an explanatory word. If every man does not participate essentially in the absolute, then everything is over. Therefore, in the sphere of the religious, genius must not be spoken of as a special gift that is bestowed only upon a few, for here the gift is that of willing, and whoever does not will should at least have the respect of not being pitied.

Ethically speaking, sin is not a state.[8] The state, however, is

IV
383

IV
382 * This is spoken ethically, for ethics does not see the state but sees how the state in the same moment is a new sin.

always the last psychological approximation to the next state. Anxiety is at this point always present as the possibility of the new state. In the state described under (a), anxiety is more noticeable; whereas in (b), it disappears more and more. But anxiety is nevertheless outside such an individual, and viewed from the standpoint of spirit, it is greater than any other anxiety. In (a), the anxiety is about the actuality of sin, out of which it sophistically brings forth possibility; whereas viewed ethically, it sins. The movement of anxiety is here the opposite of the anxiety of innocence, in which, psychologically speaking, it brings forth actuality out of the possibility of sin; whereas viewed ethically, sin is brought forth by the qualitative leap. In (b), anxiety is directed toward the further possibility of sin. If at this point anxiety decreases, we explain it by the fact that the consequence of sin conquers.

(c) The posited sin is an unwarranted actuality. It is actuality, and it is posited by the individual as actuality in repentance, but repentance does not become the individual's freedom. Repentance is reduced to a possibility in relation to sin; in other words, repentance cannot cancel sin, it can only sorrow over it. Sin advances in its consequence; repentance follows it step by step, but always a moment too late. It forces itself to look at the dreadful, but like the mad King Lear (*O du zertrümmert Meisterstück der Schöpfung* [O thou ruined masterpiece of nature])[9] it has lost the reins of government, and it has retained only the power to grieve. At this point, anxiety is at its highest. Repentance has lost its mind, and anxiety is potentiated into repentance. The consequence of sin moves on; it drags the individual along like a woman whom the executioner drags by the hair while she screams in despair. Anxiety is ahead; it discovers the consequence before it comes, as one feels in one's bones that a storm is approaching. The consequence comes closer; the individual trembles like a horse that gasps as it comes to a halt at the place where once it had been frightened. Sin conquers. Anxiety throws itself despairingly into the arms of repentance. Repentance ventures all. It conceives of the consequence of sin as suffering penalty and of perdition[10] as the consequence of sin. It is lost. Its

IV
384

judgment is pronounced, its condemnation is certain, and the augmented judgment is that the individual shall be dragged through life to the place of execution. In other words, repentance has gone crazy.

Life offers opportunities to observe what has been suggested here. Such a state is seldom found among altogether corrupt natures, but generally only among the deeper, for it requires considerable primitivity and endurance in man if he is not to fall under (a) or (b). No dialectic is capable of defeating the sophism that crazed repentance is capable of producing at every moment. Such a repentance has a dejection that in the dialectic and expression of passion is far more powerful than true repentance. (In another sense it is, of course, more impotent; yet, as anyone who has observed such cases no doubt has noticed, it is remarkable what persuasive powers, what eloquence such repentance possesses to disarm all objections and to convince all who come close to it, only to despair of itself again when this diversion is over.) To attempt to stop this horror by words and phrases is wasted effort, and whoever contemplates doing it may always be sure that his sermonizing will be like children's babble when compared with the elementary eloquence that is at the service of such repentance. The phenomenon may appear in connection with the sensuous in man (addiction to drink, to opium, or to debauchery, etc.) as well as in connection with the higher (pride, vanity, wrath, hatred, defiance, cunning, envy, etc.). The individual may repent of his wrath, and the more profound he is, the more profound is his repentance. But repentance cannot make him free; in that he is mistaken. The occasion comes; anxiety has already discovered it. Every thought trembles. Anxiety sucks out the strength of repentance and shakes its head. It is as though wrath had already conquered. Already he has a presentiment of the prostration of freedom that is reserved for the next moment. The moment comes; wrath conquers.

Whatever the consequence of sin, the fact that the phenomenon appears on a considerable scale is always the sign of a deeper nature. The phenomenon is seldom seen in life, i.e., one must be an observer to see it more often, because it can be IV
385 concealed or dispelled, and men use one or another prudential device to abort this embryo of the highest life. All that is needed in order to become like most people is to seek the advice of Tom, Dick, and Harry, and one can always secure the testimony of a few respectable people to that end. The most effective means of escaping spiritual trial [*Anfægtelse*] is to become spiritless, and the sooner the better. If only taken care of in time, everything takes care of itself. And as for spiritual trial, it may be explained as nonexistent, or at the most may be regarded as a piquant poetical fiction. In the old days, the road to perfection was narrow and solitary. The journey along it was always disturbed by aberrations, exposed to predatory attacks by sin, and pursued by the arrow of the past, which is as dangerous as that of the Scythian hordes. Now one travels to perfection by railway in good company, and before he knows it, he has arrived.

The only thing that is truly able to disarm the sophistry of sin is faith, courage to believe that the state itself is a new sin, courage to renounce anxiety without anxiety, which only faith can do; faith does not thereby annihilate anxiety, but, itself eternally young, it extricates itself from anxiety's moment of death. Only faith is able to do this, for only in faith is the synthesis eternal and at every moment possible.

It is not difficult to see that all that has been presented here belongs to the realm of psychology. Ethically, the point is to get the individual rightly placed in relation to sin. As soon as this is accomplished, the individual stands repentant in sin. According to the idea, in that very moment he has been brought to dogmatics. Repentance is the highest ethical contradiction,[11] partly because ethics requires ideality but must be content to receive repentance, and partly because repentance is dialectically ambiguous with regard to what it is to remove, an ambiguity that dogmatics for the first time removes in the Atonement, in which the category of hereditary sin becomes clear. Moreover, repentance delays action, and action is precisely what ethics requires. At last, repentance must become an object to itself, inasmuch as the moment of repentance becomes a deficit of action. It was, therefore, a genuine ethical outburst, full of energy and courage, when the elder Fichte[12] said there was no time for repentance. By this statement, however, he did not bring repentance to the dialectical point where as posited it will annul itself by new repentance and then collapse.

What has been presented in this paragraph, as elsewhere in this work, is what psychologically may be called freedom's psychological attitudes toward sin, or psychologically approximating states. They do not presume to explain sin ethically.

§2.
ANXIETY ABOUT THE GOOD
(THE DEMONIC)

Rarely is anything said in our day about the demonic. The particular accounts of it in the New Testament are generally left in abeyance. Insofar as the theologians[13] seek to explain them, they generally lose themselves in observations upon one or another unnatural sin, and they find examples where the ascendancy of the bestial over a man is such that it almost announces itself by an inarticulate animal sound or by a mimicry of animals and a brutish glance. The bestial may have acquired a pronounced form in man (the physiognomic expression—Lavater),[14] or it may in a flash, like a disappearing express messenger, suggest premonitions of what dwells within, just as the glance or gesture of the insane in a moment shorter than the shortest moment parodies, ridicules, and jeers at the rational, self-possessed, and clever man with whom he is talking. What theologians say in this respect may well be true, but the important thing is the point of the matter. Generally the phenomenon is described in such a way that it is clearly seen that the subject in question is the bondage of sin, a state that I cannot describe better than by recalling a game in which two persons are concealed under one cloak as if there were only one person, and one speaks and the other gesticulates arbitrarily without any relation to what is said. Similarly, the beast has taken on human form and now constantly jeers at him by gesticulations and farce. Yet the bondage of sin is not the demonic. As soon as sin is posited and the individual continues in sin, there are two formations, one of which is described in the foregoing section. If attention is not paid to this, the demonic cannot be defined. The individual is in sin, and his anxiety is about the evil. Viewed from a higher standpoint, this formation is in the good, and for this reason it is in anxiety about the evil. The other formation is the demonic. The individual is in the evil and is in anxiety about the good. The bondage of sin is an unfree relation to the evil, but the demonic is an unfree relation to the good.

IV
387

The demonic therefore manifests itself clearly only when it is in contact with the good, which comes to its boundary from the outside. For this reason, it is noteworthy that the demonic in the New Testament first appears when it is approached by Christ. Whether the demon is legion (cf. Matthew 8:28–34; Mark 5:1-20; Luke 8:26–39) or is dumb (cf. Luke 11:14), the phenomenon is the same, namely, anxiety about the good, for anxiety can just as well express itself by muteness as by a scream. The good, of course, signifies the restoration of freedom, redemption, salvation, or whatever one would call it.

In earlier times, there was often talk about the demonic. Here it is not important to make studies or to have made studies that would enable one to recite by rote or quote from learned and curious books. It is easy to sketch the various views that are possible and at various times have been actual. This may be of significance, because the diversity of the views may lead to a definition of the concept.

The demonic may be viewed as esthetic-metaphysical. The phenomenon then will come under the rubrics of misfortune, fate, etc. and can then be viewed as analogous to being mentally deranged at birth. Then the phenomenon is approached sympathetically. However, just as wishing is the most paltry of all solo performances, so being sympathetic in the sense in which the word is usually used is the most paltry of all social virtuosities and aptitudes. Sympathy, so far from being a good to the sufferer, is rather a means of protecting one's own egotism. Not daring in the deeper sense to think about such things, one saves oneself by sympathy. Only when the sympathetic person in his compassion relates himself to the sufferer in such a way that he in the strictest sense understands that it is his own case that is in question, only when he knows how to identify himself with the sufferer in such a way that when he fights for an explanation he is fighting for himself, renouncing all thoughtlessness, softness, and cowardice— only then does the sympathy acquire significance, and only then does it perhaps find a meaning, because the sympathetic person is different from the sufferer in that he suffers under a higher form. When sympathy relates itself in this way to the demonic, it will not be a question of a few comforting words, a mite, or a shrug of the shoulder, for if a person laments, he has something to lament about. If the demonic is a fate, it may happen to anyone. This cannot be denied, even though in our cowardly time everything possible is done to keep away lonely thoughts by diversions and the Turkish music of loud enterprises, just as in the American forests wild beasts are kept away by means of torches, shouting, and beating of cymbals. For this reason, people in our day learn to know so little about the highest spiritual trials [Anfægtelser], and so much more about the pandering conflicts between men and between man and woman, which a sophisticated soirée and society life bring with it. If true human sympathy accepts suffering as a guarantor and surety, then it must first of all make clear to itself to what extent it is fate or to what extent it is guilt. And this distinction must be drawn up with the concerned but also energetic passion of freedom, so that a person may dare to hold fast to it even though the whole world collapses, even though it may seem that by his own firmness he brings about irreparable harm.

The demonic has been viewed ethically, as something to be condemned. The terrible severity with which it has been persecuted, discovered, and punished is well known. In our

IV
388

day, we shudder at the account of it, and we become sentimental and emotional at the thought that in our enlightened
age we do not act in that manner. This may be true, but is
sentimental sympathy so much more praiseworthy? It is not
for me to judge or condemn that behavior, only to observe it.
That it was so ethically severe shows precisely that its sympathy was of a better quality. In identifying itself in thought
with the phenomenon, it has no further explanation than that
the phenomenon was guilt. Therefore it was convinced that
when all is said and done, the demoniac himself, according to
his better possibility, would in fact desire all the cruelty and
severity that was used against him.* To take an example from
a similar sphere—was it not Augustine[15] who recommended
punishment, even capital punishment, for heretics? Was it because he lacked sympathy? Or was his behavior different from
that of our own time because his sympathy had not made him
cowardly, so that he would have said about himself: God
grant that if it should come to that with me, there would be a
Church that would not abandon me but would use all its
power. Yet in our day one fears what Socrates[16] somewhere
prescribes, to be cut and cauterized by the physician in order
to be healed.

The demonic has been viewed medically-therapeutically.
And it goes without saying, *mit Pulver und mit Pillen* [with
powder and with pills] and then with enemas! Now the
pharmacist and the physician would get together. The patient
would be isolated to prevent others from becoming afraid. In
our courageous age, we dare not tell a patient that he is about
to die, we dare not call the pastor lest he die from shock, and
we dare not tell the patient that a few days ago a man died
from the same disease. The patient would be isolated. Sym-

---

* The person who is not developed ethically to the extent that he would
find comfort and relief if, even when he suffered the most, someone had the
courage to say to him, "This is not fate, it is guilt," that he would find comfort and relief when this was told to him sincerely and earnestly—such a person is not in a true sense ethically developed, because the ethical individuality
fears nothing so much as fate and esthetic rigmarole that in the cloak of compassion would trick him out of the jewel, which is freedom.

pathy would inquire about his condition. The physician would promise to issue a report as soon as possible, along with a tabulated statistical survey[17] in order to determine the average. And when one has arrived at the average, everything is explained. The medical-therapeutic view regards the phenomenon as purely physical and somatic, and as physicians often do, especially a physician in one of Hoffman's short stories,[18] takes a pinch of snuff and says: It is a serious case.

That three so different views are possible shows the ambiguity of the phenomenon and indicates that in a sense it belongs in all spheres: the somatic, the psychic, and the pneumatic. This suggests that the demonic covers a much larger field than is commonly assumed, which can be explained by the fact that a man is a synthesis of psyche and body sustained by spirit, and therefore a disorganization in one shows itself in the others. When one becomes aware of the breadth of the field of the demonic, then perhaps it will also be clear that many of those who want to deal with the phenomenon of the demonic come under the category of the demonic themselves, and that there are traces of it in every man, as surely as every man is a sinner.

Because in the course of time the demonic has denoted several different things, and at last has come to mean almost anything, it seems best to define the concept a little. Therefore, attention should be paid to the place to which we have already assigned it. In innocence there can be no question of the demonic. On the other hand, every fantastic notion of entering into a pact with evil etc., whereby a person becomes entirely evil, must be abandoned. It was because of this that the contradiction arose in the severe treatment of earlier times. People made this assumption and still wanted to punish. Nevertheless, the punishment itself was not merely a self-defense but also a means to save (either those involved by way of a milder punishment or others by way of capital punishment). But if there could be a question of salvation, the individual was not entirely in the power of evil, and if the individual was entirely in the power of evil, punishment would be a contradiction. If the question were raised as to what extent the demonic is a problem for psychology, I must reply, the demonic is a state. Out of this state, the particular sinful act can constantly break forth. However, the state is a possibility, although in relation to innocence it is an actuality posited by the qualitative leap.

The demonic is anxiety about the good. In innocence, freedom was not posited as freedom: its possibility was anxiety in the individual. In the demonic, the relation is reversed. Freedom is posited as unfreedom, because freedom is lost. Here again freedom's possibility is anxiety. The difference is absolute, because freedom's possibility appears here in relation to unfreedom, which is the very opposite of innocence, which is a qualification disposed toward freedom.

The demonic is unfreedom that wants to close itself off. This, however, is and remains an impossibility. It always retains a relation, and even when this has apparently disappeared altogether, it is nevertheless there, and anxiety at once manifests itself in the moment of contact [with the good] (see what is said above of the accounts in the New Testament).

IV
391

The demonic is *inclosing reserve* [*det Indesluttede*][19] *and the unfreely disclosed.* The two definitions indicate, as intended, the same thing, because inclosing reserve is precisely the mute, and when it is to express itself, this must take place contrary to its will, since freedom, which underlies unfreedom or is its ground, by entering into communication with freedom from without, revolts and now betrays unfreedom in such a way that it is the individual who in anxiety betrays himself against his will. Therefore, inclosing reserve in this case must be taken in a very distinct sense, for in the common use of the term it may signify the highest freedom. Brutus,[20] Henry V of England as Prince of Wales,[21] etc. were in this sense confirmed in their reserve until the time when it became evident that their inclosing reserve [*Indesluttethed*] was a pact with the good. Such an inclosing reserve was therefore identical with an expansiveness, and there was never an individuality more beautiful and noble in its expansiveness than one who is inclosed in the womb of a great idea. Freedom is precisely the expansive. In opposition to this, I maintain that κατ' ἐξοχὴν [in an eminent sense] "inclosing reserve" can be used for un-freedom. Generally, a more metaphysical expression is used for evil, namely, the negative. The ethical expression for it, when the effect is observed in the individual, is precisely this inclosing reserve. The demonic does not close itself up with something, but it closes itself up within itself, and in this lies what is profound about existence [*Tilværselsen*], precisely that unfreedom makes itself a prisoner. Freedom is always *communicerende* [communicating]²² (it does no harm even to take into consideration the religious significance of the word); un-freedom becomes more and more inclosed [*indesluttet*] and does not want communication. This can be observed in all spheres. It manifests itself in hypochondria, in capriciousness; it manifests itself in the highest passions, when in a profound misunderstanding they introduce the silent treatment.* When freedom comes into contact with inclosing reserve, it be-comes anxious. In common speech there is a very suggestive expression. It is said of a person, "He will not come out with it." Inclosing reserve is precisely muteness. Language, the word, is precisely what saves, what saves the individual from the empty abstraction of inclosing reserve. Let *x* signify the demonic, the relation of freedom to it something outside *x*. The law for the manifestation of the demonic is that against its will it "comes out with it." For language does indeed imply communication. A demoniac in the New Testament therefore says to Christ when he approaches: τί ἐμοὶ καὶ σοί [What have I to do with you], and he continues by suggesting that Christ has come to destroy him (anxiety about the good). Or a demoniac implores Christ to go another way.²³ (When anxiety is about evil, see §1, the individual has recourse to sal-vation.)

IV
392

IV
391

* It has already been stated that the demonic has a much greater compass than is generally believed. In the preceding paragraph, the formations point-ing in the other direction are indicated; here follows the second series of for-mations, and as I have presented it, the distinction can be carried out. If any-one can offer a better division, then he should choose that, but he at least ought to be cautious in this domain, because otherwise everything runs to-gether.

Life offers abundant examples of this in all possible spheres and in all possible degrees. An obdurate criminal will not make a confession (the demonic lies precisely in this, that he will not communicate with the good by suffering the punishment). There is a rarely used method that can be applied against such a person, namely, silence and the power of the eye. If an inquisitor has the required physical strength and the spiritual elasticity to endure without moving a muscle, to endure even for sixteen hours, he will succeed, and the confession will burst forth involuntarily. A man with a bad conscience cannot endure silence. If placed in solitary confinement, he becomes apathetic. But this silence while the judge is present, while the clerks are ready to inscribe everything in the protocol, this silence is the most penetrating and acute questioning. It is the most frightful torture and yet permissible. However, this is not as easy to accomplish as one might suppose. The only thing that can constrain inclosing reserve to speak is either a higher demon (for every devil has his day), or the good, which is absolutely able to keep silent, and if any cunning tries to embarrass it by the examination of silence, the inquisitor himself will be brought to shame, and it will turn out that finally he becomes afraid of himself and must break the silence. Face to face with a subordinate demon and subordinate human natures whose consciousness of God is not strongly developed, inclosing reserve conquers unconditionally, because the former is not able to endure and the latter in all innocence are accustomed to live from hand to mouth and wear their hearts on their sleeves. It is incredible what power the man of inclosing reserve can exercise over such people, how at last they beg and plead for just a word to break the silence, but it is also shameful to trample upon the weak in this manner. It is perhaps thought that such things occur only among princes and Jesuits, and in order to have a clear notion of this one must think of Domitian, Cromwell, Alba, or a general of the Jesuit order who has become almost a stock name for this. By no means, it occurs much more frequently. However, caution must be used in judging the phenomenon, for although the phenomenon is the same, the reason for it may be the very opposite, because an individuality who exercises the despotism and torture of inclosing reserve might himself wish to speak and might wait for a higher demon who could bring forth the revelation. However, the tormentor of inclosing reserve may also relate himself selfishly to his own inclosing reserve. About this I could write a whole book, although I have not been, according to the custom and the established convention among the observers of our day, in Paris and London, as if by such visits one could learn something great, more than chatter and the wisdom of traveling salesmen. If an observer will only pay attention to himself, he will have enough with five men, five women, and ten children for the discovery of all possible states of the human soul. What I have to say could indeed have significance, especially for everyone who deals with children or has any relation to them. It is of infinite importance that the child be elevated by the conception of lofty inclosing reserve and saved from the misunderstood types. In an outward respect, it is easy to determine when the moment arrives that one dares to let the child walk alone; in a spiritual respect, it is not so easy. In a spiritual respect, the task is very difficult, and one cannot exempt oneself by employing a nursemaid or by buying a walker. The art is that of constantly being present, and yet not being present, so that the child may be allowed to develop himself, and at the same time one still has a clear view of the development. The art is to leave the child to himself in the very highest degree and on the greatest possible scale, and to express this apparent relinquishing in such a way that, unnoticed, one is aware of everything. If only one is willing, time for this can very well be found, even though one is a royal officeholder.[24] If one is willing, one can do all things. And the father or the educator who has done everything else for the child entrusted to him, but has failed to prevent him from becoming closed up in his reserve, has at all times incurred a great liability.

The demonic is inclosing reserve, the demonic is anxiety about the good. Let the inclosing reserve be x and its content x, denoting the most terrible, the most insignificant, the horrible, whose presence in life few probably even dream about, but also the trifles to which no one pays attention.* What then is the significance of the good as *x*? It signifies disclosure.** Disclosure may in turn signify the highest (redemption in an eminent sense) as well as the most insignificant (an accidental remark). This must not disturb us, for the category remains the same; the phenomena have this in common—that they are demonic—although the difference otherwise is enormous enough to make one dizzy. Here disclosure is the good, for disclosure is the first expression of salvation. There is also an old saying that if one dares to utter "the word," the sorcery's enchantment is broken, and therefore the somnambulist wakes up when his name is spoken.

The collisions of inclosing reserve with regard to disclosure may be infinitely varied with innumerable nuances, because the exuberant growth of the spiritual life is not inferior to that of nature, and the varieties of the spiritual states are more numerous than those of the flowers. Inclosing reserve may wish for disclosure, wish that this might be brought about from the outside, that this might happen to it. (This is a misunderstanding, for it is a feminine relation to the freedom posited in disclosure and to the freedom that posits disclosure. Therefore unfreedom may still remain, though the condition of the inclosed person may become happier.) It may will disclosure to a certain degree but still retain a little residue in order to begin the inclosing reserve all over again. (This is the

---

* To be able to use one's category is a *conditio sine qua non* [indispensable condition] if observation in a deeper sense is to have significance. When the phenomenon is present to a certain degree, most people become aware of it but are unable to explain it because they lack the category, and if they had it, they would have a key that opens up whatever trace of the phenomenon there is, for the phenomena within the category obey it as the spirits of the ring obey the ring.[25]

** I have deliberately used the word "disclosure." I could also have called the good "transparency." If I feared that anyone might misunderstand the word "disclosure" and the development of its relation to the demonic, as if it were always a matter of something external, something tangible disclosed in the confessional, but which as something external would be of no help, I certainly would have chosen another word.

IV
395 case with subordinate spirits, who can do nothing *en gros*.) It may will disclosure, but *incognito*. (This is the subtle contradiction of inclosing reserve, examples of which are found in poet-existences.) Disclosure may already have conquered; however, at the same momemt, inclosing reserve ventures the last attempt and is ingenious enough to transform the disclosure itself into a mystification, and inclosing reserve has conquered.*

However, I dare not continue further, for how could I finish even a merely algebraic naming, let alone an attempt to describe or to break the silence of inclosing reserve in order to let its monologue become audible, for monologue is precisely its speech, and therefore we characterize an inclosed person by saying that he talks to himself. Here I shall endeavor only to give all "an understanding but no tongue," as the inclosed Hamlet[27] admonishes his two friends.

Nevertheless, I shall suggest a collision in which the contradiction is as terrible as inclosing reserve itself. What the inclosed person conceals in his inclosing reserve can be so terrible that he does not dare to utter it, not even to himself, because it is as though by the very utterance he commits a new sin or as though it would tempt him again. In order that this phenomenon may occur, the individual must be a mixture of purity and impurity, something that rarely occurs. It will most likely occur when the individual, in carrying out the terrible, is not master of himself. Similarly, a person in an intoxicated state may have done what he only faintly remembers, yet he knows that it was such a wild thing that it is almost impossible for him to recognize himself. The same may also be the case with someone who was once insane and has retained a memory of his former state. What determines IV
396 whether the phenomenon is demonic is the individual's attitude toward disclosure, whether he will interpenetrate that

IV
395 * It is readily seen that inclosing reserve *eo ipso* signifies a lie or, if one prefers, untruth. But untruth is precisely unfreedom, which is anxious about disclosure. Therefore the devil is called the father of lies.[26] That there is a great difference between lie and untruth, between lie and lie, and between untruth and untruth, I have always admitted, but the category is the same.

fact with freedom and accept it in freedom. Whenever he will not do this, the phenomenon is demonic. This must be kept clearly in mind, for even he who wishes it is essentially demonic. He has, that is to say, two wills, one subordinate and impotent that wills revelation and one stronger that wills inclosing reserve, but the fact that this will is the stronger indicates that he is essentially demonic.

Inclosing reserve is involuntary disclosure. The weaker the individuality is originally, or the more the elasticity of freedom is consumed in the service of inclosing reserve, the more likely the secret will break out at last. The slightest touch, a passing glance, etc. is sufficient for that appalling or, in relation to the content of the inclosing reserve, that comic ventriloquism to make its beginning. The ventriloquism itself may be forthrightly declarative or indirect, as when an insane man betrays his insanity by pointing to another, saying: He is most disagreeable to me; he is no doubt insane. The disclosure may declare itself in words, as when the unhappy man ends by thrusting his concealed secret upon every one. It may declare itself in facial expression, in a glance, because there is a glance by which one involuntarily reveals what is concealed. There is an accusing glance that reveals what one is almost afraid to understand, a dejected, imploring glance that does not exactly tempt curiosity to gaze into the involuntary telegraphy. With respect to the content of inclosing reserve, all of this may in turn be almost comic, as when ridiculous things, trifles, vanities, puerilities, expressions of petty envy, petty medical follies, etc. in this way reveal themselves in involuntary anxiety.

The demonic is the sudden. The sudden is a new expression for another aspect of inclosing reserve. When the content is reflected upon, the demonic is defined as inclosing reserve; when time is reflected upon, it is defined as the sudden. Inclosing reserve is the effect of the negative self-relation in the individuality. Inclosing reserve closes itself off more and more from communication. But communication is in turn the expression for continuity, and the negation of continuity is the sudden. It might be thought that inclosing reserve would have an extraordinary continuity; yet the very opposite is the case, although when compared with the vapid, enervating dissolution of oneself continually absorbed in the impression, it has the appearance of continuity. The continuity that inclosing reserve has can best be compared with the dizziness a spinning top must have, which constantly revolves upon its own pivot. In case the inclosing reserve does not drive the individuality to complete insanity, which is the sad *perpetuum mobile* of monotonous sameness, the individuality will still retain a certain continuity with the rest of human life. In relation to this continuity, the pseudocontinuity of the inclosing reserve will show itself precisely as the sudden. At one moment it is there, in the next moment it is gone, and no sooner is it gone than it is there again, wholly and completely. It cannot be incorporated into or worked into any continuity, but whatever expresses itself in this manner is precisely the sudden.

If the demonic were something somatic, it could never be the sudden. When the fever or the insanity etc. recurs, a law is finally discovered, and this law annuls the sudden to a certain degree. But the sudden knows no law. It does not belong among natural phenomena but is a psychical phenomenon—it is an expression of unfreedom.

The sudden, like the demonic, is anxiety about the good. The good signifies continuity, for the first expression of salvation is continuity. Thus, while the life of an individuality goes on to a certain degree in continuity with the rest of human life, inclosing reserve maintains itself in the person as an abracadabra of continuity that communicates only with itself and therefore is always the sudden.

In relation to the content of inclosing reserve, the sudden may signify the terrible, but the effect of the sudden may also appear to the observer as the comical. In this respect, every individuality has a little of this "suddenness," just as every individuality has something of a fixed idea.

I shall not pursue this any further, but in support of my category I call attention to the fact that the sudden is always due to anxiety about the good, because there is something that freedom is unwilling to pervade. Among the formations that lie in anxiety about evil, the sudden corresponds to weakness.

If one wants to clarify in a different way how the demonic is the sudden, the question of how the demonic can best be presented may be considered from a purely esthetic point of view. If a Mephistopheles is to be presented, he might well be furnished with speech if he is to be used as a force in the dramatic action rather than to be grasped in his essence. But in that case Mephistopheles himself is not really represented but is reduced to an evil, witty, intriguing mind. This is a vaporization, whereas a legend has already represented him correctly. It relates that the devil for 3,000 years sat and speculated on how to destroy man—finally he did discover it. Here the emphasis is upon the 3,000 years, and the idea that this brings forth is precisely that of the brooding, inclosing reserve of the demonic. If one were to vaporize Mephistopheles in the way suggested above, another form of representation might be chosen. In this case, it will appear that Mephistopheles is essentially mime.* The most terrible words that sound from the abyss of evil would not be able to produce an effect like that of the suddenness of the leap that lies within the confines of the mimical. Even though the word were terrible, even though it were a Shakespeare, a Byron, or a Shelley who breaks the silence, the word always retains its redeeming power, because all the despair and all the horror of evil expressed in a word are not as terrible as silence. Without being the sudden as such, the mimical may express the sudden. In this respect the ballet master, Bournonville, deserves great credit for his representation of Mephistopheles. The horror that seizes one upon seeing Mephistopheles leap in through the window and remain stationary in the position of the leap!

IV
398

---

* The author of *Either/Or*[28] has pointed out that Don Giovanni is essentially musical. Precisely in the same sense it is true that Mephistopheles is essentially mimical. What has happened to the mimical has happened to the musical. It has been supposed that everything could become mimical and everything become musical. There is a ballet called *Faust*.[29] Had its composer really understood what is implied in conceiving Mephistopheles as mimical, it could never have occurred to him to make a ballet of *Faust*.

This spring in the leap, reminding one of the leap of the bird of prey and of the wild beast, which doubly terrify because they commonly leap from a completely motionless position, has an infinite effect. Therefore Mephistopheles must walk as little as possible, because walking itself is a kind of transition to the leap and involves a presentiment of the possibility of the leap. The first appearance of Mephistopheles in the ballet *Faust* is therefore not a theatrical coup, but a very profound thought. The words and the speaking, no matter how short when regarded *in abstracto*, always have a certain continuity for the reason that they are heard in time. But the sudden is a complete abstraction from continuity, from the past and from the future. So it is with Mephistopheles. He is not yet visible—then he stands there, large as life, hale and hearty, and the swiftness cannot be described more strongly than by saying that he stands there in a leap. If the leap turns into a walk, the effect is weakened. Since Mephistopheles is represented in this manner, his entrance gives the effect of the demonic, which comes more suddenly than a thief in the night, for one thinks of a thief as coming stealthily. But Mephistopheles reveals his essence as well, which as the demonic is precisely the sudden. Thus in the movement forward the demonic is the sudden, thus it arises in a man, thus he himself is, insofar as he is demonic, whether the demonic has possessed him wholly or whether only an infinitesimal part of it is present in him. Thus the demonic always is, and thus unfreedom becomes anxious, and thus its anxiety moves. Hence, the tendency of the demonic toward mime, not in the sense of the beautiful but in the sense of the sudden, the abrupt, which life itself often gives opportunity to observe.

The demonic is the contentless, the boring.

In the case of the sudden, I have called attention to the esthetic problem of how the demonic may be represented. To elucidate what already has been said, I shall again raise the same question. As soon as one wants to have a demoniac speak and to have him represented, the artist who is to solve this problem must be clear about the categories. He knows that the demonic is essentially mimical; the sudden, however,

IV
399

he cannot achieve, because it interferes with his lines. He will not cheat, as if he were able to bring about the true effect by blurting out the words etc. Therefore, he correctly chooses the very opposite, namely, the boring. The continuity that corresponds to the sudden is what might be called extinction. Boredom, extinction, is precisely a continuity in nothingness. Now the number in the legend can be understood somewhat differently. The 3,000 years are not accentuated to emphasize the sudden; instead, the prodigious span of time evokes the notion of the dreadful emptiness and contentlessness of evil. Freedom is tranquil in continuity. Its opposite is the sudden, but also the quietness that comes to mind when one sees a man who looks as if he were long since dead and buried. An artist who understands this will see that in discovering how the demonic can be represented he has also found an expression for the comic. The comic effect can be produced in exactly the same way. When all ethical determinants of evil are excluded, and only metaphysical determinants of emptiness are used, the result is the trivial, which can easily have a comic aspect.*

IV
400

The contentless and the boring again signify inclosing reserve. In relation to the sudden, the determination "inclosing reserve" reflects upon the content. When I now include the determinations "contentless" and "boring," these reflect upon the content, and inclosing reserve reflects upon the form that corresponds to the content. Thus the whole conceptual determination is completed, for the form of the contentless is precisely inclosing reserve. It should be kept in mind constantly that, according to my terminology, one cannot be in-

---

* Therefore little Winsløv's[30] representation of Klister in *The Inseparables* was so profound, because he had correctly understood the comical as the boring. That a love affair, which when it is true has the nature of continuity, is exactly the opposite, namely, an infinite emptiness (not because Klister is an evil man, faithless, etc., since on the contrary he is sincerely in love, but because in his love affair he is a supernumerary volunteer, just as he is in the customhouse) has great comic effect when the accent is placed on the boring. Klister's position in the customhouse can have a comic aspect only unjustifiably, because, after all, how could Klister help it that there is no promotion? But in relation to his love, he is indeed his own master.

closed [*indesluttet*] in God or in the good, because this kind of inclosure signifies the greatest expansion. Thus the more definitely conscience is developed in a person the more expanded he is, even though in other respects he closes himself off from the whole world.

If I were now to call attention to the terminologies of the most recent philosophy, I might say that the demonic is the negative and is a nothing, like the elf maid who is hollow when seen from the back. However, I do not prefer to do this, because the terminology in and by its social intercourse has become so amiable and pliant that it may signify anything whatsoever. The negative, if I were to use this word, signifies the form of nothing, just as the contentless corresponds to inclosed reserve. But the negative has the defect that it is more externally oriented; it defines the relation to something else, which is negated, while inclosed reserve defines the state itself.

IV
401

When the negative is understood in this manner, I have no objection to its use as a designation for the demonic, provided that the negative can otherwise rid itself of all the bees that the most recent philosophy has put in its bonnet. The negative has gradually become a vaudeville character, and this word always makes me smile, just as a person smiles when in real life or in the songs of Bellmann[31] he meets one of those amusing characters who was first a trumpeter, then a minor customhouse officer, then an innkeeper, then again a mail carrier. Thus irony has been explained as the negative. Hegel was the first to discover this explanation, but strangely enough, he did not know much about irony. That it was Socrates[32] who first introduced irony into the world and gave a name to the child, that his irony was precisely inclosing reserve, which he began by closing himself off from men, by closing himself in with himself in order to be expanded in the divine, who also began by closing his door[33] and making a jest to those outside in order to talk in secret—this is something no one is concerned with. On the occasion of one or another accidental phenomena, this word "irony" is brought up, and so it is irony. Then come the parrots, who despite their survey of world history unfortunately lack all contemplation, and who know as much about the concepts as that noble youth knew about raisins, who, when asked in the test for a grocer's licence where raisins come from, answered: We get ours from the professor[34] on Cross Street.

We now return to the definition of the demonic as anxiety about the good.[35] If on the one hand unfreedom were able to close itself off completely and hypostatize itself, but if on the other hand it did not constantly will to do so* (in this lies the contradiction that unfreedom wills something, when in fact it has lost its will), the demonic would not be anxious about the good. Therefore anxiety manifests itself most clearly in the moment of contact. Whether the demonic in the single individuality signifies the terrible or whether the demonic is present only like a spot on the sun or like the little white dot in the corn, the totality of the demonic and the partly demonic have the same qualification, and the tiniest part of the demonic is anxiety about the good in the same sense as that which is totally embraced by it. The bondage of sin is, of course, also unfreedom, but as shown above, its direction is different, and its anxiety is about evil. If this is not held fast, nothing can be explained.

Unfreedom, the demonic, is therefore a state, and psychology regards it as a state. Ethics, on the other hand, sees how out of this state the new sin constantly breaks forth, for only the good is the unity of state and movement.

Freedom, however, may be lost in different ways, and so there may also be a difference in the demonic. This difference I shall now consider under the following rubrics: Freedom

IV 402

* This must constantly be maintained despite the illusion of the demonic and that of language usage, which by employing such expressions in describing this state almost tempts one to forget that unfreedom is a phenomenon of freedom and thus cannot be explained by naturalistic categories. Even when unfreedom uses the strongest possible expressions to affirm that it does not will itself, it is untrue, and it always possesses a will that is stronger than the wish. This state can be extremely deceptive, for one can bring a human being to despair by holding back and keeping the category pure over against his sophisms. One should not be afraid of this, but neither should youthful imaginative constructors try themselves in these spheres.

IV 401

IV 402

lost somatically-psychically and freedom lost pneumatically.[36] The reader will already be familiar with my extensive
use of the concept of the demonic, but it is not more extensive
than the concept will allow. It is of no use to make an ogre out
of the demonic, at which one first shudders but afterwards
ignores, since, after all, it is several hundred years since it was
found in the world. Such an assumption is a great stupidity,
but it probably has never been as widespread as in our times,
except that nowadays it manifests itself especially in the
spiritual spheres.

I. Freedom Lost Somatically-Psychically

It is not my purpose to present a pretentious and bombastic
philosophical deliberation on the relation between psyche and
body and to discuss in which sense the psyche itself produces
its body (whether this be understood in the Greek way or in
the German way) or, to recall an expression of Schelling, in
what sense the psyche itself, by an act of "corporization,"[37]
posits its body. Here I have no need of such things. For my
purpose, I shall express myself to the best of my ability: The
body is the organ of the psyche and in turn the organ of the
spirit. As soon as the serving relation comes to an end, as
soon as the body revolts, and as soon as freedom conspires
with the body against itself, unfreedom is present as the demonic. If there should be someone who has not as yet sharply
apprehended the difference between what I have developed in
this section and what was developed in the former section, I
shall state it again. As long as freedom does not defect to the
party of the rebels, the anxiety of revolution will still be present, not as anxiety about the good, but as anxiety about evil.

It will be easy to see what a multiplicity of innumerable
nuances the demonic in this sphere comprises, some of which
are so imperceptible that they are apparent only to micro-
scopic observation, and some so dialectical that the category
must be used with great flexibility in order to recognize that
the nuances belong under it. A hypersensibility and a hyper-
irritability, neurasthenia, hysteria, hypochondria, etc.—all of

these are or could be nuances of it. This makes it so difficult to talk about these things *in abstracto*, since speech itself becomes algebraic. More than this I cannot do here.

The utmost extreme in this sphere is what is commonly called bestial perdition. In this state, the demonic manifests itself in saying, as did the demoniac in the New Testament with regard to salvation: τί ἐμοὶ καὶ σοί [What have I to do with you]? Therefore it shuns every contact [with the good], whether this actually threatens it by wanting to help it to freedom or only touches it casually. But this is also enough, for anxiety is extraordinarily swift. Therefore, from such a demoniac is quite commonly heard a reply that expresses all the horror of this state: Leave me alone in my wretchedness. Or such a man says in referring to a particular time in his past life: At that time I could probably have been saved—the most dreadful reply imaginable. Neither punishment nor thunderous tirades make him anxious, yet every word that is related to the freedom scuttled and sunk in unfreedom will do so. In this phenomenon, anxiety expresses itself also in another way. Among such demoniacs there is a cohesion in which they cling to one another so inseparably and anxiously that no friendship has an inwardness that can be compared with it. The French physician Duchatelet[38] gives examples of it in his work. This sociability of anxiety will manifest itself everywhere in this sphere. The sociability in itself furnishes an assurance that the demonic is present, but insofar as there is the analogous condition as an expression of the bondage of sin, the sociability is not present, because the anxiety is that about evil.

IV
404

I shall not pursue this any farther. For me the principal thing is to have my schema in order.

II. Freedom Lost Pneumatically

IV
A 404

(a) GENERAL REMARKS. This form of the demonic is very widespread, and here we encounter the most diverse phenomena. The demonic is, of course, not dependent upon the variety of the intellectual content but upon the relation of freedom to the given content* and to the possible content commensurate with the intellectuality, because the demonic is able to express itself as indolence that postpones thinking, as curiosity that never becomes more than curiosity, as dishonest self-deception, as effeminate weakness that constantly relies on others, as superior negligence, as stupid busyness, etc.

Viewed intellectually, the content of freedom is truth, and truth makes man free.[39] For this reason, truth is the work of freedom, and in such a way that freedom constantly brings forth truth. Obviously, I am not thinking of the cleverness of the most recent philosophy, which maintains that the necessity of thought is also its freedom,[40] and which therefore, when it speaks about the freedom of thought, speaks only of the immanent movement of eternal thought. Such cleverness can only serve to confuse and to make the communication between men more difficult. On the other hand, what I am speaking about is very plain and simple, namely, that truth is for the particular individual only as he himself produces it in action. If the truth is for the individual in any other way, or if he prevents the truth from being for him in that way, we have a phenomenon of the demonic. Truth has always had many loud proclaimers, but the question is whether a person will in the deepest sense acknowledge the truth, will allow it to permeate his whole being, will accept all its consequences, and not have an emergency hiding place for himself and a Judas kiss for the consequence.

In modern times, there has been enough talk about truth; now it is high time to vindicate certitude and inwardness, not in the abstract sense in which Fichte[41] uses the word, but in an entirely concrete sense.

Certitude and inwardness, which can be attained only by and in action, determine whether or not the individual is de-

---

* In the New Testament there is the expression σοφία δαιμονιώδης [demonic wisdom] (James 3:15). As it is described there, the category does not become clear. However, if the passage in 2:19, καὶ τὰ δαιμόνια πιστεύουσι καὶ φρίσσουσι [Even the demons believe and shudder], is referred to, it is clear that in demonic knowledge there is the relation of unfreedom to the given knowledge.

monic. If only the category is held fast, everything gives way, and it will become clear, for example, that arbitrariness, unbelief, mockery of religion, etc. are not, as commonly believed, lack of content, but lack of certitude, exactly in the same sense as are superstition, servility, and sanctimoniousness. The negative phenomena lack certitude precisely because they are in anxiety about the content.

It is not my desire to use big words in speaking about the age as a whole, but he who has observed the present generation can hardly deny that the discrepancy in it and the reason for its anxiety and unrest is this, that in one direction truth increases in scope and in quantity, and partly also in abstract clarity, while in the opposite direction certainty constantly declines. What extraordinary metaphysical and logical efforts have been put forth in our time to produce a new, exhaustive, and absolutely correct proof, combining all earlier proofs, of the immortality of the soul;[42] and strangely enough, while this is taking place, certitude declines. The thought of immortality possesses a power and weightiness in its consequences, a responsibility in the acceptance of it, which perhaps will re-create the whole of life in a way that is feared. And so one saves and soothes one's soul by straining one's mind to produce a new proof. Yet, what is such a proof but a "good work" in a purely Catholic sense! Every such individuality (to stay with the example) who knows how to set forth the proof for the immortality of the soul but who is not himself convinced will always be anxious about every phenomenon that affects him in such a way that he is forced to seek a further understanding of what it means to say that a man is immortal. This will disturb him. He will be depressingly affected when a perfectly simple man talks quite simply of immortality. In the opposite direction, inwardness may be lacking. An adherent of the most rigid orthodoxy may be demonic. He knows it all. He genuflects before the holy. Truth is for him the aggregate of ceremonies. He talks of meeting before the throne of God and knows how many times one should bow. He knows everything, like the man who can prove a mathematical proposition when the letters are ABC, but not when the let-

ters are DEF. So he becomes anxious whenever he hears
something that is not literally the same. And yet, how he re-
sembles a modern speculator who has discovered a new proof
for the immortality of the soul and then, in peril of his life,
cannot produce the proof because he does not have his
notebooks with him! And what is it that both of them lack? It
is certitude.—Both superstition and unbelief are forms of unfreedom. In superstition, objectivity is conceded to be a
power—like that of Medusa's head—which can petrify subjectivity, and unfreedom does not will that the spell be broken. Mockery is the highest and apparently the freest expression of unbelief. However, what mockery lacks is precisely
certitude, and therefore it mocks. Yet how many a mocker's
existence, if only we could look into it, would recall the anxiety in which the demonic calls out: τί ἐμοὶ καὶ σοί [What
have I to do with you]? It is therefore a remarkable phenomenon that there are perhaps few who are as vain and touchy
about the applause of the moment as the mocker.

With what industrious zeal, with what sacrifice of time, of
diligence, of writing materials the speculators in our time
have wanted to produce a complete proof of God's existence
[Tilværelse]! Yet to the same degree that the excellence of the
proof increases, certitude seems to decline. The thought of
God's existence [Tilværelse], when it is posited as such for the
individual's freedom, has an omnipresence that for the prudent individuality has something embarrassing about it, even
though he does not wish to do anything evil. To live in a
beautiful and intimate companionship with this conception
truly requires inwardness, and it is a much greater feat than
that of being a model husband. How depressed such an individuality may feel when he hears a naive and simple man talk
about the existence of God. The demonstration of the existence of God is something with which one learnedly and
metaphysically occupies oneself only on occasion, but the
thought of God forces itself upon a man on every occasion.
What is it that such an individuality lacks? Inwardness. Inwardness may also be lacking in an opposite direction. The
so-called pious are often the objects of the world's mockery.

IV
407

They themselves explain this by saying that the world is evil. But this is not entirely true. If such a "pious" man is in an unfree relation to his piety, i.e., if he lacks inwardness, he is, from a purely esthetic point of view, simply comical. To that extent, the world is justified in laughing at him. If a bowlegged man wants to act as a dancing master but is unable to execute a single step, he is comical. So it is also with the religious. Sometimes one may hear such a pious person beating time, as it were, exactly like one who cannot dance but nevertheless knows enough to beat time, although he is never fortunate enough to get in step. Thus the "pious" person knows that the religious is absolutely commensurable, that it is not something that belongs only to certain occasions and moments in life, but that a man can always have it with him. However, just when he is about to make it commensurable, he is not free. It is apparent that he is softly beating time by himself and that in spite of everything he blunders and comes off badly with his heavenward glance and folded hands etc. For this reason, such an individuality is anxious about everyone who does not have this training, and in order to reassure himself, such an individuality must seize upon these grandiose observations that the world hates the pious.

Certitude and inwardness are indeed subjectivity,[43] but not in an entirely abstract sense. It really is the misfortune of the most recent knowledge that everything has become so terribly magnificent. Abstract subjectivity is just as uncertain and lacks inwardness to the same degree as abstract objectivity. When it is spoken about *in abstracto*, this cannot be seen, and so it is correct to say that abstract subjectivity lacks content. When it is spoken about *in concreto*, the content clearly appears, because the individuality who wants to make himself into an abstraction precisely lacks inwardness, as does the individuality who makes himself into a mere master of ceremonies.

(b) THE SCHEMA FOR THE EXCLUSION OR THE ABSENCE OF INWARDNESS. The absence of inwardness is always a category of reflection, and consequently every form will have a double form. Because the qualifications of the spirit are usu-

ally considered altogether abstractly, the tendency is to over-
look this. Usually immediacy is posited in opposition to reflection (inwardness) and then the synthesis (or substantiality,
subjectivity, identity, that in which this identity is said to
consist: reason, idea, spirit). But in the sphere of actuality this
is not the case. There immediacy is also the immediacy of inwardness. For this reason, the absence of inwardness is due in
the first place to reflection.

*Every form of the absence of inwardness is therefore either
activity-passivity or passivity-activity, and whether it is the one or
the other, it is in the sphere of self-reflection.* The form itself runs
through a considerable series of nuances in proportion to the
degree of the concretion of the inwardness. There is an old
saying that to understand and to understand are two things,
and so they are. Inwardness is an understanding, but *in concreto* the important thing is how this understanding is to be
understood. To understand a speech is one thing, and to understand what it refers to, namely, the personal, is something
else; for a man to understand what he himself says is one
thing, and to understand himself in what is said is something
else. The more concrete the content of consciousness is, the
more concrete the understanding becomes, and when this understanding is absent to consciousness, we have a phenomenon of unfreedom that wants to close itself off against freedom. Thus if we take a more concrete religious consciousness
that at the same time also contains a historical factor, the understanding must stand in relation to it. Here we have an
example of the two analogous forms of the demonic in this
respect. When a man of rigid orthodoxy applies all his diligence and learning to prove that every word in the New Testament derives from the respective apostle, inwardness will
gradually disappear, and he finally comes to understand
something quite different from what he wished to understand. When a freethinker[44] applies all his acumen to prove
that the New Testament was not written until the second century, it is precisely inwardness he is afraid of, and therefore he
must have the New Testament placed in the same class with

other books.* The most concrete content that consciousness can have is consciousness of itself, of the individual himself—not the pure self-consciousness, but the self-consciousness that is so concrete that no author, not even the one with the greatest power of description, has ever been able to describe a single such self-consciousness, although every single human being is such a one. This self-consciousness is not contemplation, for he who believes this has not understood himself, because he sees that meanwhile he himself is in the process of becoming and consequently cannot be something completed for contemplation. This self-consciousness, therefore, is action, and this action is in turn inwardness, and whenever inwardness does not correspond to this consciousness, there is a form of the demonic as soon as the absence of inwardness expresses itself as anxiety about its acquisition.

---

* Moreover, in the religious sphere the demonic may have a deceptive resemblance to a spiritual trial [*Anfægtelse*]. Which it is can never be determined *in abstracto*. Thus a pious, believing Christian may fall into anxiety. He may become anxious about going to Communion. This is a spiritual trial, that is, whether or not it is a spiritual trial will show itself in his relation to anxiety. On the other hand, a demonic nature can have gone so far, his religious consciousness become so concrete, that the inwardness about which he is anxious and which in his anxiety he seeks to escape is a purely personal understanding of the sacramental understanding. He is willing to go along with this, but only up to a certain point; then he breaks off and wants to relate himself only as a knower. He desires in one way or another to be more than the empirical, historically qualified, finite individuality that he is. Whoever is in a religious spiritual trial wants to go on to that from which the spiritual trial would keep him away, while the demonic, according to his stronger will (the will of unfreedom), wants to get away from it, while the weaker will in him wants to go on to it. This distinction must be maintained; otherwise one goes on and conceives of the demonic so abstractly that no such thing could ever have occurred, as though the will of unfreedom were constituted as such and the will of freedom were not always present, however weak, in the self-contradiction. Should anyone desire material dealing with the religious spiritual trial, he can find a superfluity of it in Görres's *Mysticism*.[45] However, I sincerely admit that I never had the courage to read the work completely and thoroughly, because there is such anxiety in it. But this much I have discovered, that Görres does not always know how to distinguish between the demonic and the spiritual trial. Therefore the work should be used with care.

If the absence of inwardness were brought about mechanically, all consideration of it would be wasted effort. However, this is not the case, for in every phenomenon of the absence of inwardness there is an activity, even though this begins in a passivity. The phenomena that begin with activity are more conspicuous and therefore more easily apprehended, as a result of which it is forgotten that in this activity there appears in turn a passivity, and therefore in a consideration of the demonic this contrasting phenomenon is not taken into account.

In order to show that the schema is correct, I shall now consider a few examples:

Unbelief—Superstition. These correspond completely to each other: both lack inwardness, but unbelief is passive through an activity, and superstition is active through a passivity. The one is, in a sense, the more masculine, the other the more feminine form; the content of both forms is self-reflection. Viewed essentially, both are completely identical. Unbelief and superstition are both anxiety about faith, but unbelief begins in the activity of unfreedom, and superstition begins in the passivity of unfreedom. Usually only the passivity of superstition is observed, and therefore it appears less important or more excusable, all depending upon whether esthetic-ethical or ethical categories are applied. In superstition there is a weakness that is deceptive; nevertheless, there must always be enough activity in it to preserve its passivity. Superstition is unbelieving about itself. Unbelief is superstitious about itself. The content of both is self-reflection. The comfortableness, cowardice, and pusillanimity of superstition find it better to remain in self-reflection than to relinquish it. The defiance, pride, and arrogance of unbelief find it more daring to remain in self-reflection than to relinquish it. The most refined form of such self-reflection is always the one that becomes interesting to itself by wishing itself out of this state while it nevertheless remains complacently in it.

Hypocrisy—Offense. These correspond to each other. Hypocrisy begins through an activity, offense through a passivity. Generally offense is judged more mildly, but if the individual remains in it, there must still be enough activity so that it sustains the suffering of offense and does not want to relinquish it. There is a receptivity in offense (for a tree or a stone is not offended) that is also taken into account in the annulling of offense. On the other hand, the passivity of offense finds it more enervating just to sit and, as it were, to continue letting the consequences of the offense mount up at compound interest. Therefore hypocrisy is offense at oneself, while offense is hypocrisy to oneself. Both lack inwardness and dare not come to themselves. For this reason, all hypocrisy ends by being hypocritical to oneself, because the hypocrite is offended at himself or is an offense to himself. All offense, if it is not removed, ends in hypocrisy toward others, because the offended man, through the profound activity by which he remains in offense, has turned that receptivity into something else and therefore must now be hypocritical toward others. It has also been the case in life that an offended individuality finally used this offense as a fig leaf to cover what otherwise might have required a hypocritical cloak.

Pride—Cowardice. Pride begins through an activity, cowardice through a passivity; in all other respects they are identical, because in cowardice there is just enough activity to maintain anxiety about the good. Pride is a profound cowardice, for it is cowardly enough not to be willing to understand what pride truly is. As soon as this understanding is forced upon it, it is cowardly, disintegrates with a bang, and bursts like a bubble. Cowardice is a profound pride, because it is cowardly enough not to be willing to understand even the claims of a misunderstood pride, and it manifests its pride by shrinking, as well as by taking into account the fact that it has never suffered a defeat. Therefore it is proud of pride's negative expression, namely, that it has never suffered a loss. It has also been the case in life that a very proud individuality was so cowardly as never to venture anything, cowardly enough to be as insignificant as possible, precisely in order to save his own pride. If an active-proud and a passive-proud individuality were brought together precisely in the moment when the former fell, there would be an opportunity to be convinced as to how proud the cowardly one really was.*

^{IV}
⁴¹²
(c) WHAT IS CERTITUDE AND INWARDNESS? It is no doubt difficult to give a definition of inwardness. In the meantime, I shall at this point say that it is earnestness. This is a word that everyone understands. But strangely enough, few words have less frequently been the object of deliberation. When Macbeth murdered the king, he exclaimed:

> Von jetzt giebt es nicht Ernstes mehr im Leben:
> Alles ist Tand, gestorben Ruhm und Gnade!
> Der Lebenswein ist ausgeschenkt.[46]

Macbeth was a murderer; therefore the words in his mouth were a dreadful and shocking truth. Yet every individual who has lost inwardness can truly say "The wine of life is drawn," and also "There's nothing serious in mortality; all is but toys," for inwardness is precisely the fountain that springs up unto eternal life, and what issues from this fountain is precisely earnestness. When in Ecclesiastes[47] the preacher says that "all is vanity," it is precisely earnestness that he has *in mente* [in mind]. On the other hand, when after earnestness is lost it is said that all is vanity, then this is only an active-passive expression for the same (the defiance of melancholy), or a passive-active expression (the defiance of frivolity and

---

^{IV}
⁴¹¹
* In his treatise *De affectionibus*, Descartes[48] calls attention to the fact that every passion has a corresponding passion; only with wonder this is not the case. The detailed exposition is rather weak, but it has been of interest to me that he makes an exception of wonder, because, as is well known, according to Plato's and Aristotle's views precisely this constitutes the passion of philosophy and the passion with which all philosophizing began. Moreover, envy corresponds to wonder, and recent philosophy would also speak of doubt. Precisely in this lies the fundamental error of recent philosophy, that it wants to begin with the negative instead of with the positive, which always is
^{IV}
⁴¹²
the first, in the same sense as *affirmatio* is placed first in the declaration *omnis affirmatio est negatio* [every affirmation is a negation]. The question of whether the positive or the negative comes first is exceedingly important, and the only modern philosopher who has declared himself for the positive is presumably Herbart.[49]

witticism), and so there is occasion either to weep or to laugh, but earnestness is lost.[50]

To the extent of my knowledge, I am not aware that there exists a single definition of earnestness.[51] If this were true, it would please me, not because I love the modern fluent and confluent thinking that has abolished the definition, but because in relation to existential concepts it always indicates a greater discretion to abstain from definitions, because a person can hardly be inclined to apprehend essentially in the form of definition what must be understood differently, what he himself has understood differently, what he has loved in an entirely different way, and which in the form of definition easily becomes something else, something foreign to him.[52] Whoever loves can hardly find joy and satisfaction, not to mention growth, in preoccupation with a definition of what love properly is. Whoever lives in daily and festive communion with the thought that there is a God could hardly wish to spoil this for himself, or see it spoiled, by piecing together a definition of what God is. So also with earnestness, which is so earnest a matter that even a definition of it becomes a frivolity. I do not say this because my thought is vague or because I fear that some supershrewd speculator might become suspicious of me, as if I did not quite know whereof I speak—the kind of a speculator who is as obstinate about the development of the concepts as the mathematician is about the proof, and who would say about everything else what a certain mathematician said: What does this prove? To my mind, what I say here proves much better than any conceptual development that I do know in earnest what the discussion is about.

Although I am not inclined to give a definition of earnestness or to talk about it in the jest of abstraction, nevertheless I will make a few remarks for orientation. In Rosenkranz's *Psychology*[53] there is a definition* of disposition [*Gemyt*]. On

IV
413

IV
413

* It is always a joy to assume that my reader has read as much as I. This assumption is very economical for the reader as well as for the writer.[54] So I assume that my reader is familiar with the book to which I have referred. If this is not so, I urge him to familiarize himself with it, for it is actually a com-

IV
414 page 322 he says that disposition is the unity of feeling and self-consciousness. In the preceding presentation he superbly explains "dasz das Gefühl zum Selbstbewusztsein sich aufschliesse, und umgekehrt, dasz der Inhalt des Selbstbewusztseins von dem Subjekt als der seinige gefühlt wird. Erst diese Einheit kann man Gemüth nennen. Denn fehlt die Klarheit der Erkenntniss, das Wissen vom Gefühl, so existiert nur der Drang des Naturgeistes, der Turgor der Unmittelbarkeit. Fehlt aber das Gefühl, so existiert nur ein abstrakter Begriff, der nicht die letzte Innigheit des geistigen Daseins erreicht hat, der nicht mit dem Selbst des Geistes Eines geworden ist" [that the feeling unfolds itself to self-consciousness, and vice versa, that the content of the self-consciousness is felt by the subject as his own. It is only this unity that can be called disposition. If the clarity of cognition is lacking, knowledge of the feeling, there exists only the urge of the spirit of nature, the turgidity of immediacy. On the other hand, if feeling is lacking, there remains only the abstract concept that has not reached the last inwardness of the spiritual existence, that has not become one with the self of the spirit] (cf. pp. 320, 321). If a person now turns back and pursues his definition of "feeling" as the spirit's *unmittelbare Einheit seiner Seelenhaftigkeit und seines Bewusstseins* [immediate unity of its sentience and its consciousness] (p. 242) and recalls that in the definition of *Seelenhaftigkeit* [sentience] account has been taken of the unity with the immediate determinants of nature, then by taking all of this together he has the conception of a concrete personality.

Earnestness and disposition correspond to each other in such a way that earnestness is a higher as well as the deepest expression for what disposition is. Disposition is a determi-

---

IV
413 petent book, and if the author, who otherwise distinguishes himself by his common sense and his humane interest in human life, had been able to renounce his fanatical superstitious belief in an empty schema, he could have avoided being ridiculous at times. What he says in this passage is for the most part very good. The only thing that at times is difficult to understand is the grandiose schema and how the altogether concrete discussion can correspond to it. (As an example, I refer to pp. 209-11. *Das Selbst—und das Selbst*: 1. *Der Tod*; 2. *Der Gegensatz von Herrschaft und Knechtschaft*.)

nant of immediacy, while earnestness, on the other hand, is the acquired originality of disposition,[55] its originality preserved in the responsibility of freedom and its originality affirmed in the enjoyment of blessedness. In its historical development, the originality of disposition marks precisely the eternal in earnestness, for which reason earnestness can never become habit. Rosenkranz deals with habit only in the "Phenomenology," not in the "Pneumatology"—however, habit belongs in the latter as well, and habit arises as soon as the eternal disappears from repetition. When the originality in earnestness is acquired and preserved, then there is succession and repetition, but as soon as originality is lacking in repetition, there is habit. The earnest person is earnest precisely through the originality with which he returns in repetition. It is said that a living and inward feeling preserves this originality, but the inwardness of the feeling is a fire that may cool as soon as earnestness no longer attends to it. On the other hand, the inwardness of feeling is uncertain in its mood, i.e., at one time it is more inward than at another. To make everything as concrete as possible, I shall use an example. Every Sunday, a clergyman must recite the prescribed common prayer, and every Sunday he baptizes several children. Now let him be enthusiastic etc. The fire burns out, he will stir and move people etc., but at one time more and at another time less. Earnestness alone is capable of returning regularly every Sunday with the same originality to the same thing.*

IV
415

But this same thing to which earnestness is to return with the same earnestness can only be earnestness itself; otherwise it becomes pedantry. Earnestness in this sense means the personality itself, and only an earnest personality is an actual personality, and only an earnest personality can do anything with earnestness, for to do anything with earnestness requires, first and foremost, knowledge of what the object of earnestness is.

In life there is not infrequently talk about earnestness. Someone is in earnest about the national debt, another about

---

* It was in this sense that Constantin Constantius said (in *Repetition*), "Repetition is the earnestness of existence [*Tilværelsen*]" (p. 6),[56] and that the earnestness of life is not to be like a royal riding master, even if such a man every time he mounted his horse did so with all possible earnestness.

the categories, and a third about a performance at the theater, etc. Irony discovers that this is the case, and with that it has enough to occupy itself, because everyone who becomes earnest at the wrong place is *eo ipso* comical, even though an equally comical, travestied contemporary age and the opinion of the age may be exceedingly earnest about it. Therefore, there is no measuring rod more accurate for determining the essential worth of an individuality than what is learned through the individual's own loquacity or by cunningly extracting from him the secret: What has made him earnest in life? For one may be born with disposition, but no one is born with earnestness. The phrase "What has made him earnest in life" must of course be understood, in a pregnant sense, as that from which the individuality in the deepest sense dates his earnestness. Having become truly earnest about that which is the object of earnestness, a person may very well, if he so wishes, treat various things earnestly, but the question is whether he first became earnest about the object of earnestness. This object every human being has, because it is *himself*, and whoever has not become earnest about this, but about something else, something great and noisy, is despite all his earnestness a joker, and though he may deceive irony for some time, he will, *volente deo* [God willing], still become comical because irony is jealous of earnestness. On the other hand, whoever has become earnest at the right place will prove the soundness of his spirit precisely by his ability to treat all other things sentimentally as well as jokingly, although it makes a cold shiver run down the spines of the dupes of earnestness when they see him joke about whatever made them frightfully earnest. But in regard to earnestness he will know how not to tolerate any joking, for if he forgets this, it may go with him as with Albert Magnus when he arrogantly boasted of his speculation before the deity and suddenly became stupid, or as it went with Bellerophon, who sat calmly on his Pegasus in the service of the idea but fell when he wanted to misuse Pegasus by riding the horse to a rendezvous with a mortal woman.*

* Cf. Marbach,[57] *Geschichte der Philosophie*, Pt. 2, p. 302, note: *Albertus re-*

Inwardness, certitude, is earnestness. This seems a little paltry. If at least I had said, it is subjectivity, the pure subjectivity, the *übergreifende* [encompassing] subjectivity, I would
have said something, something that no doubt would have
made many earnest. However, I can also express earnestness
in another way. Whenever inwardness is lacking, the spirit is
finitized. Inwardness is therefore eternity or the constituent of
the eternal in man.

To study the demonic properly, one needs only to observe
how the eternal is conceived in the individuality, and immediately one will be informed. In this respect, the modern age
offers a great field for observation. In our times, the eternal is
discussed often enough; it is accepted and rejected, and (considering the way in which this is done) the first as well as the
second shows lack of inwardness. But whoever has not understood the eternal correctly, understood it altogether con-
cretely,* lacks inwardness and earnestness.

Here I do not wish to be more explicit; nevertheless, I shall
indicate a number of points.

(a) Some deny the eternal in man. At the same moment, *der*

---

pente ex asino factus philosophus et ex philosopho asinus [Albert was suddenly
transformed from an ass into a philosopher and from a philosopher into an
ass]. Cf. Tennemann,[58] VIII, Pt. 2, p. 485, note. There is a more definite
account of another scholastic, Simon Tornacensis, who thought that God
must be obliged to him for having furnished a proof of the Trinity, because if
he wanted, then—*profecto si malignando et adversando vellem, fortioribus argumen-
tis scirem illam infirmare et deprimendo improbare* [if out of malice and enmity I
wished to do so, I could weaken it with stronger arguments, and disprove it
by reducing it]. As a reward for his efforts, the good man was turned into a
fool who had to spend two years learning the alphabet. See Tennemann, *Geschichte der Philosophie*, VIII, p. 314, note. Let this be as it may. Whether he
actually said this or even uttered what has been ascribed to him—the famous
blasphemy of the Middle Ages about the three great deceivers—certainly
what he lacked was not strenuous earnestness in dialectics and speculation but
an understanding of himself. This story has numerous analogies, and in our
time speculation has assumed such authority that it has practically tried to
make God feel uncertain of himself, like a monarch who is anxiously waiting
to learn whether the general assembly will make him an absolute or a limited
monarch.

* It was doubtless in this sense that Constantin Constantius[59] said of the
eternal that it is the true repetition.

Lebenswein [*ist*] *ausgeschenkt* [the wine of life is drawn], and every such individuality is demonic. If the eternal is posited, the present becomes something different from what a person wants it to be. He fears this, and thus he is in anxiety about the good. He may continue to deny the eternal as long as he wants, but in so doing he will not be able to kill the eternal entirely. Even if to a certain degree and in a certain sense he is willing to admit the eternal, he fears it in another sense and to a higher degree. Nevertheless, no matter how much he denies it, he cannot get rid of it entirely. In our day, men fear the eternal far too much, even when they recognize it in abstract words and in words flattering to the eternal. Nowadays, the various governments live in fear of restless disturbers; there are altogether too many individualities who live in fear of one restless disturber that nevertheless is the true rest—eternity. So they preach the moment, and just as the road to hell is paved with good intentions, so eternity is best annihilated by mere moments. But why do people rush around in such a terrible haste? If there is no eternity, the moment is just as long as if there were. But anxiety about the eternal turns the moment into an abstraction. Furthermore, this denial of the eternal may express itself directly or indirectly in many various ways, as mockery, as prosaic intoxication with common sense, as busyness, as enthusiasm for the temporal, etc.

(b) Some conceive of the eternal altogether abstractly. Like the blue mountains, the eternal is the boundary of the temporal, but he who lives energetically in temporality never reaches the boundary. The single individual who is on the lookout for it is a frontier guard standing outside of time.

(c) Some bend eternity into time for the imagination. Conceived in this way, eternity produces an enchanting effect. One does not know whether it is dream or actuality. As the beams of the moon glimmer in an illuminated forest or a hall, so the eternal peeps wistfully, dreamily, and roguishly into the moment. Thought of the eternal becomes a fanciful pottering around, and the mood is always the same: Am I dreaming, or is it eternity that is dreaming of me?[60]

Or some conceive of eternity purely and simply for the

imagination without this coquettish duplicity. This conception has found definite expression in the statement: Art is an
anticipation of eternal life,[61] because poetry and art are the
reconciliation only of the imagination, and they may well
have the *Sinnigkeit* [thoughtfulness] of intuition but by no
means the *Innigkeit* [inwardness] of earnestness. Some paint
eternity elaborately with the tinsel of the imagination and
yearn for it. Some envision eternity apocalyptically,[62] pretend
to be Dante, while Dante, no matter how much he conceded
to the view of imagination, did not suspend the effect of
ethical judgment.

(d) Or eternity is conceived metaphysically. A person says
Ich Ich [I-I][63] so long that he becomes the most ridiculous of
all things: the pure I, the eternal self-consciousness. He talks
about immortality until at last he himself becomes not im- ^IV 419^
mortal but immortality. Despite all this, he suddenly discovers that he has not succeeded in having immortality included in the system, and now he is intent on assigning it a
place in a supplement to the system. Considering the ridicu-
lousness of this, what Poul Møller[64] said is true, that immortality must be present everywhere. But if this be so, the
temporal becomes something quite different from what is
desired. Or eternity is conceived metaphysically[65] in such a way
that the temporal becomes comically preserved in it. From a
purely esthetic-metaphysical standpoint, the temporal is comical because it is a contradiction, and the comical always lies in
this category. If eternity is conceived purely metaphysically
and for some reason one wants to have the temporal included
in it, then it certainly becomes quite comical that an eternal
spirit retains the recollection that on several occasions he had
been in financial difficulties etc. Yet all the effort expended to
support eternity is wasted, is a false alarm, for no human
being becomes immortal or becomes convinced of his immortality in a purely metaphysical way. However, if he becomes convinced of his immortality in quite another way, the
comic will not foist itself upon him. Even though Christianity teaches that a person must render an account[66] for
every idle word he has spoken, and we understand this simply

as that total recollection of which unmistakable symptoms occasionally appear already in this life, even though the teaching of Christianity cannot be more sharply illuminated by any opposite than that of the Greek conception[67] that the immortals first drank of Lethe in order to forget, yet it by no means follows that the recollection must become directly or indirectly comical—directly by recollecting ridiculous things or indirectly by transforming ridiculous things into essential decisions. Precisely because the accounting and the judgment are essential, what is essential will have the effect of a Lethe on whatever is unessential, while it also is certain that many things will prove to be essential that one had not expected to be so. The soul has not been essentially present in the drolleries of life, in its accidental circumstances, its nooks and crannies; hence all this vanishes, except for the soul that was essentially in this, yet for him it will scarcely have comical significance. If one has reflected thoroughly upon the comic,[68] studying it as an expert, constantly keeping one's category clear, one will easily understand that the comic belongs to the temporal, for it is in the temporal that the contradiction is found. Metaphysically and esthetically it cannot be stopped and prevented from finally swallowing up all of the temporal, which will happen to the person who is developed enough to use the comic but not mature enough to distinguish *inter et inter* [between one and the other]. In eternity, on the other hand, all contradiction is canceled, the temporal is permeated by and preserved in the eternal, but in this there is no trace of the comical.

However, men are not willing to think eternity earnestly but are anxious about it, and anxiety can contrive a hundred evasions. And this is precisely the demonic.

IV
420

V

Anxiety as Saving through Faith

In one of Grimm's[1] fairy tales there is a story of a young man who goes in search of adventure in order to learn what it is to be in anxiety. We will let the adventurer pursue his journey without concerning ourselves about whether he encountered the terrible on his way. However, I will say that this is an adventure that every human being must go through—to learn to be anxious in order that he may not perish either by never having been in anxiety or by succumbing in anxiety. Whoever has learned to be anxious in the right way has learned the ultimate.

If a human being were a beast or an angel, he could not be in anxiety. Because he is a synthesis, he can be in anxiety; and the more profoundly he is in anxiety, the greater is the man—yet not in the sense usually understood, in which anxiety is about something external, about something outside a person, but in the sense that he himself produces the anxiety. Only in this sense can the words be understood when it is said of Christ[2] that he was anxious unto death, as well as the words spoken by Christ to Judas: What you are going to do, do quickly. Not even the terrifying verse that made even Luther anxious when preaching on it—"My God, my God, why hast thou forsaken me"[3]—not even these words express suffering so profoundly. For the latter signify a condition in which Christ finds himself. And the former signify the relation to a condition that is not.

Anxiety is freedom's possibility, and only such anxiety is through faith absolutely educative, because it consumes all finite ends and discovers all their deceptiveness. And no Grand Inquisitor has such dreadful torments in readiness as anxiety has, and no secret agent knows as cunningly as anxiety how to attack his suspect in his weakest moment or to make alluring the trap in which he will be caught, and no discerning judge understands how to interrogate and examine the accused as does anxiety, which never lets the accused escape, neither through amusement, nor by noise, nor during work, neither by day nor by night.

Whoever is educated by anxiety is educated by possibility, and only he who is educated by possibility is educated according to his infinitude. Therefore possibility is the weightiest of all categories. It is true that we often hear the opposite stated, that possibility is so light, whereas actuality is so heavy. But from whom does one hear such words? From wretched men who never knew what possibility is, and who, when actuality had shown that they were not good for anything and never would be, mendaciously revived a possibility that was very beautiful and very enchanting, while the foundation of this possibility was at the most a little youthful giddiness, of which they ought rather to be ashamed. Therefore this possibility that is said to be so light is commonly regarded as the possibility of happiness, fortune, etc. But this is not possibility. It is rather a mendacious invention that human depravity has dressed up so as to have a reason for complaining of life and Governance and a pretext for becoming self-important. No, in possibility all things are equally possible, and whoever has truly been brought up by possibility has grasped the terrible as well as the joyful. So when such a person graduates from the school of possibility, and he knows better than a child knows his ABC's that he can demand absolutely nothing of life and that the terrible, perdition, and annihilation live next door to every man, and when he has thoroughly learned that every anxiety about which he was anxious came upon him in the next moment—he will give actuality another explanation, he will praise actuality, and even when it rests heavily upon him, he will remember that it nevertheless is far, far lighter than possibility was. Only in this way can possibility be educative, because finiteness and the finite relations in which every individual is assigned a place, whether they be small, or everyday, or world-historical, educate only finitely, and a person can always persuade them, always coax something else out of them, always bargain, always escape from them tolerably well, always keep himself a little on the outside, always prevent himself from absolutely learning something from them; and if he does this, the individual must again have possibility in himself and himself develop that from which he is to learn, even though in the next moment that from which he is to learn does not at all acknowledge that it is formed by him but absolutely deprives him of the power.

However, in order that an individual may thus be educated absolutely and infinitely by the possibility, he must be honest toward possibility and have faith. By faith I understand here what Hegel[4] somewhere in his way correctly calls the inner certainty that anticipates infinity. When the discoveries of possibility are honestly administered, possibility will discover all the finitudes, but it will idealize them in the form of infinity and in anxiety overwhelm the individual until he again overcomes them in the anticipation of faith.

What I am saying here probably strikes many as obscure and foolish talk, because they pride themselves on never having been in anxiety. To this I would reply that one certainly should not be in anxiety about men and about finitudes, but only he who passes through the anxiety of the possible is educated to have no anxiety, not because he can escape the terrible things of life but because these always become weak by comparison with those of possibility. If, on the other hand, the speaker maintains that the great thing about him is that he has never been in anxiety, I will gladly provide him with my explanation: that it is because he is very spiritless.

If an individual defrauds possibility, by which he is to be educated, he never arrives at faith; then his faith will be the sagacity of finitude, just as his school was that of finitude. But men defraud possibility in every way, because otherwise every man, if he had merely put his head out of the window, would have seen enough for possibility to use in beginning its exercises. There is an engraving by Chodowiecki[5] that represents the surrender of Calais as viewed by four persons of different temperaments, and the task of the artist was to mirror the various impressions in the facial expressions of the four. The most commonplace life no doubt has experiences enough, but the question is that of the possibility in the individuality who is honest with himself. It is told of one Indian hermit who for two years lived on dew that he once came to the city, tasted wine, and became addicted to drink. This story, like similar stories, can be understood in different ways. It may be regarded as comic, it may be regarded as tragic. But the individuality who is educated by possibility needs but one such story. In that very moment, he is absolutely identified with the unfortunate man; he knows no finite evasion by which he may escape. Now the anxiety of possibility holds him as its prey until, saved, it must hand him over to faith. In no other place can he find rest, for every other place of rest is mere chatter, although in the eyes of men it is sagacity. Therefore possibility is absolutely educative. In actuality, no man ever became so unhappy that he did not retain a little remnant, and common sense says quite correctly that if one is cunning, one knows how to make the best of things. But whoever took possibility's course in misfortune lost all, all, as no one in actuality ever lost it. Now, if he did not defraud the possibility that wanted to teach him and did not wheedle the anxiety that wanted to save him, then he would also receive everything back, as no one in actuality ever did, even though he received all things tenfold, for the disciple of possibility received infinity, and the soul of the other expired in the finite. In actuality, no one ever sank so deep that he could not sink deeper, and there may be one or many who sank deeper. But he who sank in possibility—his eye became dizzy, his eye became confused, so he could not grasp the measuring stick that Tom, Dick, and Harry hold out as a saving straw to one sinking; his ear was closed so he could not hear what the market price of men was in his own day, did not hear that he was just as good as the majority. He sank absolutely, but then in turn he emerged from the depth of the abyss lighter than all the troublesome and terrible things in life. However, I will not deny that whoever is educated by possibility is exposed to danger, not that of getting into bad company and going astray in various ways as are those educated by the finite, but the danger of a fall, namely, suicide. If at the beginning of his education he misunderstands the anxiety, so that it does not lead him to faith but away from faith, then he is lost. On the other hand, whoever is educated [by possibility] remains with anxiety; he does not permit himself to be deceived by its countless falsifications and accurately remembers the past. Then the assaults of anxiety, even though they be terrifying, will not be such that he flees from them. For him, anxiety becomes a serving spirit that against its will leads him where he wishes to go. Then, when it announces itself, when it cunningly pretends to have invented a new instrument of torture, far more terrible than anything before, he does not shrink back, and still less does he attempt to hold it off with noise and confusion; but he bids it welcome, greets it festively, and like Socrates[6] who raised the poisoned cup, he shuts himself up with it and says as a patient would say to the surgeon when the painful operation is about to begin: Now I am ready. Then anxiety enters into his soul and searches out everything and anxiously torments everything finite and petty out of him, and then it leads him where he wants to go.

IV
425

When one or another extraordinary event occurs in life, when a world-historical hero gathers heroes about him and performs deeds of valor, when a crisis occurs and everything gains significance, then men want to have a part in it, because all of this is educative. Possibly so. But there is a simpler way in which one may become more thoroughly educated. Take the pupil of possibility, place him in the middle of the Jutland heath,[7] where no event takes place or where the greatest event is a grouse flying up noisily, and he will experience everything more perfectly, more accurately, more thoroughly than the man who received the applause on the stage of world-history if that man was not educated by possibility.

So when the individual through anxiety is educated unto faith, anxiety will eradicate precisely what it brings forth itself. Anxiety discovers fate, but just when the individual wants to put his trust in fate, anxiety turns around and takes fate away, because fate is like anxiety, and anxiety, like possibility, is a "magic" picture.[8] When the individuality is not thus transformed by himself in relation to fate, he will always retain a dialectical remnant that no finitude can remove, just as no man will lose faith in the lottery if he does not lose it by himself but is supposed to lose it by continually losing when he gambles. Even in relation to the most insignificant things, anxiety is promptly at hand as soon as the individuality wants to sneak away from something or stumble upon something by chance. In itself, it is of no significance; from the outside, from the finite, the individual can learn nothing about it. But anxiety takes swift action,[9] instantly plays the trump card of infinity, of the category, and the individuality cannot take the trick. Such an individuality cannot in an outward way fear fate, its vicissitudes and defeats, because the anxiety within him has already fashioned fate and has taken away from him absolutely all that any fate could take away. In the dialogue *Cratylus*,[10] Socrates says that it is terrible to be deceived by oneself, because one always has the deceiver present; similarly, one may say that it is fortunate to have present such a deceiver who piously deceives and always weans the child before finitude begins to bungle him. Even if in our time an individuality is not educated by possibility in this manner, our age nevertheless has an excellent characteristic for each one in whom there is a deeper nature and who desires to learn the good. The more peaceful and quiet an age is and the more accurately everything follows its regular course, so that the good has its reward, the easier it is for an individuality to deceive himself about whether in all his striving he has a beautiful but nevertheless finite goal. In these times, one does not need to be more than sixteen years old in order to recognize that whoever performs on the stage of the theater of life is like the man who traveled from Jericho[11] and fell among robbers. Whoever does not wish to sink in the wretchedness of the finite is constrained in the most profound sense to struggle with the infinite. Such a preliminary orientation is analogous to the education by possibility, and such an orientation cannot take place except through possibility. So when shrewdness has completed its innumerable calculations, when the game is won—then anxiety comes, even before the game in actuality has been lost or won, and anxiety makes the sign of the cross against the devil, and shrewdness becomes helpless and its most clever combinations vanish like a witticism compared with the case that anxiety forms with the omnipotence of possibility. Even in the most trifling matters, as soon as the individuality wants to make a cunning turn that is merely cunning, wants to sneak away from something, and the probability is that he will succeed—because actuality is not as sharp an examiner as anxiety—then anxiety is there at once. If it is dismissed because it is merely a trifle, then anxiety makes this trifle as prominent as the little place Marengo became in the history of Europe, because there the great battle of Marengo was fought. If an individuality is not weaned away from shrewdness by himself, it will never be thoroughly accomplished, because finitude always explains in parts, never totally, and he whose shrewdness always fails (and even this is inconceivable in actuality) may seek the reason for this in his shrewdness and then strive to become still more shrewd. With the help of faith, anxiety brings up the individuality to rest in providence. So it is also in relation to guilt, which is the second thing anxiety discovers. Whoever learns to know his guilt only from the finite is lost in the finite, and finitely the question of whether a man is guilty cannot be determined except in an external, juridical, and most imperfect sense. Whoever learns to know his guilt only by analogy to judgments of the police court and the supreme court never really understands that he is guilty, for if a man is guilty, he is infinitely guilty. Therefore, if such an individuality who is educated only by finitude does not get a verdict from the police or a verdict by public opinion to the effect that he is guilty, he becomes of all men the most ridiculous and pitiful, a model of virtue who is a little better than most people but not quite so good as the parson. What help would such a man need in life? Why, almost before he dies he may retire to a collection of models. From finitude one can learn much, but not how to be anxious, except in a very mediocre and depraved sense. On the other hand, whoever has truly learned how to be anxious will dance when the anxieties of finitude strike up the music

IV
427

and when the apprentices of finitude lose their minds and courage. One is often deceived this way in life. The hypochondriac is anxious about every insignificant thing, but when the significant appears he begins to breathe more easily. And why? Because the significant actuality is after all not so terrible as the possibility he himself had fashioned, and which he used his strength to fashion, whereas he can now use all his strength against actuality. Yet the hypochondriac is only an imperfect autodidact when compared with the person who is educated by possibility, because hypochondria is partly dependent upon the somatic and is consequently accidental.* The true autodidact is precisely in the same degree a theodidact,[12] as another author has said,** or to use an expression less reminiscent of the intellectual, he is αὐτουργός τις τῆς φιλοσοφίας [one who on his own cultivates philosophy]† and in the same degree θεουργός [one who tends the things of God]. Therefore he who in relation to guilt is educated by anxiety will rest only in the Atonement.

IV
428

Here this deliberation ends, where it began. As soon as psychology has finished with anxiety, it is to be delivered to dogmatics.

IV
427

* It is therefore with a higher meaning that Hamann[13] employs the word "hypochondria" when he says: "Diese Angst in der Welt ist aber der einzige Beweis unserer Heterogeneität. Denn fehlte uns nichts, so würden wir es nicht besser machen als die Heiden und Transcendental-Philosophen, die von Gott nichts wissen und in die liebe Natur sich wie die Narren vergaffen; kein Heimweh würde uns anwandeln. Diese impertinente Unruhe, diese heilige Hypochondrie ist vielleicht das Feuer, womit wir Opferthiere gesalzen und vor der Fäulnisz des laufenden *seculi* bewahrt werden müssen" [However, this anxiety in the world is the only proof of our heterogeneity. If we lacked nothing, we should do no better than the pagans and the transcendental philosophers, who know nothing of God and like fools fall in love with lovely nature, and no homesickness would come over us. This impertinent disquiet, this holy hypochondria is perhaps the fire with which we season sacrificial animals in order to preserve us from the putrefaction of the current *seculi* (century)] (vol. 6, p. 194).

** See *Either/Or*.

IV
428

† Xenophon's *Symposium* [I:5], where Socrates uses this expression about himself.

SUPPLEMENT

Key to References
164

Original Title Page
166

Selected Entries from Kierkegaard's
Journals and Papers Pertaining to
The Concept of Anxiety
169

KEY TO REFERENCES

Marginal references alongside the text are to volume and page [IV 300] in *Søren Kierkegaards Samlede Værker*, I-XIV, 1 ed., edited by A. B. Drachman, J. L. Heiberg, and H. O. Lange (Copenhagen: Gyldendal, 1901-06). The same marginal references are used in Sören Kierkegaard, *Gesammelte Werke*, Abt. 1-36 (Düsseldorf: Diederichs Verlag, 1952-69). References to Kierkegaard's works in English are to *Kierkegaard's Writings* [KW]. I-XXVI (Princeton: Princeton University Press, 1976-). Specific references to the *Writings* are given by English title and the standard Danish pagination referred to above [*Either/Or*, I, KW III (SV I 100)].

References to Kierkegaard's *Papirer* [*Pap*. I A 100; note the differentiating letter A, B, or C, used only in references to the *Papirer*] are to volume and entry in *Søren Kierkegaards Papirer*, I-XI³, 1 ed., edited by P. A. Heiberg, V. Kuhr, and E. Torsting (Copenhagen: Gyldendal, 1909-48), and 2 ed., photo-offset with two supplemental volumes, I-XIII, edited by N. Thulstrup (Copenhagen: Gyldendal, 1968-70). References to the *Papirer* in English [*JP* II 1500] are to volume and serial number in *Søren Kierkegaard's Journals and Papers*, I-VII, edited and translated by Howard V. Hong and Edna H. Hong (Bloomington: Indiana University Press, 1967-78).

References to correspondence are to the serial numbers in *Breve og Aktstykker Vedrørende Søren Kierkegaard*, I-II, edited by N. Thulstrup (Copenhagen: Munksgaard, 1953-54), and to the corresponding serial numbers in *Kierkegaard: Letters and Documents*, Translated by Henrik Rosenmeier, *Kierkegaard's Writings*, XXV [*Letters*, KW XXV, Letter 100].

References to books in Kierkegaard's own library [*ASKB* 100] are based on the serial numbering system of *Auktionsprotokol over Søren Kierkegaards Bogsamling* (Auction-catalog of Søren Kierkegaard's Book-collection), edited by H. P. Rohde (Copenhagen: Royal Library, 1967).

References in the Supplement to page and lines in the text are given as: *see 100:1-10*.

Internal references in the notes to the present work are given as: see p. 100.

Three periods indicate an omission by the editor-translator; five periods indicate omissions or fragmentariness in the Danish text.

Begrebet Angest.

En simpel psychologisk=paapegende Overveielse

i Retning af det dogmatiske Problem
om Arvesynden

af

Vigilius Haufniensis.

Kjøbenhavn.

Faaes hos Universitetsboghandler C. A. Reitzel.
Trykt i Bianco Lunos Bogtrykkeri.

1844.

THE CONCEPT OF ANXIETY.

A Simple Psychologically Orienting Deliberation

on the Dogmatic Issue
of Hereditary Sin

by

Vigilius Haufniensis.

Copenhagen.

Available at University Bookseller C. A. Reitzel.
Printed by Bianco Luno Press.

1844.

SELECTED ENTRIES FROM
KIERKEGAARD'S JOURNALS AND PAPERS
PERTAINING TO
THE CONCEPT OF ANXIETY

See xii:28:

A certain presentiment* seems to precede everything that is to happen (cf. a loose sheet [*i.e., Pap.* II A 584]); but just as it can have a deterring effect, it can also tempt a person to think that he is, as it were, predestined; he sees himself carried on to something as though by consequences beyond his control. Therefore one ought to be very careful with children, never believe the worst and by untimely suspicion or by a chance remark (a flame of hell which ignites the tinder which is in every soul) occasion an anxious consciousness in which innocent but fragile souls can easily be tempted to believe themselves guilty, to despair, and thereby to make the first step toward the goal foreshadowed by the unsettling presentiment—a remark which gives the kingdom of evil, with its stupefying, snakelike eye, an occasion for reducing them to a kind of spiritual paralysis. Of this too it may be said: Woe unto him by whom the offense comes.

In margin: *The significance of typology with reference to a theory of presentiments.—*JP* I 91 (*Pap.* II A 18) *n.d.*, 1837

See xii:28:

Frequently the reading of medical case histories can produce an effect related to presentiment—yet two factors are already present here: in a way the makings of sickness are present in the fear—for it is difficult to say which produces the other—there is a certain receptivity so strong that it is almost productive—

Also the effect which executions, for example, produce.—
The many phenomena which are evoked by the doctrine of
the sin against the Holy Spirit.—

All sin begins with fear (just as fear of a sickness is a disposition toward it—see Schubert, *Symbolik*); however, the first
human beings did not begin with it—there was no hereditary
sin.—*JP* IV 3992 (*Pap*. II A 19) *n.d.*, 1837

See xiii:1:

All existence [*Tilværelsen*] makes me anxious, from the
smallest fly to the mysteries of the Incarnation; the whole
thing is inexplicable to me, I myself most of all; to me all existence is infected, I myself most of all. My distress is enormous, boundless; no one knows it except God in heaven, and
he will not console me; no one can console me except God in
heaven, and he will not take compassion on me. —Young
man, you who still stand at the beginning of your goal, if you
have gone astray, turn back to God, and from his upbringing
you will take along with you a youthfulness strengthened for
manly tasks. You will never know the suffering of one who,
having wasted the courage and energy of youth in insubor-
dination against him, must begin to retreat, weak and
exhausted, through devastated countries and ravaged prov-
inces, everywhere surrounded by the abomination of desola-
tion, by burned-out cities and the smoking ruins of frustrated
hopes, by trampled prosperity and toppled success—a retreat
as slow as a bad year, as long as eternity, monotonously broken by the daily repeated sigh: These days—I find no satisfaction in them.—*JP* V 5383 (*Pap*. II A 420) May 12, 1839

See xiii:8-9:

                                                      May 17
If I had had faith, I would have stayed with Regine. Thanks
to God I now see that. I have been on the point of losing my
mind these days. Humanly speaking, I was fair to her;
perhaps I should never have become engaged, but from that
moment I treated her honestly. . . . If I had not honored her

higher than myself as my future wife, if I had not been prouder of her honor than of my own, then I would have remained silent and fulfilled her wish and mine—I would have married her—there are so many marriages which conceal little stories. That I did not want, then she would have become my concubine; I would rather have murdered her. —But if I were to explain myself, I would have had to initiate her into terrible things, my relationship to my father, his melancholy, the eternal night brooding within me, my going astray, my lusts and debauchery, which, however, in the eyes of God are perhaps not so glaring; for it was, after all, anxiety that made me go astray, and where was I to seek a safe stronghold when I knew or suspected that the only man I had admired for his strength was tottering.—*JP* V 5664 (*Pap*. IV A 107) May 17, 1843

See xiii:8-9:

I cannot extricate myself from this relationship, for I cannot write about it, inasmuch as the instant I want to do that I am invaded by anxiety, an impatience which wants to act.—*JP* V 5519 (*Pap*. III A 164) *n.d., 1841*

See xiii:4:

Deep within every human being there still lives the anxiety over the possibility of being alone in the world, forgotten by God, overlooked among the millions and millions in this enormous household. A person keeps this anxiety at a distance by looking at the many round about who are related to him as kin and friends, but the anxiety is still there, nevertheless, and he hardly dares think of how he would feel if all this were taken away.—*JP* I 100 (*Pap*. VIII[1] A 363) *n.d., 1837*

See xiii:7:

It is appalling to think even for one single moment about the dark background of my life right from its earliest beginning. The anxiety with which my father filled my soul, his own frightful depression, a lot which I cannot even write down. I acquired an anxiety about Christianity and yet felt powerfully attracted to it. And then what I suffered later from Peter when he became morbidly religious.

As I mentioned, it is frightful to think for a single moment of the kind of life I have led in my most hidden inwardness, literally never a word about it spoken to a single human being, of course, not even daring to write down the least thing about it—and then that I have been able to encase that life in an exterior existence of zest for life and cheerfulness. . . .—*JP* VI 6274 (*Pap.* IX A 411) *n.d.*, 1848

See xiii:12:

The thought that God tests [*prøver*], yes, tempts [*frister*] a man ("lead us not into temptation") must not horrify us. The way one looks upon it makes the crucial difference. Disbelief, melancholy, etc., immediately become anxious [*angest*] and afraid and really impute to God the intention of doing it *in order that* man shall fail. However remote it may be that the melancholy anxiety in a man would think of having such thoughts about God, yet in the profoundest sense he really does think in this way, but without knowing it or becoming aware of it, just like the hot-headed person who is said not to know what he is doing. The believer, however, immediately interprets the matter inversely; he believes that God does it *in order that* he shall meet the test [*Prøven*]. Alas, in a certain sense this is why disbelief, melancholy, anxiety, etc., so often fail in the test, because they enervate themselves in advance— it is punishment for thinking ill of God; whereas faith usually conquers.

But this is rigorous upbringing—this going from inborn anxiety to faith. Anxiety is the most terrible kind of spiritual trial [*Anfægtelse*]—before the point is reached where the same man is disciplined in faith, that is, to regard everything inversely, to remain full of hope and confidence when something happens which previously almost made him faint and expire with anxiety, to plunge fearlessly into something against which he previously knew only one means of safety, to flee, and so on.

The person with inborn anxiety can very often have even a visionary idea of God's love. But he cannot concretize his relationship to God. If his idea of God's love has a deeper ground in him and he is devoutly concerned, above all else, to nourish and preserve it, then in many ways and for a long, long time his life can go on in the agonizing suffering of getting no impression *in concreto* that God is love (for anxiety continues to be too overpowering for him and prevents him from seeing the danger, the test, the temptation, etc., in the right way, that they are for him to meet), while he still all the more firmly attaches himself to and clings to the thought: Yes, but God is love just the same.

This is a sign that he is being educated or brought up to faith. To hold fast this way to the thought that God is love just the same is the abstract form of faith, faith *in abstracto*. Then the time will come when he will succeed in concretizing his God-relationship.—*JP* II 1401 (*Pap*. X² A 493) *n.d.*, 1850

See 117·7·

The most terrible punishment for sin is the new sin. This does not mean that the hardened, confident sinner will understand it this way. But if a man shudders at the thought of his sin, if he would gladly endure anything in order to avoid falling into the old sin in the future, then the new sin is the most terrible punishment for sin.

There are collisions here (especially in the sphere of sinful thoughts) in which anxiety over the sin can almost call forth the sin.

When this is the case, a desperate wrong turn may be made. Vigilius Haufniensis has described it thus: Repentance loses its mind. As long as repentance keeps its head, what should stand eternally fast does stand fast—namely, that the sin must be overcome. But in his despair it may not enter the unhappy man's head that since the new sin is in fact the most terrible punishment of sin he perhaps ought to put up with it.

No doubt this is how to understand what quietism has taught, that a man may be saved and yet continue in sin. In deadly anxiety he trembles before the new sin—but since it is in fact the punishment, despair takes him prisoner, as if there were nothing to do.

Here we see the difference in the ways temptation [*Fristelse*] and spiritual trial [*Anfægtelse*] should be fought: in the case of temptation the right thing may be to contend by avoiding. In the case of spiritual trial one must go through it. Temptation should be avoided; try not to see or hear what tempts you. If it is spiritual trial, go straight toward it, trusting in God and Christ.

Since in our time people have no idea at all of spiritual trial, anyone who suffers from it in our time would also be regarded as a very extraordinary sinner.—*JP* IV 4023 (*Pap*. X¹ A 637) *n.d.*, 1849

See 117:7:

May 5, 1847

The difference between sin and spiritual trial [*Anfægtelse*] (for the conditions in both can be deceptively similar) is that the temptation [*Fristelse*] to sin is in accord with inclination, [the temptation] of spiritual trial [is] contrary to inclination. Therefore the opposite tactic must be employed. The person tempted by inclination to sin does well to shun the danger, but in relation to spiritual trial this is the very danger, for every time he thinks he is saving himself by shunning the danger, the danger becomes greater the next time. The sensate person is wise to flee from the sight or the enticement, but the one for whom inclination is not the temptation at all but rather an anxiety about coming in contact with it (he is under spiritual trial) is not wise to shun the sight or the enticement; for spiritual trial wants nothing else than to strike terror into his life and hold him in anxiety.—*JP* IV 4367 (*Pap*. VIII¹ A 93) May 5, 1847

See 107:7:

. . . . . It is a very special spiritual trial [*Anfægtelse*] when a person in the strictest sense sins against his will, plagued by the anxiety of sin, when he has, for example, sinful thoughts which he would rather flee, does everything to avoid, but they still come—it is a special kind of spiritual trial to believe that this is something he must submit to, that Christ is given to him to console him as he bears this cross plagued as he is by a thorn in the flesh. . . .—*JP* IV 4368 (*Pap.* IX A 331) *n.d.*, 1848

See 107:7:

The above-mentioned spiritual trial [*Anfægtelse*] is very painful and excruciating and, in addition, dialectically complicated almost to the point of madness; if it may be thought of in this way, it is, to define it teleologically, an educational torture which, whatever else, is intended to break all self-centered willfulness.

It is in fact a kind of obsession. Humanly speaking, the sufferer is completely without guilt. He himself does not, as in sin, deliberately provoke these thoughts; it is just the opposite, these thoughts plague him. In his anxiety he flees from them in every way; he perhaps strains to the point of despair all his powers of ingenuity and concentration in order to avoid not only them but even the remotest contact with anything that could be related to them. It does not help; the anxiety becomes the greater. Neither does the usual advice help—to forget, to escape, for that is just what he is doing, but it merely nourishes the anxiety. . . .—*JP* IV 4370 (*Pap.* IX A 333) *n.d.*, 1858

See 146:25:

Descartes (in his essay, *De passionibus*) observes correctly that *admiratio* has no opposite (see Article LXXX). Similarly, that *cupiditas* ought not to have its opposite in *aversio* but ought to have no opposite (see Article LXXXVII). This is important for my theory of anxiety. See JJ, p. 3 from back [i.e., *Pap*. III A 233].—*JP* V 5588 (*Pap*. IV C 10) *n.d.*, 1842-43

See 146:29:

Aristotle's view* that philosophy begins with wonder, not as in our day with doubt, is a positive point of departure for philosophy. Indeed, the world will no doubt learn that it does not do to begin with the negative, and the reason for success up to the present is that philosophers have never quite surrendered to the negative and thus have never earnestly done what they have said. They merely flirt with doubt.
*In margin:** διὰ γὰρ τὸ
θαυμάζειν οἱ ἄνθρωποι
καὶ νῦν καὶ τὸ πρῶτον
ἤρξαντο φιλοσοφεῖν.
[For it is owing to their wonder that men both now and at first began to philosophize. . . . Aristotle, *Metaphysics*, Bk A 2, 9826 12f.]
Also Plato in *Theaetetus*. μάλα γὰρ φιλόσοφον
τοῦτο τὸ πάθος, τὸ θαυμάζειν.
οὐ γὰρ ἄλλη ἀρχὴ
φιλοσοφίας ἢ αὐτή.
[For this feeling of wonder shows that you are a philosopher, since wonder is the only beginning of philosophy. Plato, *Theaetetus*, 155 d.]
See [Karl F.] Hermann, *Geschichte und System der Platonische Philosophie*, I, p. 275, note 5.—*JP* III 3284 (*Pap*. III A 107) *n.d.*, 1841

From draft to " 'Guilty?'/'Not guilty?' " in Stages on Life's Way; *see xiv:1 and 250, note 19:*

All of us have a little psychological insight, some powers of observation, but when this science or art manifests itself in its infinitude, when it abandons minor transactions on the street and in dwellings in order to scurry after its favorite: the person shut up within himself [the person of inclosing reserve]—then men grow weary.—*JP* V 5721 (*Pap.* V B 147) *n.d.*, 1844

Draft of title:

Concerning
The Concept of Anxiety
A plain and simple psychological deliberation on the
dogmatic issue of hereditary sin
by
S. Kierkegaard
M. A.
[*magister artium*][1]
—*Pap.* V B 42 *n.d.*, 1844

Addition to Pap. V B 42:

Socrates— — — — — —Hamann
+   +
400 b.Chr.   1758 after Chr.

Sokrates meine Herren war kein [Socrates was, gentlemen, no] etc.
(in *Socratic Memorabilia*).—*JP* II 1553 (*Pap.* V B 43) *n.d.*, 1844

Draft of Epigraph: *Motto*

Is it not remarkable that the greatest master of irony and the greatest humorist, separated by 2,000 years, may join together in doing and admiring what we should suppose everyone had done, if this fact did not testify to the contrary. Hamann says of Socrates: "He was great because he distinguished between what he understood and what he did not understand." If only Socrates could have had an epitaph! Many an innocent person has drained the poisoned cup, many a one has sacrificed his life for the idea, but this epitaph be-

longs to Socrates alone: Here rests Socrates, he distinguished between what he understood and what he did not understand.
    Or perhaps better simply to quote Hamann's words.—*JP* II 1554 (*Pap*. V B 44) *n.d.*, 1844

Another draft of Epigraph:

    The age of distinction is long past, because the system abrogates it. He who loves it must be regarded as an oddity, a lover of something that vanished long ago. This may well be; yet my soul clings to Socrates, its first love, and rejoices in the one who understood him, Hamann; for he has said the best that has been said about Socrates, something far more remarkable and rare than that he taught young people and made fun of the Sophists and drained the poisoned cup: Socrates was great because he distinguished between what he understood and what he did not understand.—*JP* II 1555 (*Pap*. V B 45) *n.d.*, 1844

Draft of Dedication: see 5:

To the late
Professor *Poul Martin Møller*
the happy lover of Greek culture, the admirer of Homer, the confidant of Socrates, the interpreter of Aristotle—Denmark's joy in "Joy over Denmark"*—the enthusiasm of my youth;** the confidant of my beginnings; my lost friend; my sadly missed reader
    * though "widely traveled yet always remembered in the Danish summer."
    ** the mighty trumpet of my awakening; the desired object of my feelings;
this work
is dedicated.
—*Pap*. V B 46 *n.d.*, 1844

See 7:1:

Preface

to write a book etc. [The original Preface, now No. VII in *Prefaces*, *KW* IX (*SV* V), was replaced with the present Preface.]—*Pap.* V B 47 *n.d.*, 1844

See 25:2-5:

. . . . . has taken and is taking only an inland journey from his own consciousness to the presupposition of hereditary sin in his own consciousness.—*JP* V 5726 (*Pap.* V B 47:13) *n.d.*, 1844

Deleted from final copy; see 8:3-20:

Concerning my own humble person, I frankly confess—no matter how my confession is understood—that I am fully aware that as an author I am a king without a country, and have endeavored to cut my coat from my own cloth and to be an author without any claims. If in the best sense of the word it seems too much to zealous envy that I bear a Latin name, it may serve as pleasant news that if anyone desires and I can be of service, I shall gladly assume the name Christen Madsen. Most of all I wish to be regarded as an alehouse keeper, innkeeper, or as a plain layman who walks the floor and speculates without wishing that his speculative result should be regarded as speculation. I would not for anything in the world want to be an authority, not even for the most insignificant man, because I regard being authority as the most boring of all things. But in relation to everyone else, I apply myself to be as devout in my belief in authority as the Roman was tolerant in his worship of God. When it comes to human authority, I profess to fetishism and worship anyone whomsoever with equal piety, provided it is made sufficiently clear by a proper beating of drums that he has become the authority and the *imprimatur* for the current year, whether this is decided by lottery or whether the honor is passed around, just as one of the 36 representatives takes his turn on the board of arbitration.—*Pap*. V B 72:5 *n.d.*, 1844

From draft; see 9:27:

[Thus when an author entitles the last section of the *Logic*] "actuality" which Hegel has done and the Hegelian school did again and again [the advantage is gained that it seems as if through logic the highest were already reached, or, if one prefers, the lowest].—*JP* III 3653 (*Pap*. V B 49:1) *n.d.*, 1844

From draft; see 10:10:

[when in dogmatics *faith* is called the *immediate*]*
In margin: *(and this happens every day before our eyes). —*Pap*. V B 49:2 *n.d.*, 1844

From draft; see 12:31-37:

. . . . . Even in our little Denmark men have come to the rescue of logical movement. In his "logical system," which, despite all movement, does not come further than to §23 (the beginning of the doctrine of quantity) and, despite its proud title, was not able to emancipate itself from a very subordinate existence in a periodical, Professor Heiberg nevertheless succeeded in making everything move—except the system, which comes to a halt at §23, although one might have believed that the system would have moved by itself through an immanent movement, and the more so because the author indicated in the "Preface" the course of development, namely, that the published essay was "the first contribution to a long-cherished plan of setting forth the logical system." This he wished to do, not merely for its own sake, but as a means by which he also "intended to pave the way for an esthetics, which for some time he had hoped to present." Just an example: the professor explains to us that in order to form the transition from quality to quantity "it is not enough to define quantity as unqualified being in general; it is the *annulled* quality; that is to say: quantity is not the first presuppositionless *being* but is the being which, after the quality has been presupposed and then annulled, returns to the same indeterminateness." Now this may be quite correct, but the difficulty lies in the fact that both being and quality are treated as identical. But being is no quality; logically speaking, it is rather the empty, the contentless, whereas even according to Hegel's definition, quantity is *einfache Bestimmtheit* [simple determinateness], and therefore it is not essentially being but essentially determinateness. Thus when one proceeds from being and annuls this in order to return to it again, one will never arrive at quality, and much less a new quality. —Magister Alder (in his popular lecture on Hegel's objective logic, Copenhagen 1842) makes the movement even better. He says (p. 48), "when the quality is indifferent, quantity appears as the qualifying factor." One would be tempted to answer him with an emphasis even greater than that of the Lacedemonians: when?— *Pap.* V B 49:5 *n.d.*, 1844

From draft; see 13:21:

Note. Should anyone want further explication of the unwarranted use of the negative in logic, I simply refer him to Adolf Trendelenburg, *Die logische Frage in Hegels System, zwei Streitsschriften*, Berlin 1843. Trendelenburg is well-schooled in Greek philosophy and is unimpressed by humbug.—*Pap.* V B 49:6 *n.d.*, 1844

From draft; see 16:1-20:

Sin belongs in ethics, and the mood that corresponds to its conception is ethical earnestness or, more correctly, earnestness (for it is also a confusion of language to speak of esthetical, psychological, or metaphysical earnestness). Ethics does not overcome sin metaphysically, for it knows in all earnestness that sin has endurance; it does not flee sin esthetically or mourn over it esthetically, for it abrogates sin; it does not become psychologically absorbed in it, for it knows that sin is not a state.

But there is also a difficulty about sin having a place in ethics.—*Pap.* V B 49:7 *n.d.*, 1844

From draft; see 20:3-7:

Dogmatics does not prove hereditary sin, but explains it by presupposing it.

In a scientific sense one may say about sin what the Greeks—before their consciousness matured, and as far as it was possible for paganism to rise to the conception of Providence—said of the vortex that was the origin of all things: It is present everywhere as something no one can lay hold of. No science can deal with sin satisfactorily, yet the simplest man can grasp it. Finally, dogmatics takes hold of hereditary sin and explains it by presupposing it.—*Pap.* V B 49:11 *n.d.*, 1844

From draft; see 20:18-19:

From what has been said, it may seem that sin has no place in any science, since metaphysics cannot lay hold of it, psychology cannot overcome it, ethics must ignore it, and dogmatics explains it by means of hereditary sin, which, in turn, it must explain by presupposing it. This is quite correct, but it is also correct that sin finds a place within the totality of the new science that is prefigured in the immanent science and that begins with dogmatics in the same sense that the first science begins with metaphysics.—*Pap.* V B 49:12 *n.d.*, 1844

From draft; see 22:19:

Here again we see an example of how far immanence reaches, and that with exclusive validity one succeeds only in confusing everything.*

*Note. On this point compare with *Fear and Trembling* [*KW* VI (*SV* III 93)], where the necessity of "the leap" is emphasized numerous times with respect both to the dialectical

and to pathos, which is the substance of the leap.—*JP* III 2343
(*Pap*. V B 49:14) *n.d*., 1844

From draft; see 23:8-19:

This possibility, like every possibility, cannot have the particularity of any empirical actuality. Therefore, it is important to maintain with profound psychological decisiveness: *unum noris, omnes* [if you know one, you know all]. When the possibility of sin appears in one man, it has appeared in all, and only the arena of ideal observation is left for the deliberation of the more and the less. In life, the possibility of sin occurs no more than other possibilities.—*Pap*. V B 49:15 *n.d.*, 1844

From draft; see 23:33:

In margin: and its mood should be that of contemplative, interested attention with a touch of the esthetic and the sharp contours of observation.—*Pap*. V B 49:16 *n.d.*, 1844

From draft; see 23:34-37:

If this is held fast somewhat accurately, it will become apparent that it relates to the doctrine of absolute spirit, which is dogmatics; whereas ethics is the doctrine of objective spirit, which factually and empirically has actuality as its sphere.—*Pap*. V B 49:17 *n.d.*, 1844

Deleted from draft; see 25:27:

Chapter 1.
Anxiety as the presupposition for hereditary sin and as explaining hereditary sin retrogressively in terms of its origin

§1.
Hereditary sin defined historically within dogmatics

Simple attention to the use of language convinces a person that the term "hereditary sin" is used in a double sense. By pursuing this distinction, he may clear the way for the most accurate scientific definitions. Besides, he may have the joy, satisfaction, and assurance that he has not come down like a tower watchman from distant and unknown realms, therefore always getting into conflict with common language and, without being aware of it or wanting to do so, offending the genius of language and the rightful partners in the common ownership of language—something that at times indeed happens to a scientist. For a scientist, who always needs to be reconciled to and be in reconciliation with language, tensions of this kind are most unfavorable and depressing.—*Pap.* V B 50 *n.d.*, 1844

From draft; see 33:23-24:

. . . . . for that first sin is sinfulness, and by that sin sinfulness entered into Adam, and in the same way it enters every man. By Adam's first sin, sinfulness entered into Adam and gave birth to actual sins in him. By the second man's sin, sinfulness entered into the second man and gave birth to his sins.—*Pap.* V B 53:4 *n.d.*, 1844

From draft; see 38:25-33:

. . . . . for it is a contradiction to sorrow esthetically over sinfulness. The only one who sorrowed innocently over sinfulness was Christ, and so it might seem that he sorrowed esthetically over it. But then he also carried all the sins of the world, and therefore he sorrowed ethically over sinfulness.—*Pap.* V B 53:5 *n.d.*, 1844

From draft; see 40:15-18:

. . . How many a learned theologian has not known how to explain the teachings of the Bible, the Church, the Fathers, the Symbols of the Church, as well as those of the philosophers, on hereditary sin, without having occupied himself at any time in tracing the effect of hereditary sin in his own or another man's consciousness? Nevertheless, this is the first thing that every man is assigned to do, and every man, if he carefully examines himself, possesses within himself a more complete expression for everything human than the *summa summarum* of all the knowledge that he gains in the above manner.—*Pap*. V B 53:6 *n.d.*, 1844

From draft; see 40:27:

pagan (Seneca is especially quoted)—*Pap*. V B 53:7 *n.d.*, 1844

From draft; see 41:9-12:

Even with regard to the guilt of a subsequent man, this statement seems to presume that ethics makes an unethical about-face and permits guilt to appear through a merely quantitative determination, or permits it to appear as a *deus ex machina*, although the individual was never innocent. But it would be more pretentious to apply the statement to Adam's innocence, making it the secret agent paid to overthrow him.—*Pap*. V B 53:8 *n.d.*, 1844

From draft; see 42:9-11:

As far as I know, natural scientists agree that animals do not have anxiety simply because by nature they are not qualified as spirit. They fear the present, tremble, etc., but are not anxious. They have no more anxiety than they can be said to have presentiment.—*JP* III 3557 (*Pap*. V B 53:9) *n.d.*, 1844

From draft; see 48:6:

If anyone wishing to instruct me should say, "consistent with the preceding you of course, could say, 'It [the serpent] is language,' " I would reply, "I did not say that,"—*Pap*. V B 53:11 *n.d.*, 1844

From draft; see 47:36-40:

. . . . . but this much is certain, it will not do to assume that man himself invented language or, as Professor Madvig has expressed* so superbly in a prospectus, that men reached an agreement on what language they would speak.
    In margin: *with profound irony.—*JP* III 2321 (*Pap*. V B 53:12) *n.d.*, 1844

From draft; see 50:3:

. . . . . and who are indifferent to the fact that the explanation is so inhuman that no person who has lived or who wishes to live can understand it, because it also proposes to explain him. If the explanation of Adam and his fall does not concern me as a *fabula, quae de me narratur* [story that speaks to me], one might as well forget both Adam and the explanation.—*Pap*. V B 53:13 *n.d.*, 1844

From draft; see 57:10-13:

This is again a proof that our investigation is not guilty of the Pelagian irresponsibility that is incapable of weaving the individual into the cloth of the race but instead lets each individual stick out like the end of a thread. It is easily seen that this investigation protects the concept of race in such a way that it will not deprive individuals of their power and confuse the concept of individual as well as that of race. If the sinfulness of the race is posited by Adam's sin (ἐφῷ πάντες ἥμαρτον Rom. 5:12) in the same sense as a species of web-footed birds have webbed feet, the concept of the individual is canceled, and also the concept of the race. For precisely here lies the difference between the concept of the human race and that of animal species. . . .—*Pap*. V B 53:15 *n.d.*, 1844

From draft; see 57:26-33:

Herein lies the great significance of Adam above that of every other individual in the race, a distinction that is not qualitative but quantitative, and herein lies the truth of the saying that sinfulness entered the world by Adam. The expression may seem to say too much, but just as the previous chapter reduced the meaning of the expression to the point where sin entered Adam, so there is an orthodoxy that principally stresses that sin entered the human race. If the statement that "sin entered the human race" is to be understood in the same sense as "sin entered Adam," everything becomes confused. The most comprehensive expression, sin entered the world, is obviously true, since it suggests that sin entered the world in the same sense that it entered man. For sin cannot qualitatively [but only quantitatively] enter lifeless or animal nature, and it is in this [quantitative] sense that sin entered the race by Adam.—*Pap.* V B 53:16 *n.d.*, 1844

From draft; see 58:39:

. . . It ought, on the other hand, to begin with the Atonement, and by explaining the Atonement it indirectly explains sinfulness.—*Pap.* V B 53:17 *n.d.*, 1844

From draft; see 59:10:

Some men, particularly of the Schelling school, like Schubert, Eschenmayer, Görres, Steffens,
   In margin: Jacob Böhme, Schelling.* "Anxiety, anger, hunger, suffering." These things should always be eyed with caution; now it is the consequence of sin, now the negative in God—τό ἕτερον [the other].
   *even melancholy, in his essay on freedom, quoted by Rosenkranz in his last work, p. 309 [Karl Rosenkranz, *Schelling, Vorelesungen* (Danzig: 1843; *ASKB* 766), pp. 260 ff.].—*Pap.* V B 53:18 *n.d.*, 1844

From draft; see footnote 59:36-39:

In Latin the word *alterare* is not used in this sense. As a matter of fact, the word is not used at all. According to Scheller

[*Ausführliches . . . lateinisch-deutsches Lexicon*] the word occurs once in Ovid, where another reading, *adulterare*, is now commonly used (it is rather strange that the term *adulterare* should be used in Latin to mean "distort").—*Pap*. V B 53:19 *n.d.*, 1844

From draft; see 60:27:

So it happens at times that a person believes that he has a world-view, but that there is yet one particular phenomenon that is of such a nature that it baffles the understanding, and that he explains differently and attempts to ignore in order not to harbor the thought that this phenomenon might over-throw the whole view, or that his reflection does not possess enough courage and resolution to penetrate the phenomenon with his world-view.— *Pap*. V B 53:20 *n.d.*, 1844

From draft; see 61:18:

. . . . . and psychologically speaking, the first sin always takes place in impotence; therefore, it apparently lacks, in a certain sense, accountability.—*Pap*. V B 53:21 *n.d.*, 1844

From draft; see 61:24:

In every concrete expresson of freedom, all or a part of existence [*Tilværelsen*] collaborates.—*Pap*. V B 53:22 *n.d.*, 1844

From draft; see 64:13-16:

To assume this only betrays a narrow-minded cowardice, for, on the contrary, the magnitude of anxiety is a prophecy of how wonderful perfection is; and the inability to become anxious is proof that a person is either a beast or an angel, both of whom, also according to the teaching of the Scrip-tures, are less perfect than man [I Cor. 6:3; Heb. 1:14]. The "more" in the sensuousness of woman is only a matter of indifference in itself, and in relation to the idea it is an expression of perfection, because when seen ideally, it is always seen as something overcome and appropriated in freedom.—*Pap*. V B 53:23 *n.d.*, 1844

From draft; see 66:20-35:

. . . . . she is more sensate than man; for were she more spiritual she could never have her culmination point in another. Spirit is the true independent.

Of course every religious view, like every more profound philosophical view, sees woman, despite this difference, as essentially identical with man; but it is not foolish enough to forget for that reason the truth of the difference, esthetically and ethically understood.—*JP* IV 4989 (*Pap*. V B 53:25) *n.d.*, 1844

From draft; see 66:28-35:

In a way it has always seemed remarkable to me that the story of Eve has been completely opposed to all later analogy, for the expression "to seduce" used for her generally refers in ordinary language to the man, and the other related expressions all point to the woman as weaker (easier to infatuate, lure to bed, etc.).* This, however, is easy to explain, for in Genesis it is a third power that seduced the woman, whereas in ordinary language the reference is always only to the relationship between man and woman and thus it must be the man who seduces the woman.

*Note. If anyone has any psychological interest in observations related to this, I refer him to "The Seducer's Diary" in *Either/Or*. If he looks at it closely, he will see that this is something quite different from a novel, that it has completely different categories up its sleeve, and, if one knows how to use it, it can serve as a preliminary study for a very serious and not merely superficial research. The Seducer's secret is simply that he knows that woman is anxious.—*JP* V 5730 (*Pap*. V B 53:26) *n.d.*, 1844

From draft; see 67:14:

Only the animal can remain naive in the sexual relationship; man is unable to because he is spirit, and sexuality, as the extreme point of the synthesis, promptly rebels against spirit.—*JP* III 3962 (*Pap*. V B 53:27) *n.d.*, 1844

From draft; see 67:17:

. . . . . for a moral marriage is by no means naive, and yet it is by no means immoral. This is why I always say that it is sin which makes sensuality sinfulness.—*JP* III 3963 (*Pap*. V B 53:28) *n.d.*, 1844

From draft; see 67:18-68:14:

What I shall now briefly develop I also want to present in the right mood. To offer witticisms about the sexual is a paltry art, to warn against it is not difficult, and to preach about it in the usual way is an easy task, provided the difficulty is omitted; but to speak humanly about it and say everything, and also say it morally, is very difficult. Yet it is true that as many a young person became depraved because witticism made life frivolous and turned the sexual into a joke, and just as many a young person became depraved because rigorism made life melancholy and made sexuality into sinfulness, so many a young life was ruined because no mention was made of the sexual at all. It is also true that it is ill-conceived prudishness to refrain from speaking about the sexual when all discussion about it is left to proclaimers as heterogeneous as the theater and the pulpit, each of which is embarrassed by what the other says. Psychology, on the other hand, need not be embarrassed; nevertheless, I obligate myself forthwith to draw up a number of sketches that will exhibit the prodigious conflicts that may arise in this area. Mere knowledge of the sexual is not sin, and genuine naiveté is reserved for childhood. Therefore it is high time to close the mouth of the immorality that permits itself to speak naively about the sexual.

Either one must express the immorality in sensual desire loudly and clearly, as does the Seducer in *Either/Or*—therefore his diary has a moral value—or one must penetrate all discussion of the sexual with morality and, above all, renounce naiveté. If there were poets in our day, they would have recognized the admirable opportunities found in this field. Nothing is more base, and at the same time more certain to allure a young girl, than looking at her in a way that instills in her the certainty that she has knowledge, and thus entangles her in the anxiety that this knowledge is sin. A collision as strange as this is rarely found. What entraps her is obviously her purity. She finds a place of concealment only in the person who looked at her, for he alone shares her knowledge. Her anxiety is not anxiety about sin, but anxiety about being in sin, about having already sinned. As long as the lifeless twaddle about naiveté is maintained, every innocent girl, and first of all the purest among them, will be abandoned to this art of seduction. Let our systematicians discover that such an observation is poor, since it cannot be reduced to a paragraph [in the system]—I am nevertheless convinced that whoever is interested in human beings has chosen the better part, and I am also convinced that one thing is needful above everything else, namely, to become a little more Greek in the good sense of the term, i.e., more human, and not fantastically inordinate with systematic galimatias, something that no *human being* cares about.* Psychology is what we need, and, above all, thorough knowledge of human life as well as sympathy for its interests. Herein lies the task, and until this is resolved there can be no question of completing a Christian view of life. In what sense is sensuousness sinfulness? Or, more precisely, in what sense is sexuality sinfulness? If a person every Sunday hears the proclamation of a love that is in spirit and in truth and permits the erotic to vanish as a nothing, so that the marriage relation becomes so spiritual that the sexual is entirely forgotten, then the cloister and abstinence are much

In margin: *Even though no one pays attention to this in these days, I know nevertheless that if Socrates lived now, he would have reflected [essentially the same as p. 68:6-14].

truer. If a person attends the theater in the evening, with the permission of the Church, and listens to the praise of the erotic—what can be made of all this! A person is not to enter the cloister but is to marry. Quite correct! Nevertheless, it is rather stupid to do so if the highest expression of married love is indifferent to the sexual relation. But this is where things stand, and I would like to know what has been provided in this respect in our age, which presumably has explained almost everything by means of the system but has been unable to explain the simplest of things, namely, that which almost every person is interested in, whether he has lived as a pagan or as a Christian in his marriage. Is a person to be told every Sunday in church that he is born in sin and that his mother conceived him in iniquity, and thereupon learn from the poets that their heroines had a naiveté the like of which not even Eve possessed? To my way of thinking this is nonsense, and when for a long time no alarm was raised, this must have been because our time has acquired a remarkable thoughtlessness in relation to what it means to live, and a concern for everything else, especially that which is loudly proclaimed; whereas each person should be concerned about himself and about transforming his life into a beautiful, artistically finished whole. I believed that this was the meaning of life and the meaning of the life of the single individual, with an increase of meaning in proportion to what a person could include in his life, and with a greater concreteness of this task from age to age in the historical progression. I believed that every science should direct itself to this task and that all idle knowledge debases a man and essentially wastes his time, although he may be more deeply debased and waste his time in a worse way. It is said that he who sleeps does not sin, but a man whose whole life has been absorbed in idle knowledge has nevertheless in a profound sense slept away his life. I believed that in order to grasp and to express this meaning of life it is also appropriate that the single individual who is capable of it should apply himself to studies of a scientific nature, but in such a way that such study would have its validation in an education whose ultimate expression is to impress the idea upon his own life. This is something that is not seen in our time. Instead, one sees too often a person who slovenly passes through life, performing all the common tasks of life as if they hardly concerned him; otherwise he is easily aroused when the talk turns to some stupendous idea, like an association of human talents that is supposed to accomplish the extraordinary, as if an association of men who separately are unable to accomplish something simple would be able to accomplish something difficult, a performance similar to that of the alehouse keeper who thought he would become rich by selling his beer for a penny less than he paid for it and still make a profit on the grounds that it is the quantity that does it.—*Pap.* V B 53:29 *n.d.*, 1844

From draft; see 68:38-69:3:

. . . . . merely by gazing at oneself. Psychology can easily enumerate examples of such cases, but care must be taken that it [such gazing] is not the consequence of desire.—*Pap.* V B 53:30 *n.d.*, 1844

From draft; see 70:1-8 and note:

What Socrates meant is that the erotic has been reduced to indifference and that it has become comic, and consequently one can love the ugly.—*Pap.* V B 53:31 *n.d.*, 1844

From draft; see 70:9-71:5 and note:

In Christianity, the religious has again suspended the erotic, but it is not as if this were done through an ascetic misunderstanding, as the sinful, but rather as the indifferent, because in spirit there is no difference between man and woman. Here it is not comically undifferentiated, because the tendency of Christianity is the further development of spirit, and there is therefore no time to dwell on the erotic. In paganism, however, the ultimate is not brought to completion in the deepening of the spirit, but in a positing of spirit as spirit, while nevertheless relating itself to the erotic but regarding it as comical.—*Pap.* V B 53:32 *n.d.*, 1844

From draft; see 72:3:

If the erotic is not pure, anxiety becomes anger, and if anxiety is not present at all, the erotic becomes bestiality.—*Pap.* V B 53:33 *n.d.*, 1844

From draft; see 75:6-14:

. . . . . sinfulness. [*] Especially among women there are instances of an individual who in anxiety conceives of most trivial bodily functions as sinfulness. A person may smile at this, but no one knows whether the smile will save or destroy, for if the smile contributes not to the opening of the individuality but to the closing of it, such a smile can cause irreparable harm.

[*] *In margin*: and if he now is bereft of everything that can support him in a more common view (as in the Middle Ages).

In margin: Confusion of *de te narratur fabula* [the story is told about you]—if you do likewise—if?—*Pap.* V B 53:34 *n.d.*, 1844

From draft; see 78:14-22:

. . . . . just as when certain geniuses abrogate the whole meaning of mythology in their zeal to bring every myth before their "eagle eye," to make it a capriccioso for their "mouth organ." This is the way concepts and myths are frequently prostituted in the world.—*JP* III 2802 (*Pap.* V B 53:35) *n.d.*, 1844

From draft; see 80:29-31:

. . . . . for they win neither Greek serenity nor the bold confidence of the spirit.

The sexual is not sin; when I first posit sin, I also posit the sexual as sinfulness. It does not follow as a matter of course that I sin by marrying, since on the contrary I strive to eliminate the contradiction.[*] The individual for whose arrival I am responsible does not become sinful through me but becomes that by positing sin himself and then himself positing the sexual as sinfulness.

[*] *In margin*: to transform a drive into the moral; for the sexual is the sinful only to the extent that the drive at some moment manifests itself simply as drive in all its nakedness, for this can occur only through an arbitrary abstraction from spirit.—*JP* IV 3964 (*Pap.* V B 53:38) *n.d.*, 1844

Deleted from final copy; see 82:17:

Aristotle himself defines κίνησις more precisely: It belongs neither to possibility nor to actuality. In relation to quantity it is αὔξησις [growth]—φθίσις [decay]; in relation to quality it is ἀλλοίωσις [alteration] (from this the New Testament has formed words about the Atonement   [*sic*]); in relation to time, φόρα [locomotion]. (Cf. Tennemann, *Geschichte der Philosophie*, pp. 127-28.)—*Pap.* V B 72:12 *n.d.*, 1844

From draft; see 83:5-84:3,8:

This is the way a philosopher acted with whom I once had the honor of speaking. When I ventured to point out to him one or another minor difficulty which needed consideration before it would be possible to bring off dogmatic speculation, he replied: "You may very well be right, but one should not think about it, because then he will never get around to speculating."—*JP* III 3302 (*Pap.* V B 55:3) *n.d.*, 1844

From draft; see 85:12:

If men had pursued further the ancient idea that man is a synthesis of soul and body, which is constituted by spirit, men would long since have thought more precisely with regard to sin and hereditary sin, its origin and its consequence.

Though it can be said that the spirit takes lodging in a defiled body,* and this is the most extreme expression one can employ, yet it does not follow that the spirit itself is defiled, unless this defilement is again a consequence of that relationship. But even here there is the likeness and unlikeness to Adam, together with the more detailed consideration of the possibility of freedom in the individual.

In margin: *Is this not found in Ecclesiastes or in the Psalms?—*JP* I 52 (*Pap*. V B 55:4) *n.d.*, 1844

From draft; see 86:6-8:

. . . . . for representation it is indeed something present, and nevertheless is not; something completely present, which nevertheless is not, which at this point could be expressed in this manner: they ruled India for 70,000 years.—*Pap*. V B 55:5 *n.d.*, 1844

From draft; see 88:25-26:

. . . . . for the moment is really time's atom, but not until eternity is posited, and this is why one may properly say that eternity is always in ἐν ἀτόμῳ [the moment].—*JP* III 2740 (*Pap*. V B 55:6) *n.d.*, 1844

From draft; see 90:4-5:

. . . . . more philosophically, as among the Greeks, or more historically, as when God was named the Ancient of Days [Daniel 7:9,13,22]. The eternal is indeed just as much the future.—*Pap*. V B 55:7 *n.d.*, 1844

From draft; see 90:33-91:23:

The individual is sensuously qualified, and as such he is also qualified by time in time; but he is also spirit, i.e., he is to become spirit, and as such, the eternal. Whenever the eternal touches the temporal, the future is there, for, as stated, this is the first expression of the eternal. Just as in the preceding, spirit—since it was established in the synthesis, or, rather, since it was about to be established—appeared as freedom's possibility, expressed in the individual's anxiety, so the future is now the eternal's possibility and is expressed in the individuality as anxiety.*

*Note. When I speak here of the eternal in determinants of time, it is clear that I am correct in a different sense than when logic does so, for the secret of the individual life is that the fluctuation of the movement is a state.—*Pap.* V B 55:9 *n.d.*, 1844

From draft; see 91:27-32:

It may no doubt be possible to demonstrate that a more precise and correct linguistic use links anxiety with the future. Commonly a person is not very careful in his use of language, especially because speculation has little by little formed its own language, which is used by no one but philosophers. But the art is to be able to use the same word everyone else uses. The warrant of a thinker is adequately demonstrated when the word in his mouth expresses a clear thought. Hitherto the word "anxiety" has been a kind of booty; I will now try to give the word a definite meaning, or more correctly, to affirm the word in its definite meaning.

To use a new expression for what has been said, anxiety is really the *discrimen* (ambiguity) of subjectivity. It is therefore very clear that "future" and "possibility" correspond to this; but if one speaks of being anxious about the past, this seems to invalidate my use of language, for the ambiguity of subjectivity has nothing that is past. If I were now to suggest that subjectivity is not completed all at once, and that insofar as one might speak of a reappearance of this ambiguity, then this would not be favorable to my position, assuming that it actually is justifiable to speak of anxiety about the past. But if we ask more particularly in what sense it is possible to speak of anxiety about the past, everything becomes clear.—*Pap.* V B 55:10 *n.d.*, 1844

From draft; see 93:9:

What has been developed here could also have been dealt with in Chapter I, but I have assigned it a place here because time first comes into existence [*bliver til*] with sin (just as, on the other hand, time first becomes full with the Atonement). For innocence does not really exist. . . .—*Pap.* V B 55:12 *n.d.*, 1844

From draft; see 93:28-94:1:

It is easy to show that this is the case in paganism, and that its great sin seems to be that it never arrives at the great break that constitutes sin. But the same can just as easily be shown within Christianity. To do so, a person does not need to travel to Paris and London, or to any Sodom and Gomorrah, but only to walk along the streets, and he will not have to walk far before he meets enough individuals who fit the description.—*Pap.* V B 55:13 *n.d.*, 1844

From draft; see 95:6-14:

I will cite an example and do it in a way that will exhibit its epigrammatical force, for I sincerely admit that it appears to me to be a profound epigram in which are joined two of perhaps the most brilliant minds of all time. The greatest humorist (Hamann) said of the only ironist (Socrates) that Socrates was great in that he distinguished between what he knew and what he did not know. Socrates himself has said this, and therein lies the irony. The humor lies in the reproduction as well as in the evaluating solemnity and the apparently fortuitous character of the remark. What could prevent a trivial head from repeating the same? For Socrates, this saying was the whole meaning of his life, and I know of no epitaph more fitting for him than this. There were no doubt many in the world who drained the poison-filled cup or sacrificed their lives in other ways, but there was only one who distinguished between what he understood and what he did not understand. That the best men become victims is already a terrible judgment upon the world, but this epitaph is a judgment far more terrible.—*Pap*. V B 55:14 *n.d.*, 1844

From draft; see 95:35-96:18:

It [spiritlessness] worships sometimes a dunce and sometimes a hero. But nothing impresses it more than a charlatan. However, one fetish is soon replaced by another, and while he is the fetish-man he is treated as savages treat their gods.

With paganism, as well as with all spheres of existence that correspond to it within Christianity, it is different. These lie as approximations to the qualitative leap of sin but do not reach the leap. Nevertheless, they are not innocence. We shall now consider these, and remind the reader that because they cannot be dealt with under innocence they are best dealt with here, although the present chapter treats of anxiety as the consequence of sin in the single individual.—*Pap*. V B 55:15 *n.d.*, 1844

From draft; see 97:21:

Anxiety.*

*Note. It is quite clear that Spinoza's substance signifies something else, for his substance is an inner necessity in which the fortuitous (the accidental) always disappears. Indeed, his substance is only a metaphysical expression for Christian providence, which again corresponds to fate in such a way that it is the unity of necessity and the accidental, so that for providence the accidental is, and yet in such a way that for providence nothing is accidental.—*Pap*. V B 55:17 *n.d.*, 1844

From draft; see 99:33-100:9:

The law in this story is something that no man can discover, for no one can understand fate but the man himself.—*Pap*. V B 55:18 *n.d.*, 1844

From margin of draft; see 106:3-107:5:

and the more remote the outward task is from the religious, the deeper is the deliberation—
Medieval artists who painted Venus but apprehended their task religiously.
Thus nothing outward is incommensurate with the religious. This was the misunderstanding of the Middle Ages.
—*Pap.* V B 55:24 *n.d.*, 1844

From draft; see 109:32-110:13:

In freedom's possibility, it holds true that the more profoundly this is grasped, the more profoundly and definitely the possibility of guilt appears within it, just as it holds true of immediate genius that the greater the genius the more profound the relationship to fate.

In freedom's possibility, freedom collapses. This is, as mentioned, the closest psychical approximation to the qualitative leap which posits sin. To say that the Church teaches hereditary sin, that the Catholic Church teaches it thus and the Protestant Church thus, to erect a speculative concept which explains hereditary sin and sin *at all*—this is indeed the task of the learned and wise in our time. The more concrete understanding of it in the specific individual, that is to say, the way I have to understand it, is a simpler, less complicated task, which I have chosen.

What is developed in these two paragraphs had no place in the previous chapter, because the position here described is not a state of innocence and yet does not come after the qualitative leap.—*JP* II 1248 (*Pap.* V B 55:26) *n.d.*, 1844

From draft; see 112:13-15:

Liberum arbitrium, which can equally well choose the good or the evil, is basically an abrogation of the concept of freedom and a despair of any explanation of it. Freedom means to be capable. Good and evil exist nowhere outside freedom, since this very distinction comes into existence through freedom.—*JP* II 1249 (*Pap*. V B 56:2) *n.d.*, 1844

From draft; see 113:16-114:3:

After sin has been posited, the object of anxiety is sin. The posited sin is a canceled possibility, but although posited, it is also unwarranted. Here the two forms of sin immediately appear. Sin looks back to a time before its actuality, to an imaginary possibility, and although it announces itself as posited by the individual, he will not recognize it but instead haunts like a specter, fantasylike, in nebulous regions, groping for the possibility of sin; or sin is posited, and the individual allows it to proceed in its own consequences. Both ways are forms of sin, because both exclude repentance. . . .

In margin: In the next place, the consequence of sin may lead further, and no man has sinned so much that he cannot sink still deeper.—*Pap*. V B 56:4 *n.d.*, 1844

From draft; see 114:5:

In margin: This is something that I cannot explain, unless I were to explain it as the philosophers explain the concept of "soul"—an explanation no one can understand or understand any better than if they said, soul is $a^2 + 2ab + b^2$.—*Pap*. V B 56:5 *n.d.*, 1844

From draft; see 114:30-34:

This is something that Plato already has expressed beautifully in a passage where he lets Epimetheus inquire of Jupiter whether he should distribute the ability of good and evil in the same way as poetic talent, musical talent, etc., in such a way that one becomes a poet, another an orator, etc. And Jupiter replied, No, for this ability belongs essentially to every man alike.*

*Note. The reader must pardon me for quoting in this

manner. To me, the thought has always been the important thing, and since I never use any excerpt apart from memory, I cannot without some effort recall where the passage is found, which is not worth the trouble.—*Pap.* V B 56:7 *n.d.*, 1844

From draft; see 114:35:

The two forms of sin mentioned—wanting to carry the actuality of sin back to an illusory possibility or permitting sin to pursue its course and obtain what Paul [Rom. 6:20] speaks of as freedom from righteousness—constitute the basis of all sin.

But sin is not a state.—*Pap.* V B 56:8 *n.d.*, 1844

From draft; see 122:4-8:

. . . . . an average number, so that for every generation there are so and so many measures of the demonic, and if our time has an average number, then everything is explained. Therefore it becomes so difficult to understand Christianity, for it happened only once and for all time that a human being was God. On the other hand, if an estimate can be formed of how many portions of divine gilding are assigned to each generation, perhaps *durch die Bank* [through the bank], then everything would be explained.

The medical-therapeutic view regards the phenomenon as purely physical and somatic.—*Pap.* V B 56:9 *n.d.*, 1844

From draft; see 135:2-5:

Some people are as well informed about the concept of irony as the noble youth who, when asked in a test for a grocer's licence where raisins come from, answered, "We get ours from the professor on Cross Street"—thus they get the concept from one or another professor on Cross Street.—*Pap.* V B 59 *n.d.*, 1844

From draft; see 135:6-136:10:

Now I return to the definition, anxiety about the good. V B 60
133
The loss of freedom may, however, be only a state from
which the new sin breaks forth quantitatively, for only the
good can be a unity of state and movement.

When I also use here the concepts of good and evil, then
these must be regarded quite abstractly. When freedom's possibility is anxiety about guilt, then this is anxiety about the
annulment of freedom. When the demonic is anxiety about
evil [the editors of the *Papirer* suggest that this should read
"anxiety about the good"], we have the annulled freedom
that is anxious about becoming freedom.

Perhaps this may seem strange talk to some people, for
who does not want to be free? However, the way in which a
person speaks about such things indicates that he has no conception of the crisis that arises when freedom is to be brought
into unfreedom. Wishing to be free is an easy matter, because
wishing is the most paltry and unfree of all performances.

Meanwhile, freedom may be lost in various ways, all in relation to the parts of the synthesis. It may be lost *bestially, intellectually*, and *religiously*; but no matter the way in which it is
lost or being lost, it is always lost ethically or being lost ethically.

See 136-37:

(a) *Freedom lost bestially*. This is in a sense the most dreadful
phenomenon and also the most conspicuous.[*] Whenever a
person loses freedom bestially, he stands below the level of
the beast, for originally he was designed to be above the
beast.

Life presents numerous examples of this form of the demonic. An ethical observation sees how sin always breaks

[*] *In margin*: I always speak both of the most pregnant phenomenon and of
the numerous lesser and lesser phenomena, and finally, even of the apparently insignificant approximations.

V B 60
134

forth qualitatively out of this form as new sin, while psycho-logical observation deals with the state. The essential nature of this state is anxiety about the good. Thus a demoniac in the New Testament says to Christ when he is approached by him, τί ἐμοὶ καὶ σοί ["What have I to do with you"]. This is the formula. Another demoniac begs Christ to depart and go another way. [*]

Similarly, one may hear a drunkard say, "Let me be the filth that I am." This may explain the solidarity of accessories in guilt[**] brought about by unnatural excesses, of which Duchatelet[2] gives examples. Anxiety is so great that they are able to arm themselves against it only by this mutual clinging together, which, even though false, is an expression of something good with respect to love. [†]

Such beastly lostness—which may also be found in higher spheres of life, where there is a greater mental strength to preserve it—can ruin the body, and this in turn becomes the object of medical treatment. But although medicine may be of great help, it can never know whether it helps only to bring about new sin.

I shall not pursue this form of the demonic further. It always has been in the world and cannot deceive, something that other forms may do easily.

(b) *Freedom lost intellectually.* This form [*essentially the same as 137:33-138:6*] stupid busyness that does not have the time, such as mockery etc.††

Regarded intellectually, the content of freedom is truth, and truth makes man free (John 8:32). On the other hand, truth is the work of freedom. Truth is continually brought forth. Obviously [*essentially the same as 138:10-26*] for the consequence, or does not in one way or another transform the ac-

V B 60
135

[*] *In margin*: or the demoniac asks Christ to send him away to another place.

[**] *In margin*: Hence the strange solidarity between demoniacs— Duchatelet on public prostitutes, especially those with unnatural desires.

[†] *In margin*: hypochondria.

[††] *In margin*: Even knowing that I am in an unfree relation to the truth, yet not knowing its significance for me. A demonic knowledge—the expression occurs in the Epistle of James.

tuality of truth into a possibility for himself, for this naturally alleviates anxiety.

All of the recent science offers frequent examples of this form of the demonic. A person develops the truth but is indifferent to certitude. He proves the immortality of the soul by means of a combination of all previous proofs but shrinks from the truth of immortality. He deceives both himself and others by pretending that the proof is so tremendously important and that this is what is needed, and for the sake of the proof he readily forgets immortality; for immortality itself, in all its consequences, has a power to recreate all of life, and this perhaps is what he fears. A person saves his soul by straining his mind in demonstration of the proof, and when the proof is completed, he has in a truly catholic sense made satisfaction for everything else.

Whenever inwardness, appropriation, is lacking, the individual is in an unfree relation to the truth, even though he otherwise possesses the whole truth. There is something that makes him anxious, namely, the good.

This cannot be explained often enough. Unlike the preceding form of the demonic, the intellectual form does not carry its own punishment. In the eyes of the world it is quite pleasing; nevertheless, it is anxiety about the good.

Otherwise truth may be anything whatever, but whenever inwardness is lacking, there is a qualification of the demonic. An adherent to the most rigid orthodoxy [*essentially the same as 139:32-140:7*].

See 140:7-18:

To use a simplified expression for this form of the demonic, it can be said that it is either superstition or unbelief, for in either case the individual is in untruth (unfreedom), and therefore in an unfree relation to the truth, for only faith is free in its relation to the truth. Superstition always has the truth outside itself, and therefore it does not dare to think it. Otherwise superstition is by nature entirely indifferent. While one person believes he will be saved by eating carrots, another

V B 60
136

by genuflecting before the holy, and another by his ability to repeat the categories—all of these forms are unfree, and in relation to freedom they dare not think the truth in which they would rest. The highest form of unbelief is mockery, and here the New Testament formula, τί ἐμοὶ καὶ σοί ["What have I to do with you"], cannot be applied often enough. Therefore anxiety resounds in the mockery of unbelief; the more anxious it is, the more it mocks. To the extent that mockery brings into consciousness its relation to the truth, it is ideally to be preferred to superstition. In other respects it is usually more cowardly than superstition.

Yet superstition and unbelief are such common terms: besides, our age is so sagacious that it will be neither one nor the other, but this by no means exempts it from the demonic.

See 151:7-153:11:

V B 60
136

In order to present the most common forms of the intellectual demonic of our age, I shall approach the subject somewhat differently. Like freedom, truth is the eternal.[*] If the eternal is not, there is neither truth nor freedom. The demonic can easily be recognized by an examination of the various ways in which our age deals with the eternal. Every consciousness that does not possess within itself the consciousness of the eternal is *eo ipso* demonic; it has an anxiety about the eternal, i.e., about the good.

But eternity is a very radical thought. Whenever it is posited, the present becomes something entirely different from what it was apart from it. This is something that men fear. Often enough, talk is heard about particular governments in Europe that are in fear of restless elements. I prefer to say that the entire present generation is a tyrant who lives in fear of one restless element: the thought of eternity. This thought is always suppressed; nevertheless, it is still impossible not to be in contact with it: a person will think it, and he does not dare to think it.

V B 60
137

Here the mockers meet who believe they can scare away

[*]*In margin: Inwardness is eternity.* Therefore all things can be referred to it.

the thought of eternity. They proclaim the moment but are in a frightful hurry. Why? Because they are in fear of something, and that something is eternity.

Here we find the most fantasylike conceptions. Eternity is bent into temporality, or it is left to fantasy, and now the thought of eternity becomes a fantasylike occupation* (Bettina's letters).[3]

Some teach that eternity is comic, or more correctly, that in eternity a person will preserve a comic consciousness about the temporal. This wisdom we owe especially to the last three or four paragraphs of Hegel's *Esthetics*. Here [in Denmark] it has been presented in one of the newspapers by Professor Martensen. Although the professor, after his return [from Germany], and since his first appearance in *Monthly Journal for Literature* [*Maanedsskrift for Literatur*], has invariably assured us that he has gone beyond Hegel, he certainly did not go farther in this case. After all, Martensen differs from the philosophers of promise only in that he reassures. The comic is a category that belongs specifically to the temporal. The comic always lies in *Wiederspruch* [contradiction]. But in eternity all contradictions are canceled, and the comic[**] is consequently excluded. *Eternity is indeed the true repetition*† in which history comes to an end and all things are explained.

(c) *Freedom lost religiously* [††]

    An active form (masculine)

        e.g., hypocrisy   pride

    A passive form (feminine)

        e.g., offense—He who remains in offense is

            just as demonic as the other.

            cowardice

V B 60
138

Vertically in margin: that art is an anticipation of eternal life. The apocalyptic, in which, not as in Dante, judgment ethically conceived is suspended. In every case merely a fantasy-view.

In margin: *Eternity is permitted to peep into the moment, like the glimpse of the moon in an illuminated forest or hall.

[**]*In margin:* Perhaps no one knows better what the times want than I do.

† Note. See *Repetition*, p. 142 [*KW* VI (*SV* III 254)].

[††]*In margin:* Whenever I am not free in the religious there is something demonic in it.—*Pap.* V B 60 *n.d.*, 1844.

From draft; see 142:21-25:

The more concrete the religious (consequently, the good) is, the greater is the range of nuances.—*Pap.* V B 61 *n.d.*, 1844

From draft; see 143:18-20:

There are examples of persons in anxiety about going to Communion; this, however, is not demonic but spiritual trial.—*Pap.* V B 62 *n.d.*, 1844

From draft; see 143:35-40:

There are doubtless examples in Görres, *Mystik*, but this work is so uncanny that I have never dared to read it carefully.—*Pap.* V B 63 *n.d.*, 1844

From draft; see 142:34-143:1:

Relationship to the Historical
Something demonic in wanting to attack the historical in the New Testament, as if this were the main thing.—

Yet no one has freely and openly posed the problem of doubt in relation to Christianity—Lessing might be the only one.—*JP* II 1637 (*Pap.* V B 64) *n.d.*, 1844

From draft; see 146:4;151:1:

Inwardness is earnestness.*—the remarkable words of Macbeth.[**]

When inwardness is missing, the spirit is finitized—inwardness is the eternal.— *JP* II 2112 (*Pap.* V B 65) *n.d.*, 1844

Addition to Pap. V B 65; *see 147:31-34:*

*The definition of disposition [*Gemyt*] in Rosenkranz's *Psychologie*⁴ may be used as the foundation for earnestness, provided freedom is definitely included.—*Pap.* V B 67 *n.d.*, 1844

Addition to Pap. V B 65; *see 149:34-151:8:*

[**]Therefore nothing can be said about earnestness in general. It is not pure subjectivity or any similar stupidity. Earnestness is present only in the very finest concretions (the empirical self) and as a qualification of freedom. To speak of freedom in any other sense is a misunderstanding. There is no measuring rod more accurate for the determination of the essential worth of an individuality than that of learning what in a pregnant sense made him earnest in life, for with a certain kind of earnestness one can deal with various things, except that from which an individual dates his life. Earnestness about the national debt, about one's own debt, or about astronomy, etc. A healthy spirit manifests itself precisely in being able to deal with everything else just as sentimentally as jocularly, and just as well. But in relation to earnestness, it tolerates no sentimentality and no joking. If it does that, it will happen to such a person as with Albertus* Magnus, who boasted of his speculation and suddenly became stupid.

*See somewhere in journal [i.e., *JP* V 5700 (*Pap.* IV A 174)].—*Pap.* V B 68 *n.d.*, 1844

From draft; see 152:30-154:28, also V B 61, 65:

(a) Outline
(b) What is inwardness
  1. Earnestness
  2. The eternal
  —the various conceptions of the eternal in our age

    a. Avoidance of the eternal
    b. Conceived imaginatively
    c. Conceived comically
       metaphysically
(c) The more concrete the religious is (consequently the good), the greater the range of nuances
    Positive religion
    The historical
(d) It is treated as an appendix to the system. Therefore, Poul Møller was right, that immortality must be present throughout and not brought in as an appendix to the system—
    to drink of Lethe is true to a certain degree.
       —*JP* II 2113 (*Pap.* V B 66) *n.d.*, 1844

From draft; see 147:31-148:28:

Earnestness is acquired originality
    Different from habit—it is the disappearance of self-consciousness.
    (cf. Rosenkranz, *Psychologie*)
    Therefore repetition is really—earnestness.—*Pap.* V B 69 *n.d.*, 1844

From draft; see 7:

[A note, scratched out with ink, next to the heading of what first was intended as the preface to *The Concept of Anxiety* and which afterwards was included in Kierkegaard's *Prefaces.*]
    N.B. This is not to be used because it would distract from the subject. Therefore I have written a little preface to be printed in the book.—*Pap.* V B 71 *n.d.*, 1844

Deleted from final copy; see 126:31:

As far as I am concerned, I am safeguarded in this respect by my own experience in another direction, for although I have never been accustomed to making little summaries in order to carry all my scholarly learning in my head, although I always read widely and then turn this over to my memory, although I can be totally engrossed in my own production, and although together with all this I am doing seventeen other things and talk every day with about fifty people of all ages, I swear, nevertheless, that I am able to relate what each person with whom I have spoken said the last time, next-to-the-last time, not to mention someone who is the object of particular attention—his remarks, his emotions are immediately vivid to me as soon as I see him, even though it is a long time since I saw him.—*JP* V 5731 (*Pap*. V B 72:22) *n.d.*, 1844

Deleted from final copy; see 147:2:

In the sixth letter of *The Centaur not Fabulous*, Young says a few words about *Ecclesiastes*, a work he ascribes to Solomon. Because I do not understand English, and also because no doubt there are more who understand German than English, I quote from a German translation (cf. *Einige Werke v. Dr. Edvard Young übersetzt v. J. A. Ebert,* Braunschweig and Hildesheim: 1777 [I-III, 1767-72; *ASKB* 1911], 2ᵈ D. p. 398) [the English text reads]: "I believe that wise and experienced prince, whose wisdom and experience was designed to spare future ages their own fatal experience in folly, and, closing with his *last* sentiment, the sum of his divine philosophy,* I affirm that many a philosopher may justly be reputed a fool; that as there is but one God, one trial, one great tribunal, one salvation, so there is but one wisdom; that all which, devoid of *that* assumes the name, is but folly of different colours and degrees—gay, grey, wealthy, lettered, domestic, political, civil, military, recluse, ostentatious, humble, or triumphant; and is *so* called in the language of angels, in the sole-authentic and unalterable style of *eternity*.** [Edward Young, *The Complete Works, Poetry and Prose*, ed. James Nichols, I-II (London: 1854), II, p. 521.]

*Note. The author [Young] refers to the closing words of *Ecclesiastes*: "Fear God and keep his commandments; for this is the whole duty of man. For God will bring every deed into

judgment, with every secret thing, whether good or evil" [Ecclesiastes 11:13-14].
**Note. This is a rather lengthy quotation; but if I have the patience to copy it the reader will no doubt also have the patience to read it.—*Pap*. V B 72:28 *n.d.*, 1844

Deleted from final copy; see 147:13:

The preponderant and prevailing interest in explication of and occupation with concepts in our age is something that indicates that our age is demoralized or demonized.—*Pap*. V B 72:29 *n.d.*, 1844

Deleted from final copy; see 147:36:

. . . . . and also saves the writer from the temptation of becoming important in his own eyes by writing about philosophical subjects in the same way as one would publish a book that was not intended for schoolchildren, saying that the main forms of the conjugation of *amo* [I love] are *amavi, amatum, amare*.—*Pap*. V B 72:30 *n.d.*, 1844

Deleted from final copy; see 151 note:

What a shame that Professor Heiberg has the obsession that he is the man to correct things. How fortunate that the professor now has taken up astronomy; now anyone writing about religious issues may hope to be spared his corrections. This is the happiest thought that his gilded New Year gift has brought to me, who am neither theoretical nor practical nor an also-astronomer.—*Pap*. V B 72:31 *n.d.*, 1844

Deleted from final copy; see 152:37:

Bettina's letters[5] may be cited as an example of this.—*Pap*. V B 72:32 *n.d.*, 1844

Deleted from final copy; see 154:17:

The whole wisdom of the superiority of the comic we owe to the three or four last paragraphs in Hegel's *Esthetics*, although it has also been presented with bravura by one who long since has gone beyond Hegel; and while he astonished women and children with his discourse, he would not as much as intimate that it was Hegel's.—*Pap*. V B 72:33 *n.d.*, 1844

EDITORIAL APPENDIX

ACKNOWLEDGMENTS

The present volume is included in a general grant from the National Endowment for the Humanities. The grant includes a gift from the Danish Ministry of Cultural Affairs. A grant for special research expenses has been received from the A. P. Møller og Hustru Chastine McKinney Møllers Fond.

Acknowledgment is made to Gyldendals Forlag for permission to absorb notes to Søren Kierkegaard, *Begrebet Angest, Samlede Værker*, I-XIV, ed. A. B. Drachman, J. L. Heiberg, and H. O. Lange (Copenhagen: 1901-06), IV; to Eugen Diederichs Verlag for permission to absorb notes to Søren Kierkegaard, *Der Begriff Angst, Gesammelte Werke*, I-XXXVI, ed. Emanuel Hirsch (Düsseldorf: 1956-69), XI-XII; to Jacob Hegner Verlag for permission to absorb notes to Søren Kierkegaard, *Der Begriff der Angst, Philosophisch-Theologische Schriften*, ed. Hermann Diem and Walter Rest, commentary by Niels Thulstrup (Cologne and Olten: 1956).

The book collection and the microfilm collection of the Kierkegaard Library, St. Olaf College, have been used in preparation of the text and of the supplement and appendix.

Robert L. Perkins, Niels Thulstrup, John Elrod, Gregor Malantschuk, and Per Lønning, members of the International Advisory Board for *Kierkegaard's Writings*, have given helpful criticism of the manuscript on the whole and in detail.

The translator-editor is indebted to Howard V. Hong for valuable suggestions and criticisms of the manuscript.

Thanks are expressed to Ruth Storvick for typing the manuscript, to Olin Storvick for checking Greek and Latin quotations, and to Sanford G. Thatcher and Gretchen Oberfranc for guiding the manuscript through the press.

Reidar Thomte
Concordia College
Moorhead, Minnesota

COLLATION OF *THE CONCEPT OF ANXIETY* IN THE DANISH EDITIONS OF KIERKEGAARD'S COLLECTED WORKS

Vol. IV Ed. 1 Pg.	Vol. IV Ed. 2 Pg.	Vol. 6 Ed. 3 Pg.	Vol. IV Ed. 1 Pg.	Vol. IV Ed. 2 Pg.	Vol. 6 Ed. 3 Pg.
276	306	102	310	342	133
277	307	103	311	343	134
279	309	105	312	344	134
280	309	105	313	345	135
281	313	109	314	346	136
282	313	109	315	348	137
283	314	110	316	349	138
284	316	111	317	350	139
285	317	112	318	351	140
286	317	113	319	352	141
287	318	113	320	353	142
288	320	114	321	355	143
289	321	115	322	356	144
290	322	116	323	357	145
291	322	117	324	358	145
292	323	118	325	359	146
293	325	118	326	360	147
294	326	119	327	361	148
295	327	120	328	362	149
296	328	121	329	364	150
297	329	122	330	365	151
298	329	122	331	365	152
299	330	123	332	367	153
300	331	123	333	368	154
301	332	124	334	369	155
302	333	125	335	370	156
303	334	126	336	371	157
304	335	127	337	373	158
305	336	128	338	374	159
306	338	129	339	375	160
307	339	130	340	376	160
308	340	131	341	377	161
309	341	132	342	378	162

Vol. IV Ed. 1 Pg.	Vol. IV Ed. 2 Pg.	Vol. 6 Ed. 3 Pg.	Vol. IV Ed. 1 Pg.	Vol. IV Ed. 2 Pg.	Vol. 6 Ed. 3 Pg.
343	379	163	386	426	202
344	381	164	387	427	203
345	382	165	388	428	204
346	383	166	389	430	205
347	384	167	390	430	205
348	385	168	391	431	206
349	386	169	392	433	207
350	387	170	393	434	208
351	387	170	394	435	209
352	388	171	395	436	210
353	389	172	396	437	211
354	390	173	397	439	212
355	391	173	398	440	213
356	392	174	399	441	214
357	393	175	400	442	215
358	394	176	401	443	216
359	395	177	402	444	217
360	396	178	403	445	218
361	397	178	404	447	219
362	398	179	405	447	220
363	399	180	406	449	221
364	400	181	407	450	222
365	402	182	408	451	223
366	403	183	409	452	224
367	404	184	410	453	224
368	405	185	411	455	226
369	406	186	412	456	226
370	407	187	413	457	227
371	408	187	414	458	228
372	410	188	415	459	229
373	411	189	416	460	230
374	412	190	417	461	231
375	413	191	418	462	231
376	414	192	419	463	232
377	415	193	420	464	233
378	417	194	421	465	234
379	419	196	422	465	234
380	420	197	423	467	235
381	420	197	424	468	236
382	421	198	425	469	237
383	422	199	426	470	238
384	424	200	427	471	239
385	425	201	428	473	240

NOTES

TITLE PAGE.   The subtitle presents the subject as "hereditary sin." The deliberation is "simple," not speculative. The argument deals with the "dogmatic issue," not with metaphysics. The emphasis is not upon the actuality of sin, but on sin as a possibility, i.e., on how a human being must be qualified if sin is to be a psychological possibility. The Biblical background is Genesis 3.

The term "hereditary sin" (Danish, *Arvesynd*; German, *Erbsünde*), as used here, is analogous to the English term "original sin." Something is lost from the Danish, and from *The Concept of Anxiety* in particular, if "original sin" is used rather than a literal translation of the Danish *arvesynd*. Documentation for the term "hereditary sin" is found in *The Smalcald Articles:* "Hoc peccatum hereditarium tam profunda et tetra est corruptio naturae, ut nullius hominis ratione intelligi possit, sed ex Scripturae patefactione agnoscenda et credenda sit [This hereditary sin is so deep and horrible a corruption of nature that no reason can understand it, but it must be learned and believed from the revelation of Scriptures], Ps. 51:5; Rom. 5:12 ff.; Ex. 33:3; Gen. 3:7 ff." (*The Smalcald Articles*, The Third Part of the Articles, I. Of Sin, *Triglot Concordia, The Symbolical Books of the Ev. Lutheran Church* [St. Louis: Concordia Publishing House, 1921], pp. 476-77).

The name Vigilius Haufniensis means "watchman of Copenhagen." The original draft has S. Kierkegaard as the author; see Supplement, p. 177 (*Pap.* V B 42). *Concluding Unscientific Postscript* states:

> *The Concept of Anxiety* differs essentially from the other pseudonymous works in that its form is direct and even somewhat didactic [*docerende*]. Perhaps the author thought that at this point a communication of knowledge might be needful before a transition could be made to the development of inwardness. The latter task pertains to someone who is presumed essentially to possess knowledge and who does not merely need to know something but rather needs to be influenced. The somewhat didactic form of the book was undoubtedly the reason it found a little favor in the eyes of the *docents* as compared with the other pseudonymous works. I cannot deny that I regard this favor as a misunderstanding, wherefore it pleased me that a merry little book was published simultaneously by Nicolaus Notabene. The pseudonymous books are generally ascribed to one writer, and now everyone who had hoped for a didactic author suddenly gave up hope upon seeing light literature from the same hand. (*KW* XII; *SV* VII 229, ed. tr.)

The pseudonymity of *The Concept of Anxiety* is weak, not formal as in

Philosophical Fragments. In such pseudonymous works as *Philosophical Fragments, Concluding Unscientific Postscript, The Sickness unto Death,* and *Practice in Christianity,* Kierkegaard's name appears on the title page as the person responsible only for publication. This is not the case with *The Concept of Anxiety.* A journal entry of 1844 refers to the pseudonym: "Some people may be disturbed by my sketch of an observer in *The Concept of Anxiety.* It does, however, belong there and is like a watermark in the work. After all, I always have a poetic relationship to my works, and therefore I am pseudonymous. At the same time as the book develops some theme, the corresponding individuality is delineated. For example, Vigilius Haufniensis delineates several, but I have also made a sketch of him in the book" (*JP* V 5732; *Pap.* V A 34, *n.d.,* 1844). See pp. 54-56.

EPIGRAPH. Johann Georg Hamann (1730-1788), a German philosopher, theologian, and literary critic from Königsberg, was known by the epithet "Magus in Norden." His originality was recognized by Kant and Hegel, and he influenced such men as Johann Gottfried von Herder, Friedrich Heinrich Jacobi, Jean Paul Richter, Johann Wolfgang von Goethe, and Søren Kierkegaard, who owned his *Schriften,* I-VIII[1-2] (Berlin: 1821-43; *ASKB* 536-44). The quotation is from *Sokratische Denkwürdigkeiten, Schriften,* II, p. 12. In an age of unbelief, Hamann was a fervent believer in Christianity. He maintained that the Enlightenment had both misunderstood and misrepresented Socrates, whom he regarded as a forerunner and prophet of, rather than as a rational alternative to, Christ. Like Socrates, Hamann believed that man is the crucial problem in philosophy. Of his works, *Socratische Denkwürdigkeiten* (Amsterdam: 1759) is probably the best known. Hamann's relevance for contemporary thought is found in his views on language and sexuality, both of which he treats within a supernaturalistic context. He maintained that language and cognition, no less than the body, arise from a sexual act.

In the final manuscript Kierkegaard's initials appeared under the epigraph, but they were scratched out with pencil before the book went to press (*Pap.* V B 72:2). Two other sketches were made for an epigraph but were discarded. See Supplement, pp. 177-78 (*Pap.* V B 44, 45). Cf. Plato, *Apology,* 20 d-e, 21 d.

DEDICATION. Poul Martin Møller (1794-1836) had been a professor of philosophy at the University of Copenhagen. Kierkegaard attended his lectures on the history of ancient philosophy and had probably read the chapter on Aristotle that was published in the first edition of the posthumous works of Møller, *Efterladte Skrifter,* I-III (Copenhagen: 1839-43; *ASKB* 1574-76). The second edition (1848) contains an uncompleted translation into Danish of Aristotle's περὶ ψυχῆς (*De Anima*). Møller had understood and helped the young Kierkegaard, whose admiration and friendship for his teacher is expressed in the dedication and much more personally in the draft to the dedication. See Supplement, p. 178 (*Pap.* V B 46).

"Joy over Denmark" ["*Glæde over Danmark*"] is a poem by Møller, written when he was a ship's chaplain, a period during which he visited the Far East. A few weeks after Møller's death, Kierkegaard heard a recitation of "Joy over Denmark" in the Royal Theater; returning home, he wrote in his journal: "I went over to hear Nielsen [an actor] give a reading of 'Joy over Denmark' and was strangely moved by the words:

Remember the traveler far away.

Yes, now he has gone far away—but I at least will surely remember him" (*JP* V 5305; *Pap.* II A 216, April 2, 1838).

The dedication to Møller is in itself evidence that *The Concept of Anxiety* is not strictly pseudonymous. By means of the pseudonym and the abbreviations in the dedication, Kierkegaard concealed the privacy of his relationship to Møller. Møller's greatest literary contribution was an essay on the possibility of proofs of the immortality of the soul (*Efterladte Skrifter*, II, pp. 158-272), an essay that Kierkegaard read thoroughly. Kierkegaard later developed some of its suggestions and ideas in *The Concept of Anxiety*, and therefore this particular work is dedicated to Møller, the reader "sadly missed," who would have recognized the actualization of his most important ideas in *The Concept of Anxiety*.

PREFACE AND INTRODUCTION

1. Kierkegaard discarded the first preface he wrote for *The Concept of Anxiety*. See Supplement, p. 210 (*Pap.* V B 71). It was later included as No. VII in a book called *Prefaces, KW* IX (*SV* V).

2. See John 3:29.

3. Possibly an allusion to Goethe's ballad *"Der Sänger"*: "I sing as birds are wont to sing,/That live in woodland bowers" [Ich singe wie der Vogel singt],/ [Der in den Zweigen wohnet]. "The Minstrel," in E. H. Zeydel, *Goethe the Lyrist* (Chapel Hill: University of North Carolina Press, 1955), pp. 97-98.

4. See Genesis 12:3.

5. See Matthew 6:34.

6. A reference to H. L. Martensen's dissertation, *De autonomia conscientiae sui humanae* (Copenhagen: 1837; *ASKB* 648), which was issued in a Danish translation in 1841 with the title *Den menneskelige Selvbevidstheds Autonomie i vor Tids dogmatiske Theologie* (*ASKB* 651). The translator, L. V. Petersen, states in the introduction that "it was the first work to appear in this country [Denmark] in the new speculative trend and heralded the era in theology from which we have begun to reckon."

7. A reference to J. L. Heiberg's *Urania* (Copenhagen: 1844; *ASKB* U 57), an astronomical annual that was published at Christmas 1843 as "a New Year's gift." Kierkegaard joked about the fact that the first 1,000 copies of the first printing were sold out in two months, but that copies of the second printing could be had at one-eighth of the price of those of the first (*Prefaces, KW* IX; *SV* V 25-26).

8. "A currency of doubtful value" and "authority for the current year" (see p. 8) refer, of course, to the Danish Hegelianism of that day. See Søren Kierkegaard, *Der Begriff Angst*, in *Gesammelte Werke*, I-XXXVI, ed. Emanuel Hirsch (Düsseldorf: Eugen Diederichs Verlag, 1956-69), XI-XII, p. 240, note 2.

9. See Matthew 7:21.

10. The source of this exclamation is unknown. It is composed of Italian and German words: *Bravo, bravissimo* may be translated "bravo, bravo, bravo"; *schwere Noth* means "severe need," and *Gottsblitz* means the "lightning of God."

11. Compare the last paragraph of the draft. See Supplement, pp. 179-80 (*Pap.* V B 72:5).

12. See I Corinthians 2:3.

13. The *decanus*, or chairman, of the philosophical faculty of the university placed his *imprimatur* upon all dissertation manuscripts before their publication. In Holberg's comedy *Erasmus Montanus*, Per, the parish clerk, asks Erasmus, the Latin student who has just returned from Copenhagen, "Who is *Imprimatur* this year?" Per takes the word to refer to the professor rather than to the practice of accepting manuscripts as qualified dissertations.

14. *Wissenschaft der Logik*, I, Book Two, Section Three, *Georg Wilhelm Friedrich Hegel's Werke, vollständige Ausgabe*, I-XVIII, ed. Ph. Marheineke et al. (Berlin: 1832-40; *ASKB* 549-65), IV, pp. 184 ff.; *Jubiläumsausgabe* [*J.A.*], I-XXVI (Stuttgart: 1927-40), IV, pp. 662 ff.; *Hegel's Science of Logic*, tr. A. V. Miller (London: Allen & Unwin; New York: Humanities Press, 1969), pp. 529 ff. A marginal note in the draft adds: "which Hegel has done and the Hegelian school did again and again." See Supplement, p. 180 (*Pap.* V B 49:1). Hegel divided his treatment of logic into the doctrine of *Being*, the doctrine of *Essence*, and the doctrine of the *Notion*. Actuality is treated as the last part of the doctrine of essence. Whereas classical and formal logic do not deal with actuality, Hegel's logic is principally ontological, and he himself calls the first part of his logic "ontological logic." *Philosophische Propädeutik*, Course III, Part Two, Division One, *Die Logik*, §§15-53, *Werke*, XVIII, pp. 149-58; *J.A.*, III, pp. 171-80.

Influenced by Adolf Trendelenburg, Kierkegaard maintained that if actuality is treated as part of logic, both actuality and logic are confused. For Kierkegaard, actuality comprises the accidental, whereas Hegel maintains that it pertains to necessity. Kierkegaard's position allows for freedom, which belongs in the realm of actuality.

15. A marginal note in the draft suggests that this happens every day before our eyes. See Supplement, p. 180 (*Pap.* V B 49:2). Here the polemic is not directed primarily against Hegel but against the Danish Hegelians Rasmus Nielsen and H. L. Martensen. Hegel had criticized F. H. Jacobi for defining faith as "immediate Knowledge." *Geschichte der Philosophie*, III, Part Three, Section A, 2, *Werke*, XV, pp. 543-45; *J.A.*, XIX, pp. 543-45; *Hegel's Lectures on the History of Philosophy*, I-III, tr. E. S. Haldane and Frances H. Simson, (London: Routledge & Kegan Paul; New York: Humanities Press, 1955), III, pp. 417-19. See *Fear and Trembling, KW* VI (*SV* III 118).

16. The Danish word *ophæve* corresponds to the German word *aufheben*, which usually is translated "annul," "sublate," or "cancel." Hegel maintains that *aufheben* is one of the most important concepts in philosophy. The term has two meanings: (1) to preserve, to maintain, and (2) to abolish, to do away with. Thus what is annulled is at the same time preserved. In the Hegelian triad, the synthesis both preserves and abolishes the difference between the thesis and antithesis. This twofold activity is expressed by the word "annul" *(aufheben)*. See *Hegel's Science of Logic*, pp. 106-7, and Kierkegaard's criticism in *Postscript, KW* XII *(SV* VII 126-27).

17. Possibly a reference to the Danish Hegelian P. M. Stilling's *Philosophiske Betragtninger over den spekulative Logiks Betydning for Videnskaben* (Copenhagen: 1843), pp. 45-46, where the word "atonement" (reconciliation) is used for speculative knowledge. For Kierkegaard, the word "atonement" *(Forsoning)* has definite religious connotations.

18. Kant maintained that self-evident and universal understanding is possible by virtue of analysis of concepts such as those that are central to logic and geometry. However, he was a skeptic in that he insisted that things-in-themselves are unknowable. The content of our knowledge is derived from experience, but the mind conceives and thinks its experiences according to its own a priori rational ways. Although things-in-themselves do exist and we can think them, we cannot know them as we know the phenomenal world.

19. Hegel does not use the term "manifestation" but "self-revelation" *(Selbstoffenbarung)*. See Hegel, *Encyclopädie der philosophischen Wissenschaften im Grundrisse*, Part Three, *Die Philosophie des Geistes*, §383 and *Zusatz, Werke*, VII², pp. 27-29; *J.A.*, X, pp. 33-35; *Hegel's Philosophy of Mind*, tr. William Wallace, *Zusätze*, tr. A. V. Miller (Oxford: Clarendon Press, 1970), pp. 16-18. It is of interest that Miller in *Zusatz* to §383 uses "manifestation" (Kierkegaard's term) for *Selbstoffenbarung*. See *Fragments, KW* VII *(SV* IV 243).

20. Schelling maintained that "intellectual intuition" is the organ of all transcendental thinking. Intellectual intuition is akin to the artist's intuition. The identity of the ideal and the real is expressed in man, who is identical with nature and is also the vehicle by which nature reaches its highest development. The intellectual intuition, also called "the organic conception," is the faculty of seeing unity in plurality, identity in diversity. To intuit an object and to produce it are the same. See F. W. Schelling, *Vorlesungen über die Methode des academischen Studium* (Tübingen: 1830; *ASKB* 764), p. 98 (Lecture IV, end); *System des transcendentalen Idealismus* (Tübingen: 1800), pp. 146-69; *Sämmtliche Werke*, I-XIV, ed. K.F.A. von Schelling (Stuttgart and Augsburg: 1856-61), Part One, III, pp. 369 ff. See *Fragments, KW* VII *(SV* IV 243).

21. In the Christian sense, "logos" is "the word" (John 1:1). In philosophy logos stands for "thought," and in logic it is the true doctrine of logos. The reference is possibly to Stilling, *Philosophiske Betragtninger*, p. 11.

22. In Hegelian philosophy, a concept that presents itself to thought provokes a contradictory concept, the antithesis, which is the negation of the first concept or thesis. Thesis and antithesis unite to form a new thought, the synthesis. In Hegelian dialectic, the negative is the principle of motion as well as the creative principle. See Supplement, p. 181 *(Pap.* V B 49:6).

23. Kierkegaard caricatures the Hegelian philosophy by inserting *ergo* between two statements from Hegel's *Logic*: (1) "The German language has preserved essence in the past participle [*gewesen*] of the verb 'to be'; for essence is past—but timelessly past—being" [Die Sprache hat im Zeitwort: Seyn, das Wesen in der vergangene Zeit: gewesen behalten; denn das Wesen ist das vergangene aber zeitlos vergangenen Seyn]; (2) "Essence is sublated [annulled] being" [Das Wesen ist das aufgehobene Seyn]. *Wissenschaft der Logik*, I, Book Two, Section One, *Werke*, IV, pp. 3, 8; *J.A.*, IV, pp. 481, 486; *Hegel's Science of Logic*, pp. 389, 394.

24. *Lulu*, a romantic opera by C. F. Güntelberg (Copenhagen: 1824).

25. I Corinthians 9:26.

26. The Danish terms *Tilværelse* (vb. *være til*) and *Eksistens* (vb. *eksistere*) are both translated into English by the word "existence" (vb. "to exist"). *Tilværelse* corresponds to the German word *Dasein* (*was da ist*), and it usually denotes the outer observable existence in time and space. To make more explicit the distinction between "existence" in the existential sense and "existence" as the outward observable existence, the German word *Dasein* might well be used for the latter.

27. Hegel uses the term "the other" rather than the expression "necessary other." See *Wissenschaft der Logik*, II, Section Three, Chapter 3, *Werke*, V, p. 340; *J.A.*, V, p. 340; *Hegel's Science of Logic*, p. 834.

28. See *Grundlinien der Philosophie des Rechts*, §§18, 139 *Zusatz*, *Werke*, VIII, pp. 54, 186-88; *J.A.*, VII, pp. 70, 202-4; *Hegel's Philosophy of Right*, tr. T. M. Knox (Princeton: Princeton University Press, 1961), pp. 28, 92-93.

29. Anne Louise Germaine (Necker) Staël-Holstein said that the most insignificant men appear clever when they are acquainted with speculative philosophy (*De Allemagne* [Paris: 1814], III, Chapter 8).

30. The term "system" always refers to Hegel's system.

31. See Matthew 25:21-23.

32. "A dog, while carrying a piece of meat across the river, caught sight of his own image floating in the water, and thinking that it was another prize, carried by another dog, decided to snatch it. But his greed was disappointed; he let go the meat that he held in his mouth, and failed besides to grasp the meat for which he strove" (*The Aesopic Fables of Phaedrus*, tr. B. E. Perry, *Loeb Classical Library*, Book I, no. 4).

33. See Supplement, pp. 181-82 (*Pap*. V B 49:7).

34. "It is plain, Gorgias, that Polus is well equipped to make speeches, but he failed to accomplish what he promised Chaerophon. . . . For it is obvious from what Polus has said that he is much better versed in what is called rhetoric than in dialogue" (*Gorgias*, 448 d-e, tr. W. D. Woodland, *The Collected Dialogues of Plato*, ed. Edith Hamilton and Huntington Cairns [New York: Pantheon Books, 1961]).

35. See Galatians 3:19, 21, 24.

36. The draft explains virtue by the addition of καλοκαγαθία (*Pap*. V 49 B 8). The Greek word is composed of καλός [beautiful] and ἀγαθός [good].

The word καλοκαγαθία was used of masculine perfection. See *Ethica Nicomachea*, Book I, Chapter 8.

37. See II Corinthians 5:17.

38. "Recollection is the ethnical view of life" (*Repetition*, KW VI; SV III 189). "Generally every ethnical teaching, including pure philosophy (in contrast to that which deceitfully has blended with Christianity) comes to the same point—that knowledge (wisdom) is virtue. Socrates presented this thesis; later, all Socratics. —Christian teaching is the opposite—that virtue is knowledge. From this comes the expression—to do the truth. —At the same time, it is still always a problem for Christianity to establish on the basis of spirit an existence [*Existents*] which is indifferent with respect to knowledge so that one could be perfect although completely ignorant. The question is whether knowledge is accented first or last. But even then a very dialectical deliberation is necessary" (*JP* I 895; *Pap*. IV C 86).

39. In *Stromateis*, Clement of Alexandria states several times that he presents Christian doctrine in a concealed form, in order that the uninitiated might not misuse and abuse it. He does not refer to heretics.

40. This page number is from the original edition of *Repetition, KW* VI (*SV* III 189).

41. Under the caption "The Delight that Determines the Judgment of Taste Is Independent of all Interest," Kant says: "Everyone must allow that a judgment on the beautiful which is tinged with the slightest interest is very partial, and not a pure judgment of taste. One must not in the least be presupposed in favor of the real existence of the thing, but must preserve a complete indifference in this respect, in order to play the part of judge in matters of taste" (Immanuel Kant, *Critik der Urtheilskraft* [2 ed., Berlin: 1793; *ASKB* 595], I, §2, pp. 5-7; *The Critique of Judgment*, tr. J. C. Meredith [Oxford: Oxford University Press, 1952], p. 42).

42. This page number is from the original edition of *Repetition, KW* IV (*SV* III 254).

43. In his yearbook *Urania*, pp. 97-102, J. L. Heiberg discusses *Repetition*, but he completely misinterpreted the nature of the book. He understood "repetition" to be something that refers to the phenomena of nature, whereas Kierkegaard deals with repetition in the realm of spirit, in the life of the individual. "In the entire book I have said nothing about repetition in the phenomena of nature. I have dealt with repetition within the realm of freedom. It is significant that among the Greeks freedom was not posited as freedom; therefore its first expression became recollection, for only in recollection did freedom have eternal life. The modern view must be precisely that of expressing freedom with a view toward the future, and here repetition belongs" (*Pap*. IV B 111, p. 273). From the subtitle of the book, "A Venture in Experimenting Psychology," Heiberg ought to have recognized that *Repetition* has nothing to do with the phenomena of nature. At first Kierkegaard intended to publish a polemical answer to Heiberg, and he made a draft (*Pap*. IV B 110) for that purpose. However, he decided against publication, especially because the pseudonymous author of *Repetition*, like Clement of Alexandria, writes

"in such a way that the heretics cannot understand it." In view of such a statement, Kierkegaard would have been out of character if he had replied to Heiberg (*Pap.* IV B 109).

44. See K. Hase, *Hutterus redivivus*, tr. A.L.C. Listow (Copenhagen: 1841), §38 ff., §73 ff. The auction-catalog lists the German edition (4 ed., Leipzig: 1839; *ASKB* 581).

45. See Supplement, p. 182 (*Pap.* V B 49:11).

46. The reference is no doubt to Democritus, who maintained that "atoms are unlimited in size and number, and they are borne along in the whole universe in a vortex, and thereby generate all composite things" (*Diogenes Laertius*, tr. H. D. Hicks [Loeb Classical Library], IX 44).

47. The reference is to Schleiermacher's *Der Christliche Glaube*, I-II (3 ed., Berlin: 1835; *ASKB* 258); *The Christian Faith*, ed. H. R. Mackintosh and J. S. Stewart (Edinburgh: T. T. Clark, 1956). Kierkegaard undoubtedly gained insights from Schleiermacher's deliberations on hereditary sin.

48. See Supplement, p. 182 (*Pap.* V B 49:12). The "first ethics" has metaphysics as its presupposition and is expressed in the Greek thought of recollection. It assumes that there is no absolute distinction between the world of ideas and the world of sense, and that the world of sense participates in the world of ideas. Man has the possibility of recollecting himself back into metaphysical reality. The first ethics is altogether ideal and proposes to bring ideality into actuality. It is the ethics of law. It is a chastiser that demands, and by its demands it only judges and does not bring forth life. The "second ethics," which is Christian ethics, has the new science, dogmatics, as its presupposition. It assumes that man is a sinner, that sin constitutes a complete break in the harmonious development of man, and that there is no way back to metaphysical reality. The new science does not interpret the disharmony as ignorance or weakness, but as sin; it offers a condition for overcoming sin, not by restoration of the former harmony, but by a new beginning. Because the new ethics proceeds from the assumption that man is a sinner, it places its demands upon man. Its ideality in no sense consists in making ideal demands, but in a penetrating consciousness of actuality, namely, the actuality of sin. Kierkegaard presents this ethics in *Works of Love* and in "Imitation" in *Practice in Christianity*. See *Works of Love*, II A, *KW* XVI (*SV* X), and *Practice in Christianity, KW* XX (*SV* XII).

49. Emanuel Hirsch, in a notation to his translation of *The Concept of Anxiety (Der Begriff Angst*, p. 243), suggests a comparison of Kierkegaard's presentation of hereditary sin with that of Schleiermacher. The following are paragraph headings in Schleiermacher, *The Christian Faith*, pp. 283-314:

§70. The sinfulness which is present in an individual prior to any action of his own, and has its ground outside his own beginning, is in every case a complete incapacity for good, which can be removed only by the influence of Redemption.

§71. Original sin, however, is at the same time so really the personal guilt of every individual who shares in it that it is best represented as the corporate act and the corporate guilt of the human race, and that the recognition of it as such is likewise recognition of the universal need of redemption.

§72. While the idea that we have thus developed cannot be applied in precisely the same way to the first human pair, we have no reason for explaining universal sinfulness as due to an alteration in human nature brought about in their persons by the first sin.

§73. In all men original sin is always issuing in actual sin.

§74. There is no difference in worth between men in regard to sin, apart from the fact that it does not in all stand in the same relationship to redemption.

50. According to Aristotle, theoretical philosophy has three branches: mathematics, physics, and first philosophy. The latter treats of being *qua* being. First philosophy, which Aristotle also called theology (*Metaphysics*, 1026 a), is the highest theoretical science or philosophy and deals with the universal characteristics of knowable reality, as well as with the principles of its organization in their universality. See *Metaphysics*, Book V, 1. Kierkegaard proceeds to apply the term "first philosophy" to Hegel's speculative system, "that totality of science which we might call ethnical, whose essence is immanence."

51. Kierkegaard attended Schelling's lectures on the philosophy of revelation (*Philosophie der Offenbarung*) in Berlin during the winter semester 1841-1842. Although he took extensive notes, the distinction that Schelling made between negative and positive philosophy in his fifth lecture is not recorded among them. At the beginning of the lecture course, Kierkegaard wrote, "I am so happy to have heard Schelling's second lecture—indescribably. I have been pining and thinking mournful thoughts long enough. The embryonic child of thought leapt for joy within me, as in Elizabeth, when he mentioned the word 'actuality' in connection with the relation of philosophy to actuality" (*JP* V 5535; *Pap.* III A 179, *n.d.*, 1841). By February he was through with Schelling and wrote to his friend Emil Boesen in Copenhagen, "Schelling talks endless nonsense both in an extensive and an intensive sense" (*Letters, KW* XXV, Letter 69).

52. See Leibniz, *Opera Philosophica*, ed. J. E. Erdmann (Berlin: 1840; *ASKB* 620), p. 78; *Philosophical Fragments, KW* VII (*SV* IV 209); Kierkegaard's draft, Supplement, pp. 182-83 (*Pap.* V B 49:14).

53. See Supplement, p. 183 (*Pap.* V B 49:15).

54. See the marginal note in the draft, Supplement, p. 183 (*Pap.* V B 49:16).

55. Hegel arranged the sciences in three groups: (1) the sciences of Subjective Spirit: anthropology, phenomenology, and psychology; (2) the sciences of Objective Spirit: law (*Rechtslehre*), morality of conscience (*Morallehre*), and moral law and social ethics (*Sittlichkeitslehre*); and (3) the sciences of Absolute Spirit: art, religion, and philosophy. See *Hegel's Philosophy of Mind*, §§387 ff. Karl Rosenkranz entitled his work on psychology *Psychologie oder die Wissenschaft vom subjektiven Geist* (Königsberg: 1837; *ASKB* 744).

56. See Supplement, p. 183 (*Pap.* V B 49:17).

1. Kierkegaard first presents the traditional concepts of hereditary sin as found within the historic Christian church. He regards the Roman Catholic view as dialectical-fantastic and considers the view of the "federal theology" to be historical-fantastic. Between the conceptions of the Greek Church and the Protestant Church lie the interpretations of Augustine and Tertullian. Unfortunately, the traditional concepts do not attempt to explain what Adam's sin signified for Adam himself but deal only with the consequences of Adam's sin for the race. The inadequacy of the dogmatic conceptions of Christianity lies in their tendency to make sin an ontological qualification of man's substance. Compare the first paragraph of §1 in the draft, Supplement, pp. 183-84 (*Pap.* V B 50). A notation from the journal of 1850 speaks of the paradoxical character of "hereditary sin":

> *That "Hereditary Sin" is "Guilt"*
> is a real paradox. How paradoxical is best seen as follows. The paradox is formed by a composite of qualitative heterogeneous categories. "Hereditary" is a category of nature. "Guilt" is an ethical category of spirit. How can it ever occur to anyone to put these two together, the understanding says—to say that something is hereditary which by its very concept cannot be hereditary.
> It must be believed. The paradox in Christian truth always involves the truth as before God. A superhuman goal and standard are used—and with regard to them there is only one relationship possible—that of faith. (*JP* II 1530; *Pap.* X² A 481, *n.d.*, 1850)

As a student, Kierkegaard had attended H. N. Clausen's lectures on dogmatics in 1833-1834, and his notes from these lectures are found in *Papirer* XII. Both Clausen and Kierkegaard made use of G. B. Winer, *Comparative Darstellung des Lehrbegriffs der verschiedenen christlichen Kirchenparteien . . .* (Leipzig: 1837; *ASKB* 178).

2. Kierkegaard takes the expression from Thomas Aquinas. See *Pap.* XIII, p. 134; *Hutterus redivivus*, §80, 4, §81.

3. "Federal theology" was developed in Holland by Joh. Coccejus in the middle of the seventeenth century. It divided dogmatics into a double covenant (*foedus*): the covenant of works (state of innocence) and the covenant of grace (after the fall). Adam, as a plenipotentiary for the whole race, established the first covenant. See *Hutterus redivivus*, §26, 10.

4. Part III, Art. I, 3.

5. Kierkegaard has προτοπατορικόν instead of πρωτοπατορικόν.

6. The term "vice of origin" (*vitium originis*) is used by Tertullian in *De Anima*, 41, and the designation has been used since his time. A distinction is made between the fall (*peccatum originale originans*) and hereditary sin brought forth by the fall (*peccatum originale originatum* [*derivatum*]), which in shortened form is called original sin (*peccatum originale*). *Hutterus redivivus*, §84,1. See also Schleiermacher, *The Christian Faith*, §71.

7. See *Formula of Concord*, Part II: *Solid Declaration*, I, 10, and *Apology of the*

Augsburg Confession, II, 15-23. See Supplement, pp. 201-02 (*Pap.* V B 56:7n.). The Latin on p. 27 is a case in point. Cf. *Pap.* XIII, p. 137.

8. See *Apology of the Augsburg Confession*, II, 38 and 47.

9. See *Formula of Concord*, Part II: *Solid Declaration*, I, 9ff., and *The Augsburg Confession*, I, 2.

10. See Romans 5:12-14 and *Formula of Concord*, Part II: *Solid Declaration*, I, 8-9.

11. Dracon (ca. 624 B.C.), an Athenian lawgiver, recorded the old laws of punishment. Although it was not the first Athenian code, it was the first comprehensive code. It was regarded as intolerably harsh, punishing trivial crimes with death. Solon repealed all but the laws dealing with murder. Plutarch, *Solon*, 17.

12. Pelagius (fifth century) denied the notion of hereditary sin and maintained that every man, like Adam before the fall, is born without sin. Socinius (sixteenth century) rejected the traditional doctrines of hereditary sin. "Philanthropic individualism" is a reference to the radical moral-religious individualism associated with the philanthropic movement of J. B. Basedow.

13. " 'This,' namely, that man is both himself and the race, is spoken of as man's perfection, that ideal of man that can be actualized within the development of the human race in time where man has not as yet entered into relation with the eternal and where the highest ideal is that of serving the race. This is confirmed by the statement, 'viewed as a state,' where state signifies precisely the result of the synthesis that is brought about when the individual incorporates in himself the development of the race. 'Man's perfection' also expresses his advantage over the animal. In the animal world, the particular specimen does not contribute to the species, nor does the species contribute to the specimen. That the sentence in question is to be understood in this way is obvious from what follows, namely, that man's perfection is a contradiction. The contradiction is that man is at once both himself and the race, i.e., as individual he receives the contributions of the race in its development, while he, in turn, makes his contributions to coming generations. Thus the contradiction places man over against a task. He is to combine his own existence with that of the race. This task is an historical movement. Here again lies a contradiction, because the individual is born at a particular time in history and must begin his development entirely anew, while he at the same time repeats the development of the race" (Gregor Malantschuk, *Frihedens Problem i Kierkegaards Begrebet Angest* [Copenhagen: Rosenkilde og Bagger, 1971], pp. 17-18, ed. tr.).

14. Movement in which both nature and end are one and the same, and in which the essential development of the individual embodies the tension between being both himself and the race, is defined as historical movement.

15. "As head of the human race by nature, by generation" is an expression found in older works on Lutheran dogmatics. The expression "by covenant" belongs to the federal theology. See C. G. Bretschneider, *Handbuch der Dogmatik der evangelisch-lutherischen Kirche*, I-II (4 ed., Leipzig: 1838; *ASKB* 437-38), II, pp. 70-71; *Hutterus redivivus*, §85,6.

16. For Kierkegaard, "quality" signifies the unique character of an appearance [*Erscheinung*] and its concept. He maintains that the transition from one quality to another can take place only by a "leap." Hegel also speaks of a qualitative leap but on the basis of quantitative change. "On the qualitative side, therefore, the gradual, merely quantitative progress, which is not in itself a limit, is absolutely interrupted; the new quality in its merely quantitative relationship is, relatively to the vanishing quality, an indifferent, indeterminate other, and the transition is therefore a *leap*; both are posited as completely external to each other." In the case of morality, Hegel maintains that "there occurs the same transition from quantity into quality, and different qualities appear to be based on a different magnitude. It is through a more and less that the measure of frivolity or thoughtlessness is exceeded and something quite different comes about, namely, crime, and thus right becomes wrong and virtue vice" (*Wissenschaft der Logik*, I, Book One, Section III, Chapter 2 B, *Werke*, III, pp. 448, 451; *J.A.*, IV, pp. 458, 461; *Hegel's Science of Logic*, pp. 368, 370–71). Over against Hegel, Kierkegaard maintains that the leap has no place whatever in logic, that it does not take place by necessity but by freedom, and that the transition from virtue to vice is never a quantitative process. For the "leap" see *Philosophical Fragments*, KW VII (*SV* IV 236-49).

17. Schelling maintains over against Hegel that there is a qualitative difference between Absolute Spirit and nature. But the absolute manifests itself in two potencies: the ideal (mind) and the real (extended nature). The origin of the sensible world is due to a cosmic fall, a falling or breaking away from the Absolute. See F.W.J. Schelling, *Darstellung meines Systems der Philosophie* (1801), §§23 ff., *Sämmtliche Werke*, I-XIV, ed. K.F.A. von Schelling (Stuttgart and Augsburg: 1856-61), Part Four, I, pp. 123 ff.; *Ideen zu einer Philosophie der Natur* (1797), *Sämmtliche Werke*, Part Two, I, p. 313; *Philosophie und Religion* (1804), *Sämmtliche Werke*, Part Six, I, pp. 38 ff.

18. "One merely needs to recall Hegel's beautiful expression in the first part of his *Logic*, where he indicates that a quality by a change in its quantity passes over into another quality" (Karl Rosenkranz, *Psychologie oder die Wissenschaft vom subjectiven Geist*, p. 332). Kierkegaard knew of Rosenkranz's view of Schelling through two works by Rosenkranz, *Sendschreiben an P. Leroux über Schelling und Hegel* (Königsberg: 1843) and *Vorlesungen über Schelling* (Danzig: 1843; *ASKB* 766).

19. Kierkegaard insists that there is no qualitative difference between Adam's sin and the first sin of any subsequent individual. The quality is posited by the individual's own action. An undated journal entry from 1844 reads: "There is really only one single quality—individuality. Everything revolves around this, and this is also why everyone understands qualitatively with regard to himself what he understands quantitatively with regard to others. This constitutes individuality, but not everyone wants to have it" (*JP* II 1986; *Pap.* V A 53, *n.d.*, 1844).

20. "Sin" signifies actual sin; "sinfulness" expresses the greater possibility for new and actual sins, a possibility that never constitutes the actuality of sin. Traditional conceptions have not been aware of or distinguished between the actuality of sin as actual sin and the possibility of sin as hereditary sin.

21. In J. L. Heiberg's vaudeville *Recensenten og Dyret* (*The Reviewer and the Beast*), Trop, a *studiosus perpetuus* (perpetual student) of jurisprudence, says: "I can at any time obtain a testimonial to the fact that I have almost been close to taking my law examination."

22. Even before D. F. Strauss, H. N. Clausen had used the designation "Mosaic myth" about the Genesis account. *Katholicismens og Protestantismens Kirkeforfatning, Lære og Ritus* (Copenhagen: 1825; *ASKB* A I 42), p. 521.

According to Hegel, the incidents of the myth of the fall "form the basis of an essential article of the creed, the doctrine of original sin in man and his consequent need of succour" (*Hegel's Logic*, §24 *Zusatz* 3). Kierkegaard maintains that Hegel treated the story as a "myth of the understanding." Such a myth is based on the assumption that it adequately expresses the eternal in temporal qualities and that its truth can be grasped by the understanding. Over against Hegel's position, Kierkegaard affirms the paradoxicality of Christian truths, including that of hereditary sin, which involves a transcendence that is incapable of being grasped by reason.

23. It is impossible to translate the Danish rhyme, "Pole-een-Mester, Pole-to-Mester, . . . Politi-Mester." I am indebted to Walter Lowrie for his excellent substitution.

24. See the more extensive presentation in the draft, Supplement, p. 184 (*Pap.* V B 53:4).

25. See Romans 5:12-21; I Corinthians 15:21-22.

26. These were boys from an orphanage in Copenhagen who were dressed in blue uniforms. When admitted to the orphanage, each boy was given a number, and the boys addressed one another by number rather than by name.

27. Philipp Marheineke, *Grundlehren der christlichen Dogmatik* (2 ed., Berlin: 1827; *ASKB* 644), p. 260. Marheineke finds support in the most recent philosophy (Hegelianism), which defines innocence, a state in which there is no distinction between good and evil, as the state of immediacy.

28. "Man *must not remain what he is immediately*; he must pass beyond the state of immediacy: that is the notion or conception of Spirit." See Hegel, *Vorlesungen über die Philosophie der Religion*, II, Part Three, II, 3, *Werke* (2 ed., 1840; *ASKB* 564-65), XII, p. 259; *J.A.*, XVI, p. 259; *Lectures on the Philosophy of Religion*, I-III, tr. E. B. Speirs and J. B. Sanderson (London: Routledge & Kegan Paul; New York: Humanities Press, 1962), III, p. 47.

"When man's condition is immediate and mentally undeveloped, he is in a situation in which he ought not to be and from which he must free himself. This is the meaning of the doctrine of original sin [*Erbsünde*] without which Christianity would not be a religion of freedom" (*Grundlinien der Philosophie des Rechts*, §18 *Zusatz*, *Werke*, VIII, p. 54; *J.A.*, VII, p. 70; *Hegel's Philosophy of Right*, p. 231).

29. Hegel states: "Upon a closer examination of the myth of the Fall . . . we find an expression of a universal relation of knowledge to spiritual life. In its immediacy the spiritual life is next qualified as innocence and simple confidence. But the essence of spirit is that the immediate state is to be annulled, for spiritual life differs from natural life, and more particularly from animal life in that it does not remain as being-in-itself, but that it is for-itself. This

standpoint is in turn likewise to be annulled, and spirit by itself will return to unity" (*Encyclopädie*, Part One, *Die Logik*, §24 *Zusatz* 3, *Werke*, VI, p. 55, ed. tr.; *J.A.*, VIII, p. 93; *Hegel's Logic*, tr. William Wallace [Oxford: Clarendon Press, 1975], §24, pp. 42-43). Wallace's translation does not bring out the distinctive terminology of Hegel that is so essential for understanding Kierkegaard's argument.

30. "But even if we take up an empirical, and external attitude, it will be found that there is nothing at all that is immediate, that there is nothing to which only the quality of immediate belongs to the exclusion of that of mediation; but that which is immediate is likewise mediated, and that immediacy itself is essentially mediated" (Hegel, *Philosophie der Religion*, I, Part One, B, III, 2, a, β, *Werke*, XI, p. 158; *J.A.*, XV, p. 174; *Lectures on the Philosophy of Religion*, I, p. 162).

31. "This pure being is after all a *pure abstraction*, and therefore *absolutely negative*; regarded immediately it is nothing" (*Encyclopädie*, Part One, *Die Logik*, §87, *Werke*, VI, p. 169, ed. tr.; *J.A.*, VIII, p. 207; *Hegel's Logic*, p. 127).
"Pure being and pure nothing are, therefore, the same." Hegel, *Wissenschaft der Logik*, Book One, Section One, Chapter 1, C, *Werke*, III, p. 78; *J.A.* IV, p. 88; *Hegel's Science of Logic*, p. 82.

32. The editors of Kierkegaard's *Samlede Værker* suggest that "it" refers to "immediacy" and not to "innocence" on the ground that "innocence" is found nowhere in Hegel's *Logic*. However, Thulstrup points out that this is not quite true, for the term "innocence" appears several times in the *Logic*, also in the very place where Hegel deals with the Mosaic myth. See *Encyclopädie*, Part One, *Die Logik*, §24 *Zusatz* 3, *Werke*, VI, pp. 53-59; *J.A.*, VIII, pp. 91-97; *Hegel's Logic*, pp. 41-45.

33. See *Upbuilding Discourses*, *KW* V (*SV* IV 24-26).

34. Romans 3:19.

35. Psalm 51:7. This passage was used as part of the baptismal liturgy.

36. See John 1:29; Supplement, p. 184 (*Pap.* V B 53:5).

37. Leonhard Usteri, *Entwickelung des paulinischen Lehrbegriffes mit Hinsicht auf die übrigen Schriften des neuen Testamentes* (4 ed., Zürich: 1832); *Udvikling af det Paulinske Lærebegret . . .* , tr. W.J.J. Boethe (Copenhagen: 1839; *ASKB* 850).

38. Franz Baader's doctrine of will and freedom rests on the assumption that the will can become conscious of its freedom and determination only through a choice necessitated by external incitements of various kinds. Baader also applied this concept to Adam in Paradise. See Franz Baader, *Vorlesungen . . . über religiöse Philosophie* (Munich: 1827; *ASKB* 395); *Sämmtliche Werke*, I-XVI (Leipzig: 1851-60), I, §35, pp. 249-50.

39. See Supplement, pp. 184-85 (*Pap.* V B 53:6).

40. In the siege of Pelusium, Cambyses, the Persian king, placed animals sacred to the Egyptians in the front of his army. See Polyaenus, *Strategemata*, 7, 9.

41. *Augsburg Confession*, II, 1.

42. See Supplement, p. 185 (*Pap.* V B 53:8).

43. Genesis 2:17, 3:5.

44. For another description of paradisiacal innocence, see *Upbuilding Discourses*, KW V (SV IV 24 ff.).

45. See *Christian Discourses*, KW XVIII (SV X 113).

46. The editors of Kierkegaard's *Samlede Værker* assume that the term "the possibility of possibility" is a slip of the pen and that the intended reading is "the possibility of freedom." The assumption is hardly tenable. The term must be understood in relation to its context. When man is psychically qualified in unity with his naturalness, and spirit is *sleeping*, human freedom does not manifest itself. Anxiety is the qualification of the dreaming spirit, and when spirit becomes *awake*, the difference between oneself and the other is posited. In the dreaming state, spirit has a presentiment of the freedom that follows when consciousness is awakened. This presentiment of freedom, this state of anxiety, is spoken of as "freedom's actuality as the possibility of possibility." It is also spoken of as "entangled freedom, where freedom is not free in itself but is entangled, not by necessity, but in itself." See p. 49.

47. See Supplement, p. 185 (*Pap.* V B 53:9). A journal entry reads: "The nature of hereditary sin has often been explained, and still a primary category has been lacking—it is anxiety [*Angst*]; this is the essential determinant. Anxiety is a desire for what one fears, a sympathetic antipathy; anxiety is an alien power which grips the individual, and yet he cannot tear himself free from it and does not want to, for one fears, but what he fears he desires. Anxiety makes the individual powerless, and the first sin always occurs in weakness; therefore it apparently lacks accountability, but this lack is the real trap" (*JP* I 94; *Pap.* III A 233, n.d., 1842).

48. See *The Sickness unto Death*, KW XIX (SV XI 127-28).

49. Genesis 2:17.

50. A board upon which were pasted letters of the alphabet. Each letter was illustrated by an animal whose name begins with that letter.

51. A superficial reading of this paragraph might suggest that Kierkegaard is at the same time both affirming and denying monogenesis. However, this paragraph must be understood in the context of §2 (pp. 29-35). Kierkegaard's anthropological postulate, "the relationship of generation," affirms that every human being as an individual is both himself and the race. The race does not begin anew with every individual, for in that case there would be no race. Were the race descended from several pairs—an assumption that is dismissed by the statement that nature does not favor a meaningless superfluity—every particular Adam would have been a statue by himself, qualified by the indifferent determination (number), and every particular man would have been himself, not himself and the race.

52. Genesis 3:1.

53. See Supplement, p. 186 (*Pap.* V B 53:12).

54. See the sentence deleted from the draft, Supplement, p. 185 (*Pap.* V B 53:11). It appears that Kierkegaard conceived of the serpent as a symbol of language.

55. James 1:13-14.

56. Augustine in the *City of God*, XIV, 23, raised the question of whether there would have been procreation in Paradise if no one had sinned. Follow-

ing Jacob Böhme, Franz Baader suggested the possibility of the androgynous nature of man prior to the fall.

57. See Genesis 2:25.

58. *Liberum arbitrium*, freedom of indifference or the ability of the will to choose independently of antecedent factors. Kierkegaard states: "A perfectly disinterested will (*equilibrium*) is a nothing, a chimera; Leibniz demonstrates this superbly in many places; Bayle also acknowledges this (in opposition to Epicurus)" (*JP* II 1241; *Pap.* IV C 39, *n.d.*, 1842-43). See also *Pap.* IV C 31 ff., and Leibniz, *Theodicee, Opera philosophica*, I-II, ed. J. E. Erdmann (Berlin: 1840; *ASKB* 620), §311, §319-20, II, pp. 595, 597-98.

59. See the deleted continuation in the draft, Supplement, p. 186 (*Pap.* V B 53:13).

60. A man had a daughter called Clever Elsie. He tried to get her married, and at length a man called Hans came and wooed her but stipulated that if she was not really smart, he would not have her. After the meal, Elsie was sent to the cellar to fetch beer. As she was filling the pitcher, her eyes fell upon a pickax above her on the wall. She said to herself, "If Hans and I get married and have a child, when he grows up and is sent to the cellar to fetch beer, the ax may fall upon his head and kill him." And she wept and screamed. When she did not return with the beer, the mother sent the maid to see why Clever Elsie did not return, but when Clever Elsie had told her story, the maid sat down and screamed with her. At length, all the members of the family gathered in the cellar and wept and screamed with Elsie, saying: "What a clever Elsie we have!" When at last Hans came to the cellar and was told of the tragedy that was in store for their son, he said: "Come, more understanding is not needed for my household." "Die Kluge Else," *Kinder- und Haus-Märchen. Gesammelt durch die Brüder Grimm*, I-III (2 ed., Berlin: 1819-22; *ASKB* 1425-27), I, no. 34; *The Complete Grimm's Fairy Tales*, tr. Margaret Hunt and James Stern (New York: Pantheon Books, 1944), pp. 171-72.

61. The traditional date for the creation of the world was 4000 B.C. Nebuchadnezzar lived about 600 B.C. The round number 4000 is arbitrary. Daniel 4:25, 33.

62. Soldin was an absent-minded bookseller in Copenhagen, notorious for his many distractions. Once when a customer entered the bookstore, Soldin was standing on a ladder reaching for a book. Imitating the voice of Soldin, the customer said a few words to the bookseller's wife. Turning on the ladder, Soldin said, "Rebecca, is it I who is speaking?"

CHAPTER II

1. Romans 8:22.

2. See Chapter IV §2.

3. Luke 18:11.

4. See Supplement, p. 186 (*Pap.* V B 53:15).

5. See Supplement, pp. 186-87 (*Pap.* V B 53:16).

6. The Greek word ἀποκαραδοκία is translated *Forlængsel* in the Danish

Bible, and *ängstliche Harren* in the German Bible. The term occurs twice in the New Testament, in Romans 8:19 and in Philippians 1:20, where it is associated with hope. Kierkegaard uses the word twice in *The Concept of Anxiety*, on pages 53 and 57-58. The word is used once in the *Postscript*, *KW* XII (*SV* VII 164), and twice in *The Concept of Irony*, *KW* II (*SV* XIII 173, 258). It does not appear in the Danish index to the *Papirer*.

7. See the continuation of this statement in the draft, Supplement, p. 187 (*Pap.* V B 53:17).

8. The first and second editions of *Begrebet Angest* and the first edition of *Samlede Værker* use the term *Endeligheden* (finitude). The second edition of *SV* has substituted *Elendigheden* (misery), which must be a misprint, because no account of this change is made in the text-critical supplement to the second edition. German editions translate the word as *Endlichkeit*. Walter Lowrie in his translation (*The Concept of Dread*) uses the phrase "man's pitiful condition," which alters the meaning of the whole passage. For the reference to Baader, see *Vorlesungen in spekulative Dogmatik* (Stuttgart, Tübingen: 1828-38; *ASKB* 396), XVII, *Sämmtliche Werke*, I-XVI (Leipzig: 1851-60), VIII, pp. 143 ff.

9. See Supplement, p. 187 (*Pap.* V B 53:18).

10. Referring to Plato's *Parmenides*, Hegel says: "That which enables the Notion to advance itself is the already mentioned *negative* which it possesses within itself; it is this which constitutes the genuine dialectical element. Dialectic in this way acquires an entirely different significance from what it had when it was considered as a separate part of logic and when its aim and standpoint were, one may say, completely misunderstood. Even the *Platonic* dialectic in the Parmenides itself and elsewhere even more directly, on the other hand, aims only at abolishing and refuting limited assertions through themselves, and, on the other hand, has for results simply nothingness. Dialectic is commonly regarded as an external, negative activity which does not pertain to the subject matter itself, having its ground in mere conceit as a subjective itch for unsettling and destroying what is fixed and substantial, or at least having for result nothing but the worthlessness of the object dialectically considered" (*Wissenschaft der Logik*, I, Introduction, *Werke*, III, p. 43; *J.A.*, IV, pp. 53-54; *Hegel's Science of Logic*, pp. 55-56). Specific reference is made to the Platonic ἕτερον in Hegel's *Geschichte der Philosophie*, II, Part One, Section One, Period 1, Chapter II, A, 1, *Werke*, XIV, p. 233; *J.A.*, XVIII, p. 233; *History of Philosophy*, II, p. 64.

11. Schelling, *Philosophische Untersuchungen über das Wesen der menschlichen Freiheit*, *Sämmtliche Werke*, IV, p. 291.

12. "To think only of oneself is the most painful state for a healthy man. Man does not remain in himself [*an sich*]. Johannes Müller writes, 'I am happy only when I produce.' In his creative activity man is not occupied with himself, but with something outside himself. Because of this, God is called the Great Blissful One" (H.E.G. Paulus's edition of Schelling's lectures in Berlin, *Die endlich offenbar gewordene positive Philosophie der Offenbarung* [Darmstadt: 1843], pp. 476-77, ed. tr.).

13. Philipp Marheineke, *Zur Kritik der Schellingschen Offenbarungsphilosophie* (Berlin: 1843; *ASKB* 647), p. 47.

14. See Supplement, pp. 187–88 (*Pap.* V B 53:19). In the translation an uncommon, older English form (see *OED*) is used to signal the special additional meaning of the Danish term.

15. See the continuation of this statement in the draft, Supplement, p. 188 (*Pap.* V B 53:20).

16. See Supplement, p. 188 (*Pap.* V B 53:21).

17. See the continuation of this statement in the draft, Supplement, p. 188 (*Pap.* V B 53:22).

18. In *Erasmus Montanus*, III, 5, Jasper, the bailiff, says about Erasmus Montanus, "Oh, it's terrible: My hair stands on end when I think of it. I can't remember all that I heard, but I know that among other things he said that the earth was round. What can I call such a thing Monsieur Jeronimus? That is nothing else than overthrowing all religion and leading folk away from the faith. A heathen certainly cannot speak worse" (*Comedies by Holberg,* tr. Oscar James Campbell Jr. and Frederick Schenck [New York: American Scandinavian Foundation, 1935]).

19. See Supplement, pp. 188–89 (*Pap.* V B 53:23).

20. Kierkegaard takes a position opposite to that of Hegel, who maintained that beauty and spirit are identical in a perfect work of art.

21. Genesis 3:6.

22. See the addition in the draft, Supplement, p. 189 (*Pap.* V B 53:25).

23. See Supplement, p. 189 (*Pap.* V B 53:26).

24. See Supplement, p. 190 (*Pap.* V B 53:27).

25. See Supplement, p. 190 (*Pap.* V B 53:28).

26. Instead of beginning the paragraph with the preceding words, the draft has a much longer presentation. See Supplement, pp. 190–93 (*Pap.* V B 53:29). Compare the following journal entry: "An example of dialectic in regard to guilt and innocence. An old sensualist, yet still witty and ironical (a diplomat) guides some young girls into an exhibition of Greek sculpture. There are some young men in the company. One of the young girls, the most innocent of them all, blushes, not because she is disturbed, but because there is something in the old scoundrel's countenance which wounds her modesty. But this blush does not escape his notice; in his face she reads his thoughts. In that same moment one of the young men looks at her—she is mortified; she cannot speak to anyone about it, and she becomes melancholy" (*JP* II 1526; *Pap.* IV A 121, *n.d.*, 1843).

27. Matthew 23:4.

28. See Supplement, p. 193 (*Pap.* V B 53:30).

29. "The beautiful will not tolerate to be kissed, but the ugly like it, because they believe they are called beautiful for the sake of their soul" (*Memorabilia*, II, 6, 32-33; *Xenophontis Memorabilia*, ed. F. A. Bornemann [Leipzig:1829; *ASKB* 1211], pp. 137-38).

30. See Supplement, p. 193 (*Pap.* V B 53:31).

31. See Supplement, pp. 193–94 (*Pap.* V B 53:32).

32. See Galatians 3:28.

33. "What do you think, Critobulus, happens to you when you kiss a beautiful face? Do you not believe you lose your freedom in no time, and are made a slave, begin to spend great sums on pleasure which do not benefit you, never have time at your disposing which a gentleman should have, and are forced to things which a true man should not care about?" (*Memorabilia*, I, 3, 8).

34. The quotation is from Pierre Bayle, *Dictionaire*, article "Puteanus," note J. Kierkegaard owned the German translation of the *Dictionaire, Herrn Peter Baylens . . . Historiches und Kritisches Wörterbuch, nach der neuesten Auflage von 1740 ins Deutsche übersetzt; auch mit einer Vorrede und verschiedenen Anmerkungen sonderlich bey anstössigen Stellen versehen, von Johann Christoph Gottscheden*, I-IV (Leipzig: 1741-44; *ASKB* 1961-64). It was through reading Leibniz that Kierkegaard became aware of Bayle.

35. Athenaeus (ca. 200 A.D.), *Deipnosophista*, Book V.

36. Plutarch, *Pericles*, 24,2; *Plutarks Levnetsbeskrivelser*, tr. Stephan Tetens, I-IV (Copenhagen: 1800-11; *ASKB* 1197-1200), II, pp. 210-11.

37. Socrates says about his wife, "I have taken her because I am convinced that if I can handle her, my relation to the rest of mankind will cause me no trouble" (*Symposium*, II, 10; *Xenophontis Opera*, I-IV, ed. G. A. Thieme, [Leipzig: 1801-04; *ASKB* 1207-10], IV).

38. Originally the relationship had the nature of a spiritual fellowship, and this is no doubt what Kierkegaard refers to.

39. A significant addition in the draft adds meaning to the text. See Supplement, p. 194 (*Pap.* V B 53:33).

40. See Exodus 20:5; Deuteronomy 5:9.

41. See the section on "Quantitative Infinity," *Wissenschaft der Logik*, I, Book One, Section Two, Chapter I, C, *Werke*, III, pp. 263 ff.; *J.A.*, IV, pp 273 ff.; *Hegel's Science of Logic*, pp. 225 ff.

42. See the continuation of this statement in the draft, Supplement, p. 194 (*Pap.* V B 53:34).

43. An animal with the legs of a frog and the tail of a salamander, which, according to the zoology of that day, passed through a development opposite to that of a frog and eventually became a fish.

44. Kant maintained that man does not have an innate evil will and that man's sensate nature is not evil. Evil consists in the fact that man derives his strongest incentives from self-love and self-interest and not from the unselfish moral law. "For despite the fall, the injunction that we ought to become better men resounds unabatedly in our souls; hence this must be within our power, even though that *we* are able to do is in itself inadequate and though we thereby only render ourselves susceptible of higher, and for us, inscrutable assistance. It must indeed be presupposed throughout that a seed of goodness still remains in its purity, incapable of being extirpated or corrupted; and this seed certainly cannot be self-love, which, when taken as the principle of all our maxims, is the very source of evil" (Immanuel Kant, *Die Religion innerhalb der Grenzen der blossen Vernuft* [Königsberg: 1793], p. 47; *Religion within the Limits of Reason Alone*, tr. Theodore M. Greene and Hoyt H. Hudson [New York: Harper & Row, 1960], pp. 40-41).

For Hegel, evil consists essentially in asserting one's own subjective peculiarity over against the universal. "Once self-consciousness has reduced all otherwise valid duties to emptiness, and itself to the sheer inwardness of the will, it has become the potentiality of either making the absolutely universal its principle, or equally well of elevating above the universal the self-will of private particularity, taking that as its principle, and realizing it through its action, i.e., it has become potentially evil" (*Philosophie des Rechts*, §139, *Werke*, VIII, pp. 184-85; *J.A.*, VII, pp. 200-201; *Hegel's Philosophy of Right*, p. 92). See also *Philosophie der Religion*, I-II (2 ed., 1840; *ASKB* 564-65), II, Part Three, II, 3, *Werke*, XII, p. 261; *J.A.*, XVI, p. 261; *Lectures on the Philosophy of Religion*, III, p. 49.

Both Hegel and Kant maintain that man possesses within himself the possibility of knowing and actualizing the good, something that is contrary to the Christian position.

45. A possible reference to N.F.S. Grundtvig's subjective interpretation of Nordic mythology or to his mythological interpretation of romantic philosophers of Schelling's school. See N.F.S. Grundtvig, *Nordens Mythologie* (Copenhagen: 1832; *ASKB* 1949), p. 114.

46. Kierkegaard's remark is directed against the Danish Hegelian P. M. Stilling's *Philosophiske Betragtninger over den spekulative Logik* (Copenhagen: 1812), p. 12. See also J. L. Heiberg's introductory lecture to the course in logic, *Indlednings-Foredrag til det logiske Kursus, Prosaiske Skrifter*, I-XI (Copenhagen: 1861-62), I, p. 472. For Hegel, "Know yourself" is an absolute command, but it is not meant to promote mere self-knowledge of the individual's particular capacities, character, inclinations, and weaknesses, for such self-knowledge is negative in its relation to the absolute, and consequently evil. Self-knowledge is that of the most concrete and universal knowledge of man's spirit as it expresses itself in the history of the race and in the state. See Hegel, *Encyclopädie*, Part Three, *Die Philosophie des Geistes*, §377 and *Zusatz*, *Werke*, VII², pp. 3-5; *J.A.*, X, pp. 9-11; *Hegel's Philosophy of Mind*, pp. 1-2.

47. *Hutterus redivivus*, §130, 7, states that in the Resurrection the sexual difference is retained, but *excluso semine et lacte* [with the exclusion of semen and milk].

48. According to Luke 20:34-36, angels are without sex. See K. G. Bretschneider, *Handbuch der Dogmatik der evangelisch-lutherischen Kirche*, I-II (4 ed., Leipzig: 1842; *ASKB* 437-38), I, §101,2.

49. Sinlessness is attributed to the human nature of Christ. See *Ibid.*, II, §136.

50. Terence, *Phormio*, II, 1, 1. 265; *Terentses Skuespil*, tr. F. H. Guldberg, I-II (Copenhagen: 1805; *ASKB* 1293-94), II, p. 251. The proposition becomes a principle in Kierkegaard's psychological method. It is based on the assumption that one in a sense is all. The principle is reaffirmed in the *Postscript*, which states that speculative philosophy is indifferent to what it means to be an existing subject. At the most, it deals with the pure idea of mankind. Existence-communication, on the contrary, understands something entirely different by *unum* in the principle *unum noris omnes* and something different by "yourself" in the dictum "know yourself" and indicates thereby that the

words do not refer to anecdotal differences between Peter and Paul. See *Post-script, KW* XII (*SV* VII 498, also 306, 309). Kierkegaard's opposition to Hegel is expressed in a journal entry: "The excellence of Plato's *Republic* is that he did not make the state higher than the individual, least of all in the manner of Hegelian jargon. In order to describe the individual, he describes the state; he describes a democrat by describing democracy; he constructs a state for the individual, *unum noris omnes*—this is the proper human ideality; otherwise we get the confusion that many by being many produce something entirely different from what each one is individually" (*JP* III 3327; *Pap.* VII¹ A 70, *n.d.*, 1846). See Supplement, p. 183 (*Pap.* V B 49:15).

51. Hegel speaks of the *Heiterkeit* and *Wehmut* (sadness, melancholy) of Hellenism. See "*Gymnasial-Reden*," September 29, 1809, *Vermischte Schriften, Werke*, XVI, p. 139; *J.A.*, III, p. 237. He also speaks of *Heiterkeit* in Greek religion. See *Philosophie der Religion*, II, Part Two, Division II, II, C, a, *Werke*, XII, p. 131; *J.A.*, XVI, p. 131; *Lectures on the Philosophy of Religion*, II, p. 261.

52. See the addition in the draft, Supplement, pp. 194-95 (*Pap.* V B 53:38).

CHAPTER III

1. The lesser logic is one of the few places where Hegel deals with the category of transition. The onward movement of the notion is neither a transition into nor a reflection of something else. It is a kind of development. "Transition into something else is the dialectical process within the range of Being: reflection (bringing something else into light) in the range of essence. The movement of the notion is *development:* by which that only is explicit which is already implicitly present" (*Encyclopädie*, Part One, *Die Logik*, §161 and *Zusatz, Werke*, VI, pp. 317-18; *J.A.*, VIII, p. 355, *Hegel's Logic*, pp. 224-25).

Kierkegaard maintains that Hegelian logic is unable to account for transition: "Ancient philosophy, the most ancient in Greece, was preeminently occupied with the question of the motion whereby the world came into existence [*blev til*], the constitutive relationship of the elements to each other. —The most recent philosophy is especially occupied with motion—that is motion in logic. . . . Modern philosophy has never accounted for motion" (*JP* III 3294; *Pap.* IV A 54, *n.d.*, 1843).

"Hegel has never done justice to the category of transition. It would be significant to compare it with the Aristotelian teaching about κίνησις [change]." *In margin:* "See Tennemann, III, p. 125; he translates the word as *change*" (*JP* I 260; *Pap.* IV C 80, *n.d.*, 1842-43).

Kierkegaard distinguishes between dialectical transitions in the realm of thought and pathetical transitions, which take place in the realm of freedom and which involve a leap. "Can there be a transition from a quantitative qualification to a qualitative one without a leap? And does not the whole of life rest in that?" (*JP* I 261; *Pap.* IV C 87, *n.d.*, 1842-43). "Every qualification for which being [*Væren*] is an essential qualification lies outside of immanental thought, consequently outside of logic" (*JP* I 196; *Pap.* IV C 88, *n.d.*, 1842-43).

242 Notes to Page 81

Finally, compare this significant notation: "The category to which I intend to trace everything, and which is also the category lying dormant in Greek Sophistry if one views it world-historically, is motion (κίνησις), which is perhaps one of the most difficult problems in philosophy. In modern philosophy it has been given another expression—namely, transition and mediation" (*JP* V 5601; *Pap.* IV C 97, *n.d.*, 1842-43). The concept of κίνησις is most systematically treated in the "Interlude" of *Philosophical Fragments, KV* VII (*SV* 236-39).

2. These were Greek monks who by gazing at their own navels induced an ecstatic state in themselves, through which they believed they could look into divine glory. In an earlier journal entry Kierkegaard wrote: "There is nothing more dangerous for a man, nothing more paralyzing, than a certain isolating self-scrutiny, in which world-history, human life, society—in short, everything—disappears, and like the navel gazers . . . in an egotistical circle one constantly stares only at his own navel" (*JP* II 1971; *Pap.* II A 187, Nov. 3, 1837).

3. According to Hegel, the concept of essence, when deprived of all its concretions, is identical with "nothing." On nothing and presuppositionlessness, see, for example, Hegel's *Wissenschaft der Logik, Werke*, III, pp. 63, 68; *J.A.*, IV, pp. 73, 78.

"But if no presupposition is to be made and the beginning itself is taken *immediately*, then its only determination is that it is to be the beginning of logic, of thought as such. All that is present is simply the resolve, which can also be regarded as arbitrary, that we propose to consider thought as such. Thus the beginning must be an *absolute*, or what is synonymous here, an *abstract* beginning; and so it *may not presuppose anything*, must not be mediated by anything nor have a ground; rather it is to be itself the ground of the entire science. Consequently, it must be purely and simply *an* immediacy, or rather merely *immediacy* itself. Just as it cannot possess any determination relatively to anything else, so too it cannot contain within itself any determination, any content; for any such would be a distinguishing and an interrelationship of distinct moments, and consequently a mediation. The beginning therefore is *pure being*" (*Hegel's Science of Logic*, p. 70).

"As yet there is nothing and there is to become something. The beginning is not pure nothing, but a nothing from which something is to proceed; therefore being, too, is already contained in the beginning. The beginning, therefore, contains both, being and nothing, is the unity of being and nothing; or is non-being which is at the same time being, and being which is at the same time non-being" (*Hegel's Science of Logic*, p. 73).

Among references to the theme of nothing and presuppositionlessness, Kierkegaard's journals include a sketch of Hegel and Socrates:

The Dialectic of Beginning
Scene in the Underworld

Characters: Socrates
Hegel

Socrates sits in the cool [of the evening] by a fountain, listening.

Hegel sits at a desk reading Trendelenburg's *Logische Untersuchungen*, II, p. 198, and walks over to Socrates to complain.

Socrates: Shall we begin by completely agreeing or disagreeing about something which we call a presupposition.

[*Sic*] Hegel:

Socrates: With what presupposition do you begin?

Hegel: None at all.

Socrates: Now that is something; then you perhaps do not begin at all.

Hegel: I not begin—I who have written twenty-one volumes?

Socrates: Ye gods, what a hecatomb you have offered!

Hegel: But I start with nothing.

Socrates: Is that not with something?

Hegel: No—the inverse process. It becomes apparent only at the conclusion of the whole process, when I have treated all the sciences, history, etc.

Socrates: How shall I be able to surmount this difficulty, for many remarkable things must certainly have happened which would captivate me. (Misuse of the oratorical element.) You know that I did not allow even Polos to talk more than five minutes at a time, and you want to talk XXI volumes.

JP III 3306 (*Pap*. VI A 145) *n.d.*, 1845.

4. For Aristotle the term means any kind of change. See Supplement, p. 195 (*Pap*. V B 72:12).

5. Kierkegaard's knowledge of the Pythagoreans and the Eleatics is from Tennemann, *Geschichte der Philosophie*, I-XII (Leipzig: 1798-1819; *ASKB* 815-26), I, pp. 53-208. See Kierkegaard's excerpts from this work (*Pap*. IV C 3).

6. "Must we not even refuse to allow that in such a case a person is saying something, though he may be speaking of nothing? Must we not assert that he is not even saying anything when he sets about uttering the sounds 'a thing that is not'?" (Plato, *Sophist*, 237 e, tr. F. M. Cornford [*The Collected Dialogues of Plato*, ed. Edith Hamilton and Huntington Cairns]). The rest of the dialogue is a refutation of the position that non-being is an absolute contradiction of being. "When we speak of 'that which is not,' we do not mean something contrary to what exists, but only something that is different" (*ibid.*, 257 b). The Stranger in the *Sophist* concludes: "Whereas we have not merely shown that things that are not, are, but we have brought to light the real character of 'non-being.' We have shown that the nature of the Different has existence and is parcelled out over the whole field of existent things with reference to one another; and of every part of it that is set in contrast to 'that which is' we have dared to say that precisely that *is really* 'that which is not' " (*ibid.*, 258 d-e).

7. Socrates speaks of rhetoric and Sophistry as semblances and false imitations of legislation and justice (*Gorgias*, 464 b ff.).

8. The reference is to the helmet of Hades, which made the wearer invisible. In the battle against Ares (Mars), Athene placed the helmet on her head (*Iliad*, 5, 845).

9. See *Johannes Climacus, or De omnibus dubitandum est*: "For example, during a discussion of the importance of having doubted as a prerequisite for philosophy, he heard the following remark: 'We ought not waste time doubting but should just begin right away with philosophy' " (*KW* VII; *Pap*. IV B1, p. 143). See Supplement, p. 195 (*Pap*. V B 55:3).

10. The translator prefers "experimental dialectic" but has adopted the terminology established for the entire edition of *Kierkegaard's Writings*. See note to subtitle of *Repetition, KW* VI.

11. In *Parmenides*, ἄτοπον signifies the moment [τὸ ἐξαίφνης] and involves the category of transition discussed below. "The instant [moment] seems to indicate a something from which there is a change in one direction or the other. For it does not change from rest, nor from motion, while it is still moving, but there is this strange instantaneous nature, something interposed between motion and rest, not existing in any time, and into this and out from this, that which is in motion changes into rest, and that which is at rest changes into motion" (*Parmenides*, 156 d, tr. H. N. Fowler, *Loeb Classical Library*).

12. The editors of *Samlede Værker* state that Kierkegaard's translation is incorrect and that it should read "neither being separated nor combined," inasmuch as the meaning is that the moment is also the transition in the case of separation and combination.

13. A conventional term for a hackney. It was the popular conveyance from Copenhagen to Deer Park.

14. The editors of *Samlede Værker* state that it would be more correct to translate this passage, "Is not *to be* participation of being in the present time," and that Plato means to say no more than that *to be* is present tense and consequently expresses being in the present. H. N. Fowler translates the passage: "But is to be anything but participation in existence together with present time" (*Parmenides, Loeb Classical Library*). Gregor Malantschuk (*Frihedens Problem*, p. 42) points out that Kierkegaard follows the translation by Schleiermacher, which reads: "Ist aber das Sein wohl etwas anderes als Theilhabung an einem Wesen in der gegenwärtigen Zeit" (*Platons Werke* I-VI [2 ed., Berlin: 1817-18; *ASKB* 1158-61], II, 1, p. 151). In the first edition, Schleiermacher had translated, "Heist denn Sein etwas anderes, als das Sein an sich haben in der gegenwärtigen Zeit." In a notation about "The Concept of Category," Kierkegaard adds: "The definition of being which Plato gives in *Parmenides*, §151, the last words: Being is nothing other than participation in an essence in time present" (*JP* III 3324; *Pap*. IV C 70, *n.d.*, 1842-43). He understands Plato's "being" (*Væren*) as something that occurs in the present time in the sensuous world, as well as something that participates in the ideas; or in other words, for anything to be called being it must, in addition to participating in essence, have touched the now, which is a determination of time.

15. A reference to Hegelian philosophy, which begins with pure being as

the most extreme abstraction and from this proceeds toward continually more concrete determinations. For example: "Eternity is not before or after time, not before the creation of the world, nor when it perishes; rather is eternity the absolute present, the Now, without before and after" (*System der Philosophie*, Part Two, *Die Naturphilosophie*, §247 *Zusatz, Werke*, VII¹, p. 26; *J.A.*, IX, p. 52; *Hegel's Philosophy of Nature*, tr. A. V. Miller [Oxford: Clarendon Press, 1970], §247 *Zusatz*, p. 15).

Schelling, too, defines the eternal as "the constant now." Both Hegel and Schelling follow an old tradition in philosophy. See also Augustine, *Confessions*, XI, 10-11; Aristotle, *Physics*, 221 b; Plato, *Timaeus*, 37 c-38 b.

16. See the continuation of this statement in the draft, Supplement, pp. 195-96 (*Pap.* V B 55:4).

17. Hegel's view of time is set forth briefly in *Hegel's Philosophy of Nature*: "The dimensions of time, *present, future*, and *past*, are the *becoming* of externality as such, and the resolution of it into the difference of being as passing over into nothing, and of nothing as passing over into being. The immediate vanishing of these differences into *singularity* is the present as *Now*, which, as singularity, is exclusive of the other moments, and at the same time completely *continuous* in them, and is only this vanishing of its being into nothing and of nothing into its being. The *finite* present is the *Now* fixed as being and distinguished as the concrete unity, and hence as the affirmative, from what is *negative*, from the abstract moments of past and future, but this being is itself only abstract, vanishing into nothing. Furthermore in nature where time is a *Now*, being does not reach the *existence* of the difference of these dimensions; they are of necessity, only in subjective imagination, in *remembrance*, and *fear* or *hope*. But the past and future of time as being in nature, are space, for space is negated time; just as sublated space is immediately the point, which developed for itself is time" (*System der Philosophie*, Part Two, *Die Naturphilosophie*, §259 and *Zusatz, Werke* VII¹, pp. 57-61; *J.A.*, IX, pp. 83-87; *Hegel's Philosophy of Nature*, pp. 37-40).

18. Kierkegaard has the reference from Hegel's *Philosophie der Geschichte*, Part One, Section Two, *Werke*, IX, p. 200; *J.A.*, XI, p. 222; *Philosophy of History*, tr. J. Sibree (New York: Collier, 1902), p. 231.

19. See Hegel's analysis of the sensuous consciousness as that which is tied to the *now* and the *here. Phänomenologie des Geistes*, A, I, *Werke*, II, pp. 73-84; *J.A.*, II, pp. 81-92; *The Phenomenology of Mind*, tr. J. P. Baillie (New York: Harper Torchbook, 1967), pp. 149-60.

20. The presence of the gods as immediately intervening (Terence, *Phormio*, III, 1, l. 345).

21. The Danish word *Øiblikket* (the moment) is figurative in the sense that it is derived from *Øiets Blik* (a blink of the eye). Cf. the German word *Augenblick*.

22. The reference is to Esaias Tegner's *Frithjof's Saga* (Stockholm: 1825) IX, p. 71, and to a pictorial illustration on the title page. See *JP* III 3800 (*Pap.* I A 136).

23. I Corinthians 15:52. See Supplement, p. 196 (*Pap.* V B 55:6).

24. See *Philosophical Fragments*, *KW* VII (*SV* IV 239).

25. Plato uses recollection as a proof of the immortality of the soul. Our perceptions of the beautiful, the good, etc. among the phenomena of nature are explained only by a knowledge of such universal concepts recollected from an earlier existence (*Tilværelse*) (*Phaedo*, 72e ff.).

26. The philosopher's task is that of dying away from the pleasures of the body and from sensuousness in the broadest sense; through such dying away he would enter into "eternity" (*Phaedo*, 64 a ff.). See Supplement, p. 196 (*Pap.* V B 55:7).

27. Galatians 4:4.

28. See Supplement, pp. 196-97 (*Pap.* V B 55:9).

29. See Supplement, p. 197 (*Pap.* V B 55:10). In this notation Kierkegaard translates the term *discrimen* as "ambiguity."

30. *"Wie die Alten den Tod gebildet"* [How the Ancients Pictured Death], *Gotthold Ephraim Lessing's sämmtliche Schriften*, I-XXXII (Berlin: 1825-28; *ASKB* 1747-62), III, pp. 75-159.

31. See Kierkegaard's discourse, "At the Side of a Grave," in *Three Discourses on Imagined Occasions*, *KW* X (*SV* V 226 ff.).

32. See the continuation of this statement in the draft, Supplement, p. 198 (*Pap.* V B 55:12).

33. See Supplement, p. 198 (*Pap.* V B 55:13).

34. Kierkegaard uses an idiomatic folk phrase about sparks from burning flax straw. When the fire was almost extinguished and only a few sparks followed one by one, the spectators would say, "There come the school children." Finally, when the last spark appeared, they would say, "There went the schoolmaster."

35. Reference to Socrates and Hamann. See the epigraph to *The Concept of Anxiety* and Supplement, pp. 198-99 (*Pap.* V B 55:14).

36. I Corinthians 2:4.

37. See Matthew 5:13; Luke 14:14. A verbatim translation of the Greek word μωρανθῇ is "becomes dumb"; μωρός, "dumb."

38. See Supplement, p. 199 (*Pap.* V B 55:15).

39. Hegel speaks in several places of *Fatum* as identical with "necessity." See *Philosophie der Geschichte*, Part Two, Section Two, Chapter 2, *Werke*, IX, p. 301; *J.A.*, XI, p. 323; *Philosophy of History*, p. 326 (where *Fatum* is incorrectly translated as "fact" rather than as "fate"); *Philosophie der Religion*, II, *Anhang, Beweise vom Daseyn Gottes*, no. 16, *Werke*, XII, p. 505; *J.A.*, XVI, p. 44; *Lectures on the Philosophy of Religion*, III, p. 314; *Encyclopädie*, Part One, *Die Logik*, §147 *Zusatz*, *Werke*, VI, pp. 293-98; *J.A.*, VIII, pp. 331-36; *Hegel's Logic*, pp. 207-11.

40. I Corinthians 8:4. In the Danish New Testament: "an idol is nothing in the world."

41. See Supplement, p. 199 (*Pap.* V B 55:17).

42. Hegel states that "By *genius*, we are to understand the particular nature of a man which, in every situation and circumstance, decides his action and destiny. I am in fact a duality: on the one hand, what I know myself to be according to my *outward* life and *general* ideas, and on the other hand, what I

am in my *inner* life which is determined in a *particular* manner. This particular nature of my inwardness constitutes my *destiny*: for it is the oracle on whose pronouncement depends every resolve of the individual; it forms the objective element which asserts itself from out of the individual's character" (*Encyclopädie*, Part Three, *Philosophie des Geistes*, §405 *Zusatz* 3, *Werke*, VII², p. 161; *J.A.*, X, p. 167; *Hegel's Philosophy of Mind*, p. 100). See also *Vorlesungen über die Æsthetik*, Part One, Chapter 3, C, 1, b, *Werke*, X¹, pp. 365-69; *J.A.*, XII, pp. 381-85; *Hegel's Aesthetics*, I-II, tr. T. M. Knox (Oxford; Clarendon, 1975), I, pp. 281-88.

43. That something is *an sich* means in Hegelian terminology that it is not dependent upon something else. For Kant, on the other hand, *an sich* signifies an object that exists independently of the forms of human apprehension. Applied to the genius, this means that, immediately determined, he has his own laws and purposes within himself and not outside of himself.

44. On June 14, 1800, Napoleon defeated the Austrian army in the battle of Marengo. On December 2, 1805, he defeated the Austrian and Russian armies at Austerlitz. When the sun rose over Moscow on September 7, 1812, Napoleon is reputed to have said, "Where is the sun of Austerlitz."

45. See Supplement, p. 199 (*Pap.* V B 55:18), for additions in the draft.

46. See Plutarch, *Caesar*, 38.

47. In this paragraph, which deals with the relation of the genius to religiousness, Kierkegaard speaks in a concealed way about himself. Talleyrand was of noble birth, but because he had a clubfoot his life was intended for a position in the church. This position Talleyrand forsook in order to pursue an entirely secular career. Kierkegaard suggests that Talleyrand's deformity might have been a divine sign, and that if he had disdained the temporal and immediate and had turned instead to himself and the divine, a religious genius might have emerged.

48. For Kierkegaard there is no such a thing as a genius in religiousness, like a genius in poetry or a genius in mathematics. By the term "religious genius," he means not one with profound virtuosity for religiousness but one who is a genius and also a religious person. See pp. 107-10; "The Difference between a Genius and an Apostle," *KW* XVIII (*SV* XI 95-109).

49. The Carpocratians were a second-century Gnostic sect. They believed that a person must participate in all of human experience, even the worst and most condemnable, before he can attain perfection. Kierkegaard detects a variation of this view in Hegel's thought, in which evil is a necessary transitional link with the good and consequently is not a radical evil. As a theological student, Kierkegaard had written in his journal: "May it not seem right to do as that ancient sect (see Church History) did—go through all the vices simply to have experience of life" (*JP* IV 4391; *Pap.* I A 282, *n.d.*, 1836).

50. The repetition of the sacrifice in the Old Testament becomes for Kierkegaard an indication of its imperfection, as well as an indication that the "actual relation of sin is not posited." See Hebrews 9:12-28, a passage that Lutherans affirmed against the Catholic sacrifice of the mass. Kierkegaard calls attention to this confessional distinction.

51. Possibly a reference to N.F.S. Grundtvig's review of world-historical

surveys, *Udsigt over Verdens-Krøniken, fornemlig i det Lutherske Tidsrum* (Copenhagen: 1817; *ASKB* 1970). It may also refer to Hegel's *Philosophy of History*.

52. See *Protagoras*, 320 ff.

53. In the *Postscript*, Kierkegaard calls attention to the questionable nature of the absolute inwardness of the monastic movement, because its inwardness created for itself a conspicuous and very distinct outwardness. See, for example, *KW* XII (*SV* VII 351-54).

54. A lucky fellow.

55. A paraphrase of Matthew 25:21 and Luke 17:33.

56. Talleyrand is reputed to have said to the Spanish envoy Isquierdo, "La parole a été donnée à l'homme pour désguiser sa pensées [Speech was given to man to conceal his thoughts]." Edward Young writes in *Love of Fame*, I, 207-8: "Where nature's end of language is declined / And men talk only to conceal the mind." In an undated journal entry from 1844, Kierkegaard writes, "Men do not seem to have acquired speech in order to conceal their thoughts (Talleyrand, and before him Young in *Night Thoughts* [*sic*]) but in order to conceal the fact that they have no thoughts" (*JP* I 623; *Pap.* V A 19, 1844).

57. See the continuation of this statement in the draft, Supplement, p. 200 (*Pap.* V B 55:26).

58. On the "religious genius," see note 48 above.

CHAPTER IV

1. See Supplement, pp. 200-201 (*Pap.* V B 56:2). The reference is to Leibniz, *Theodicy*, §§319-20; see p. 236, note 58.

2. All of these terms signify lazy reasoning and refer to the fatalistic view that effects are entirely dependent upon fate, that they are what they are regardless of what a person does. Cf. *JP* III 2361 (*Pap.* IV A 12); Leibniz, *Theodicy*, §55.

3. See the draft of §1, Supplement, p. 201 (*Pap.* V B 56:4).

4. In Mozart's *Don Juan*, tr. Laurids Kruse (Copenhagen: 1822), II, last scene.

5. See the continuation of this statement in the draft, Supplement, p. 201 (*Pap.* V B 56:5).

6. *Murmicoleon formicarius.*

7. "To this belongs, for example, what is called talent or genius, and certainly not only genius for fine arts and the sciences, but also genius for action. It sounds harsh, but it is nevertheless no less true that just as by nature countless people are incapable of the highest function of the spirit, so countless people are never able to act beyond law with freedom and elevation of spirit, because this is granted only to a few who are chosen. Therefore, even from the outset free actions are made impossible by an unknown necessity which compels men to accuse or extol first the favor or disfavor of nature, and then the destiny of fate" (F.W.J. Schelling, *System des tranzendentalen Idealismus* [Tübingen: 1800], 4, A. Zweiter Satz, p. 351; *Sämmtliche Werke*, Part One, III, p. 549). Emanuel Hirsch states that "Schelling's words express with un-

equaled sharpness the view that Kierkegaard as an ethical, religious, and Christian author combats as the fundamental corruption, namely, the telescoping of the ethical concept of the single individual into the esthetic concept of the single individual, when the concept of the single individual is used in the sense of something distinctive" (*Der Begriff Angst*, tr. Emanuel Hirsch [Düsseldorf: Eugen Diederichs Verlag, 1958], p. 263, ed. tr.).

8. See Supplement, p. 202 (*Pap.* V B 56:8).

9. *King Lear*, IV, 6. Kierkegaard quotes from *Shakespeare's dramatische Werke*, I-XII, tr. A. W. v. Schlegel and L. Tieck (Berlin: 1839-40; *ASKB* 1883-88), XI.

10. In *The Point of View*, KW XXIII (*SV* XIII 567), Kierkegaard states that in the crisis of his life he was on the way to perdition. See Matthew 7:18. See also Supplement, pp. 173-74 (*Pap.* X¹ A 637).

11. See *Fear and Trembling*, KW VI (*SV* III 146).

12. J. G. Fichte's answer to an open letter from F. H. Jacobi in *Nachgelassene Werke*, I-III, ed. I. H. Fichte (Bonn: 1834-35; *ASKB* 489-91), III, p. 349: "To be occupied with incessant self-examination of one's own character in general and by way of preparation for a general confession is quite useless, just as if the world were not replete with other tasks and actions. Instead, a person should permit his weak side to be forcefully touched and uncovered by life; but the hidden corner of life that is as yet untouched and stirred up by his reflection is itself partly sin, for it is idleness, and partly through an excessive humility does he bring along all manner of impurities when he definitely and consciously searches himself. Let us be content with a simple fidelity to the divine within us and follow where it leads us, and not cultivate by one's own piety an artificial self-remorse that is not of oneself" (ed. tr.). The same thought is expressed both in *Die Anweisung zum seligen Leben* and in *Die Grundzüge des gegenwärtigen Zeitalters, Johann Gottlieb Fichte's* [*sic*] *sämmtliche Werke*, I-VIII, ed. I. H. Fichte (Berlin: 1845-46; *ASKB* 492-99), V, p. 565; VII, p. 14.

13. Kierkegaard may have had in mind Hermann Olshausen, who in his *Biblischer Kommentar über sämmtliche Schriften des Neuen Testaments*, I-IV (3 ed., Königsberg: 1837-40; *ASKB* 96-100), I, pp. 284-302, gives a detailed exposition of each account. When Kierkegaard refers to the synoptic Gospels, he usually quotes one variant, but in this case he quotes all three accounts. From 1760, Johann Salomo Semler had successfully advocated a naturalistic-medical interpretation of the demonic possessions of the New Testament.

14. Johann Caspar Lavater, *Physiognomische Fragmente*, I-IV (Leipzig and Winterthur: 1775-78; *ASKB* 613-16).

15. Appealing to the Scripture "compel them to come in" (Luke 14:23), Augustine, speaking in Carthage in A.D. 411, advocated that force be used against the heretical Donatists as a duty of love in order to bring them to the true faith (*Contra Candentium*, I, 28). However, he did not speak of punishment. This thought was expressed by Tertullian in *Scorpiace*, II.

16. See *Gorgias*, 479 a.

17. See Supplement, p. 202 (*Pap.* V B 56:9).

18. Kierkegaard owned E.T.A. Hoffmann's *Auserwählte Schriften*, I-X

(Berlin: 1827-28; *ASKB* 1712-16), and *Erzählungen*, I-V (Stuttgart: 1839; *ASKB* 1717-21). The particular expression has not been located. The reference may be to a physician in *Die Doppelgänger, ibid.*, I.

19. Inclosing reserve is a prominent subject of Kierkegaard's psychology. See Supplement, pp. 176-77 (*Pap.* V B 147).

20. Kierkegaard has in mind Brutus of Shakespeare's *Julius Caesar.*

21. Shakespeare, *Henry IV*, first part.

22. The term *communicere* (German, *kommunizieren*) is used for receiving the sacrament of the Eucharist. In the text, Kierkegaard refers to the religious meaning of the word.

23. Possibly a reference to Mark 5:17, where the people, when they saw how the demoniac had been healed, begged Jesus to depart from their neighborhood.

24. See Supplement, pp. 210-11 (*Pap.* V B 72:22).

25. Reference to Oehlenschläger's *Aladdin.*

26. John 8:44.

27. "And whatsoever else shall hap tonight / Give it an understanding but no tongue" (*Hamlet*, I, 2). Kierkegaard quotes Schlegel and Tieck's German translation, "allem einen Sinn und keine Zunge."

28. *KW* III (*SV* I 29-30).

29. The reference is to the ballet master Antoine Auguste Bournonville, who presented his own ballet *Faust* in Copenhagen and who himself danced the part of Mephistopheles. The ballet was presented for the first time in 1832. Kierkegaard writes in his journal: "The leap with which Bournonville, in the role of Mephistopheles, always enters and bounds into a motionless pose is commendable. This leap is an element which ought to be noted in an understanding of the demonic. The demonic is namely the sudden.

"Another aspect of the demonic is the boring, as little Winsløv so excellently interpreted it, whereby it passes into the comic (the way in which, as Pepin in *Charlemagne*, he said, 'Patience'—. See his Klister in *De Uadskillelige.*" (*JP* I 732; *Pap.* IV A 94).

30. C. Winsløv played (1827-1834) the role of Klister (the word "Klister" means glue) in J. L. Heiberg's vaudeville *De Uadskillelige.*

31. Karl Michael Bellmann (died 1795) was a Swedish author known for his description of Swedish folk life.

32. For a distinction between Hegel's conception of irony and that of Socrates, see Kierkegaard's *The Concept of Irony, KW* II (*SV* XIII); Hegel's *Geschichte der Philosophie*, Part One, Section One, Period 1, Chapter II, B, 1, *Werke*, XIV, pp 60 ff.; *J.A.*, XVIII, pp. 62 ff.; *History of Philosophy*, I, pp. 398 ff. See also *Vermischte Schriften*, "*Über Solgers nachgelassene Schriften und Briefwechsel*," I, Section IV, 4, *Werke*, XVI, p. 487; *J.A.*, XX, p. 183.

33. Matthew 6:6.

34. The Danish term *Professor* in this anecdote may be a garbling of the word *Provisor* (provisioner).

35. Note that the rubrics of the draft are different from those of the published text. See Supplement, pp. 203-07 (*Pap.* V B 60).

36. "Freedom lost somatic-psychically and freedom lost pneumatically" is changed from "freedom lost bestially, freedom lost intellectually, and freedom lost religiously" (*Pap.* V B 72:24, *n.d.*, 1844).

37. Schelling uses the term *Korporisation* in *Philosophische Untersuchungen über das Wesen der Menschlichen Freiheit* (1809), *Sämmtliche Werke*, Part One, VII, p. 387.

38. Parent-Duchatelet was the author of *De la prostitution de la ville de Paris.* No accurate reference to Kierkegaard's statement has been found.

39. John 8:32.

40. "A freedom involving no necessity, and mere necessity without freedom, are abstract and in this way untrue formulae of thought. Freedom is no blank indeterminateness; essentially concrete, and unvaryingly self-determinate, it is so far at the same time necessity" (Hegel, *Encyclopädie*, Part One, *Die Logik*, §35, *Werke*, VI, pp. 72-73; *J.A.*, VIII, pp. 110-11; *Hegel's Logic*, pp. 54-56).

41. J. G. Fichte, *Über den Begriff der Wissenschaftslehre*, *Werke*, I, pp. 40 ff.; *Bestimmung des Menschen*, *Werke*, II, p. 225.

42. In 1831, Ludwig Feuerbach published his work on death and immortality, *Gedanken über Tod und Unsterblichkeit*, in which he maintained that as a result of Hegel's philosophy, the doctrine of individual immortality could no longer be accepted. Against this position, Karl Friedrich Göschel presented his essay on the immortality of the human soul in light of speculative philosophy, *Von den Beweisen für die Unsterblichkeit der menschlichen Seele im Lichte der spekulativen Philosophie*. In Denmark, the debate about the immortality of the soul found expression in the most important of Poul Martin Møller's works, an essay on the possibility of proofs for the immortality of the soul, *Tanker om Muligheden af Beviser for Sjælens Udødelighed med Hensyn til den derhen hørende nyeste Literatur*, *Efterladte Skrifter*, I-III (Copenhagen: 1839-43; *ASKB* 1574-76), II, pp. 158-272. Møller's work was of significance for Kierkegaard's understanding of the issue. "The episode Poul Møller includes in his essay on the immortality of the soul in the latest issue of *Maanedsskrift* is very interesting; perhaps it will become the usual thing to mitigate the more strictly scholarly-scientific tone with lighter portions which, however, bear forth life much more fully, and in the area of knowledge will be somewhat comparable to the chorus, to the comic portions of romantic dramas" (*JP* V 5201; *Pap.* II A 17, Feb. 4, 1837).

43. See Supplement, pp. 209-10 (*Pap.* V B 66).

44. Kierkegaard might have had in mind Bruno Bauer, *Kritik der evangelischen Geschichte der Synoptiker* (Critique of the Evangelical History of the Synoptics), I-III (Leipzig: 1841-42). See Supplement, p. 208 (*Pap.* V B 64); *Postscript, KW* XII (*SV* VII 74).

45. Joseph von Görres, *Die christliche Mystik*, I-IV[1-2] (Regensburg and Landshut: 1836-42; *ASKB* 528-32). See Supplement, p. 208 (*Pap.* V B 63, VIII[1] A 93; IX A 331, 333).

46. "from this instant/There's nothing serious in mortality;/All is but toys;/renown and grace is dead:/The wine of life is drawn, and the mere lees/Is left

this vault to brag of" (*Macbeth*, II, 3). Kierkegaard quotes from *Shakespeare's dramatische Werke*, tr. A. W. von Schlegel and L. Tieck, XII, p. 301 (II, 2).

47 Ecclesiastes 1:2.

48. "When our first encounter with an object surprises us and we judge it to be new and very different from what we have previously known, or from what we supposed it ought to be, this causes us to wonder and be astonished. Since this can happen before we have any idea of whether the object is beneficial to us or not, it seems that wonder is the first of all passions, and it has no opposite; for if the object which presents itself has nothing in it that surprises us, we are not moved by it at all, and we consider it without passion" (Descartes, *Tractatus de Passionibus Animæ*; *Passiones, sive Affectus Animæ*, Part II, Article LIII, *Opera Philosophica*, Editio ultima [Amsterdam: 1685; *ASKB* 437], p. 27). See Supplement, pp. 175-76 (*Pap.* IV C 10, III A 107). Kierkegaard collapses the title and appropriately changes the case of Affectus.

49. In *Allgemeine Metaphysik*, I-II (Königsberg: 1828-29), II, §§201-4, Johann F. Herbart affirms, over against Kant and the idealistic philosophy, that objective reality and the definite being [*Sein*] of things are independent of the perceptive subject, and thus something that excludes all negation.

50. See Supplement, pp. 211-12 (*Pap.* V B 72:28).

51. See Supplement, p. 209 (*Pap.* V B 68).

52. See the addition to this statement in the draft, Supplement, p. 212 (*Pap.* V B 72:29).

53. Kierkegaard owned the first edition of Karl Rosenkranz, *Psychologie oder die Wissenschaft vom subjektiven Geist* (Königsberg: 1837; *ASKB* 744). Rosenkranz's definition of *Gemüt* differs from that of Hegel, who speaks of *Gemüt* as "this shrouded undetermined totality of the bearing of the spirit upon the will, in which a man in even so general and indefinite manner has a satisfaction within himself" (*Philosophie der Geschichte*, Part Four, Section One, Chapter 1, *Werke*, IX, p. 425; *J.A.*, XI, p. 447, ed. tr.). In another place, Hegel indentifies *Gemüt* with the "Inwardness [*Innigkeit*] of the Spirit's perceptibility" (*Æsthetik*, Part Two, Section Three, Chapter 1, 2, *Werke*, X², p. 149; *J.A.*, XIII, p. 149, ed. tr.).

54. See Supplement, p. 212 (*Pap.* V B 72:30).

55. See Supplement, p. 210 (*Pap.* V B 69).

56. See *Repetition*, *KW* VI (*SV* III 175).

57. G. O. Marbach, *Geschichte der Griechischen Philosophie . . . und Geschichte der Philosophie des Mittelalters* (Leipzig: 1838-41; *ASKB* 642-43).

58. W. G. Tennemann, *Geschichte der Philosophie*, I-XII (Leipzig: 1798-1819; *ASKB* 815-26). According to the legend, when Bellerophon attempted to ride Pegasus to heaven, he was thrown by the horse. Kierkegaard may have confused this legend with the story in Euripides' *Stheneboea*, in which Bellerophon, returning from Lycia to Tiryns, persuaded the queen of Tiryns, who was responsible for his having to battle the Chimaera, to mount Pegasus with him on the pretence that he would return her love. Upon reaching the open sea, he hurled her into the waves.

59. See *Repetition*, *KW* VI (*SV* III 254), and the addition in the draft, Supplement, p. 212 (*Pap.* V B 172:31).

60. The draft mentions Bettina's letters as an example. Anna Elisabeth von Arnim (1785-1859), called Bettina, the sister of Clemens Brentano, wrote a volume of imaginary letters (1835) under the title *Goethes Briefwechsel mit einem Kinde* (Goethe's Correspondence with a Child). See Supplement, p. 212 (*Pap*. V B 60; 72:32).

61. "True art is an anticipation of the blessed life" (Poul M. Møller, *Efterladte Skrifter*, 1 ed., II, p. 217). See p. 251, note 42; Supplement, p. 207 (*Pap*.V B 60 p. 137); *Postscript, KW* XII (*SV* VII 268 fn.).

62. A reference to J. L. Heiberg's apocalyptic comedy, *En Sjæl efter Døden* (1841), and H. L. Martensen's review of the same in the daily paper *Fædrelandet*.

63. A reference to Fichte's philosophy, where the *I* (*ich*) is conceived partly as empirical and partly as essentially absolute and identical with the Absolute.

64. Poul M. Møller, in the essay on immortality, *Efterladte Skrifter*, 1 ed., II, pp. 188-200. See p. 251, note 42.

65. A reference to the review by Martensen mentioned in note 62 above. See Supplement, p. 207 (*Pap*. V B 60 p. 137).

66. Matthew 12:36.

67. "And so, Glaucon, the tale was saved, as the saying is, and was not lost. And it will save us if we believe it, and we shall safely cross the river of Lethe, and keep our soul unspotted from the world. But if we are guided by me, we shall believe that the soul is immortal and capable of enduring all extremes of good and evil, and so we shall hold ever to the upward way and pursue righteousness with wisdom always and ever, that we may be dear to ourselves and to the gods both during our sojourn here, and where we receive our reward, as the victors in the game go about and gather theirs. And thus both here and in that journey of a thousand years, whereof I have told you, we shall fare well" (Plato, *Republic*, 621 b-d, Paul Shorey's translation in *The Collected Works of Plato*).

68. See Supplement, p. 213 (*Pap*. V B 72:33). The reference is to H. L. Martensen.

CHAPTER V

1. "*Das Märchen von einem, der auszog, das Fürchten zu lernen*" (*Kinder- und Haus-Märchen. Gesammelt durch die Brüder Grimm*, I, no. 4, p. 14; "The Story of the Youth Who Went Forth to Learn What Fear Was," *The Complete Grimm's Fairy Tales*, pp. 29-39).

2. Matthew 26:37, 38; Mark 14:33, 34; John 12:27, 13:27.

3. Mark 15:34.

4. Kierkegaard does not quote Hegel. He may have had in mind such passages from Hegel as "Faith must be defined as the witness of the spirit to absolute Spirit, or as a certainty of the truth" or "faith may be defined as being the witness of the Spirit to Spirit, and this implies that no finite content has any place in it" (*Philosophie der Religion*, Part One, C, I, 2, *Werke*, XI, pp. 206, 213; *J.A.*, XV, pp. 222, 229; *Lectures on the Philosophy of Religion*, I, pp. 212, 218).

5. Although innocent of the accusations against him, the French Calvinist

Jean Calas was executed in 1762. Daniel Chodowiecki, a German painter and engraver, made an engraving showing Calas taking leave of his family. Later, Chodowiecki made an engraving in which he pictures the four temperaments watching "Les adieux de Calas." Kierkegaard has confused the surrender of Calais with the "Farewell of Calas."

6. See *Phaedo*, 117b.

7. When Kierkegaard had completed his theological examination, he took a trip to Jutland to see the place where his father was born. At that time he wrote in his journal (1840): "The heath must be particularly adapted to developing vigorous spirits; here everything lies naked and unveiled before God, and here is no place for a lot of distractions, those many odd nooks and corners where the consciousness can hide, and from which earnestness often has a hard time recovering vagrant thoughts. Here consciousness must come to definite and precise conclusions about itself. Here on the heath one must truly say, 'Whither shall I flee from thy presence?' " (*JP* III 2830; *Pap.* III A 78).

8. The Danish *Heksebrev* means literally "witch's letter," which is a magiclike set of picture segments of people and animals that recombine when unfolded and turned. The figure is used also in *Either/Or*, II, *KW* IV (*SV* II 231-32): "The person who lives ethically has seen himself, knows himself, penetrates his whole concretion with his consciousness, does not allow vague thoughts to rustle around inside him, or let tempting possibilities distract him with their juggling; he is not like a 'magic' picture that shifts from one thing to another, depending on how one turns it."

9. "Whoever is educated by anxiety is educated by possibility, and only he who is educated by possibility is educated according to his infinitude. Therefore possibility is the weightiest of all categories" (p. 156).

10. Socrates says, "I have long been wondering at my own wisdom. I cannot trust myself. And I think that I ought to stop and ask myself, what am I saying? For there is nothing worse than self-deception—when the deceiver is always at home and always with you it is quite terrible, and therefore I ought often retrace my steps and endeavor to 'look fore and aft' in the words of the aforesaid Homer" (*Cratylus*, 428 d, Jowett's translation in *The Collected Dialogues of Plato*).

11. Luke 10:30. In the parable the man travels from Jerusalem to Jericho.

12. The reference is to *Either/Or*, II, *KW* IV (*SV* II 243). "Autodidact" means self-taught; "theodidact," taught by God. See I Thess. 4:9: "concerning the love of the brethren you have no need to have anyone write to you for you yourselves have been taught by God to love one another." Here Paul uses the term θεοδίδακτοι.

13. "In volume VI, p. 194, of his works [J. G. Hamann, *Schriften*, I-VIII (Berlin: 1821-43; *ASKB* 536-44)], Hamann makes an observation which I can use, although he neither understood it as I wish to understand it nor thought further about it: [text as in note, p. 162]" (*JP* I 96; *Pap.* III A 235, *n.d.*, 1842).

SUPPLEMENT

1. *Magister artium* (*liberalium*)—master of the liberal arts—was conferred by the philosophical faculty of the University of Copenhagen. The degree was equivalent to that of doctor, the degree conferred by the other faculties. In 1854, the magister degree was replaced by the degree of doctor of philosophy, and all persons holding the *magister artium* degree were declared to be *doctores philosophiae*.

2. See K. Rosenkranz, *Psychologie*, p. 334.

3. See p. 253, note 60.

4. See p. 137 and note 38.

5. See p. 253, note 60.

BIBLIOGRAPHICAL NOTE

For general bibliographies of Kierkegaard studies, see:
Jens Himmelstrup, *Søren Kierkegaard International Bibliografi.* Copenhagen: Nyt Nordisk Forlag Arnold Busck, 1962.
Aage Jørgensen, *Søren Kierkegaard-litteratur 1961-1970.* Aarhus: Akademisk Boghandel, 1971.
Kierkegaard: A Collection of Critical Essays, ed. Josiah Thompson. New York: Doubleday (Anchor Book), 1972.
Søren Kierkegaard's Journals and Papers, I, ed. and tr. Howard V. Hong and Edna H. Hong, assisted by Gregor Malantschuk. Bloomington: Indiana University Press, 1967.
For topical bibliographies of Kierkegaard studies, see ibid., I-IV (1967-75).

INDEX

corruption, 58
courage, to believe, 117; to understand, 102
cowardice, 79, 121, 144-45
creation, 46-47, 53, 57-59, 73, 78, 83
Crites, Stephen D., xi
Critobulus, 70, 239
cupiditas, 176
curiosity, 39, 57, 138
cynic, 70

Daniel, Book of, 196
Dante, Alighieri, 207
Dasein, 226
death, 45, 92-93, 96, 121
deceiver, 150, 160
dedication, *The Concept of Anxiety*, 5, 178, 222-23
defiance, 108, 116, 145-46
definition, categorical, 12; dogmatic, 35, 79; of sentience, 148
deity, 59, 86, 150. *See also* God
delusion, 56
Democritus, 228
demon, 119, 125, 132
demoniac, 124, 204, 250
demonic, the, 118-36, 202-08, 249; as anxiety about the good, 123, 135, 203; as the boring, 132-33, 250; category of, 138; concept of, 119, 122; as the contentless, 132-33; defined, 119, 122-23, 135; forms of, 124, 137, 141-42, 144; as inclosing reserve, 123-29; as the negative, 134; in New Testament, 124; as noncommunication, 124-25; spheres of, 137-38; as the sudden, 129-32, 250; views of, 119-23, 202. *See also* knowledge
Descartes, René, vii-ix, xi, 146, 175, 252
desire, 66, 73. *See also* concupiscence
despair, 105, 169, 173, 175, 200
determinability, 37-38
determinant, ethical and metaphysical, 133; quantitative, 114

determinations (determinateness, determine), 61, 63, 69, 92, 105, 133, 181, 234; conceptual, 133; dialectical, 42, 102; psychological, 42; quantitative, 30-31, 33-34, 38, 43, 52, 54, 56, 59, 74, 90, 93, 114, 185; of time, 84, 87
Deuteronomy, 239
devil, 62, 125, 128
dialectic, 82-83, 116, 238, 242; Hegelian, 225, 237
dialectical, the, 11, 15, 25, 32, 40, 42-43, 59, 84, 92, 96, 102-03, 118, 136, 160, 227, 241
didactic, the, 221
Diogenes Laertius, 228
disbelief, 172. *See also* unbelief
disclosure, 123, 126-29; category of, 127
discrimen, 90-91; *discrimen rerum*, 50
disposition, 37, 47, 148-49, 209; defined, 148. *See also* Gemüt
divine, the, 102-03, 134
dizziness, 61, 130, 158
dogmatics, 9-10, 12, 20-24, 58, 60, 79, 180, 183, 221; and Adam, 33, 36; and ethics, 12, 39; and faith, 10, 18; and Hegel, 35; and hereditary sin, iii, 14, 19-20, 23, 119, 182; and psychology, 58, 77, 162; and repetition, 18; science of, 12, 19-20, 23
Don Giovanni, xiii, 113, 131, 248
doubt, ix, 11, 25, 146, 176, 208, 244
Dracon, 27, 231
drive, 80; sexual, 69, 76, 79, 195
Duchatelet, Alexandre Jean B. B. (Parent-), 137, 204, 251

eager longing, 53, 57, 236-37
earnestness, 146-54, 210; as certitude and inwardness, 138-41, 146, 151, 153, 208-09; defined, 147; and disposition, 148-49, 209; as mood corresponding to sin, 15-16, 181; and personality, 149
Ecclesiastes, 146, 196, 212, 252

266 *Index*

ADVISORY BOARD

KIERKEGAARD'S WRITINGS

Library of Congress Cataloging in Publication Data

Kierkegaard, Søren Aabye, 1813-1855.
    The concept of anxiety.

    Translation of Begrebet Angest.
    Bibliography: p.
    Includes index.
    1. Sin, Original.   2. Psychology, Religious.   3. Anxiety.
I. Thomte, Reidar.   II. Anderson, Albert, 1928-   III. Title.
BT720.K52   1980   233'.14   79-3217
ISBN 0-691-07244-2